THE SUBJECT
IS
WRITING

THE SUBJECT IS WRITING

essays by teachers and students

edited by
WENDY BISHOP

**Boynton/Cook
Heinemann
Portsmouth, NH**

Boynton/Cook Publishers, Inc.
A subsidiary of Reed Elsevier Inc.
361 Hanover Street
Portsmouth, NH 03801–3912

Library of Congress Cataloging-in-Publication Data
The subject is writing : essays by teachers and students /
    edited by Wendy Bishop.
        p.   cm.
    ISBN 0–86709–314–5
    1. English language—Rhetoric—Study and teaching.   2. Rhetoric—
Problems, exercises, etc.   3. English language—Rhetoric.
4. Readers—Rhetoric.   I. Bishop, Wendy.
PE1404.S85   1993   92-39430
808'.042'07—dc20   CIP

Cover design by T. Watson Bogaard
Printed in the United States of America
95 96 97   10 9   8   7   6   5   4   3

Contents

Preface

This book is for writing students and their teachers. By gathering these essays together, I hope to invite you into an ongoing discussion and to illustrate a small but important premise: writing is the subject of writing classes.

In journals, at conferences, and in department meetings, I often hear assertions that writing classes have no "content," especially when compared to literature classes or other classes in other disciplines where famous texts by famous authors are commonly under discussion. Those of us who write, who teach writing, and who love writing and reading a variety of texts know that the *contentless* claim is simply not true. Student texts are valuable texts.

Maxine Hairston (1986) believes, as I do, that "a writing course has its own content, and that is the students' and teacher's writing and the writing process itself" (p. 188). I believe her statement fully because I know my second best hours as a writer are spent talking to writers, researching writing, and responding to writing. My best hours as a writer, of course, are spent writing, since *talk about* will never substitute for *writing about*. It is clear that we learn to write better by attempting writing and by thinking through writing.

I know that not everyone shares my enthusiasm for writing and talking about writing. Still, I feel that shared enthusiasm—that of committed writing teachers and freshly engaged writing students in this text—will offer you needed classroom support, writing advice, and the encouragement to begin and continue your own journey as a writer. I'd like to think that you might learn, in our company and the company of your writing class, the lesson shared by poet Marvin Bell: "I always feel better when I write, when I go to my study out back under the wild cherry tree. It only takes a few minutes before I say, 'Why didn't I come out here sooner?' It feels wonderful" (Murray, 1990, p. 190).

Of course that wonderful feeling isn't easy to achieve, but I believe it is worth pursuing. The writing teachers in this book are all trying to create a new kind of writing classroom, one that makes students ask "Why didn't I come here sooner?" At the same time, in their essays they examine the institutional constraints that still exist to slow the development of better writing instruction.

You may be in a writing class because you were told you needed to be there, and we still need to convince you to stay willingly. On the other hand, you may have already discovered that writing has a special place in your life because writing is *for* you as well as for those you write to. Toni Morrison claims:

> Writing was the only work I did that was for myself and by myself. In the process, one exercises sovereignty in a special way. All sensibilities are engaged, sometimes simultaneously, sometimes sequentially. While I'm writing, all of my experience is vital and useful and possibly important. (Murray, 1990, p. 8)

In the writing classes described in these essays and created by you and your peers and your teacher, writing is for you and for others, work you do alone and work you do together, work that engages you and that authorizes your view and your experiences, work that remains central to your sense of self—important *work*.

The five parts of this book are not intended to restrict your reading; move freely between them. To invite you into the process of writing, essayists in Part I share their literacy autobiographies, their stories of coming into writing. Part II introduces you to four teachers talking about writing classrooms. You may want to read about several of these classrooms as you start working with your own writing teacher to develop a classroom community. Part III looks in detail at classroom activities like forming and maintaining peer groups, keeping a journal, and developing greater fluency with composing activities like generating ideas and revising. Essayists in Part IV continue to look at the act of composing and offer advice for successful negotiation of classrooms and of writing tasks. Part V asks you to consider issues in writing instruction. If you've ever felt like rebelling against teachers' suggestions, if you've ever felt uncertain about what is being asked of you in the writing classroom or even in the university community, or if you've ever wondered what is at stake in writing in particular genres or for particular audiences, these essays will help you develop preliminary responses to some of those big questions.

None of these authors offers you pat answers. None intends his or her view to be the only way to look at writing. But all are trying to share their commitment to writing.

The essays in this textbook were reviewed before publication in writing classrooms around the country. Students responded to the essay drafts, and suggested revisions to authors who then revised, trying to improve the essays in light of those suggestions. These are, then, not esoteric academic journal essays but, we hope, essays in the best sense, exploratory and earnest communications from writers to readers. And you'll notice that our essay writing—like your essay writing—takes many forms.

Time for Thanks

John Updike wrote: "Writing well involves two gifts—the art of adding and the art of taking away. Of the two, the first is more important, since without it the second could not exist" (Murray, 1990, p. 187).

Clearly *The Subject is Writing* represents a group effort in the best sense. I need to thank all the essayists who added to this book, sharing the gift of their work. Next, the quality of an editor's life depends directly on her publishers. Bob Boynton responded to the idea of this textbook with enthusiasm and speed. Peter Stillman supported the book through every draft and revision. He has been a true writer's editor, contributing his expertise and sharing his fund of teaching, travel, and horse raising stories. I can't thank him enough for his attention to my ideas and for his support of student writers.

The following teachers and their writing students helped with the manuscript drafts: thanks to Susan Barron, Anne Bower, Roger Casey, Gay Lynn Crossley, Beth Daniell, Kevin Davis, Kim Haimes-Korn, Rich Haswell, Ruth Johnson, Ann Kalinak, Carolyn Kremers, Pat MacEnulty, Michael McMahon, Ruth Mirtz, Dean Newman, Elsie Rogers, Mary Jane Ryals, Jim Strickland, Craig Stroupe, Gretchen Thies, Cindy Wheatley-Lovoy, Ron Wiginton, Thia Wolf, and Trisha Yarborough. In addition, all the members of my Summer 1991 teacher education course shared thoughtful responses as well. Two cats, two kids, a husband, five palm trees, and two computers have also put up with me—they're not responsible for this book—but their good spirits reside, I hope, within it.

Works Cited

Hairston, Maxine (1986). Using Nonfiction Literature in the Composition Classroom. In B. T. Peterson (Ed.), *Convergences: Transactions in Reading and Writing*. Urbana, IL: National Council of Teachers of English. (pp. 179–188).

Murray, Donald M. (1990). *Shoptalk: Learning to Write With Writers*. Portsmouth, NH: Boynton/Cook Heinemann.

Part I

Growing into Writing

These essays show how our daily lives as well as our writing class-rooms affect us as writers. Carolyn Kremers takes you on a journey from her earliest years as a student writer to her current life as a writing teacher. Brad Usatch analyzes his writing voice, discovering that he sounds decidedly different when he composes what he thinks of as his "art" writing and his "academic" writing. Brad finds his writing habits began as early as 7 years of age. Audrey Brown covers 11 years of her own writing development. Starting with childhood journal entries and moving to college papers, she considers how her writing voice changed as she changed. These writers all picked differ-ent lenses for examining the past—11, 15, and 35 years.

You too have an important history of writing, one you will want to explore even as you continue to write today's papers and share them with your peers and teacher. I expect you'll connect with some of these writers' experiences, but I also expect you'll have your own, different account to share, that is, your writing life as seen through your life lens. You might share your thoughts in a literacy autobiog-raphy, in journal entries, during classroom discussions, or in confer-ence with your teacher. When reading these essays and talking about your own writing past, I hope you'll notice how all of us start writing courses already informed by significant writing experiences. All of us, too, have the ability to grow, more fully, into our writing.

1

Learning to Sing

Carolyn Kremers

Carolyn Kremers grew up in Colorado, where the outdoors crept into her and never left. She received her M.F.A. in Creative Writing from the University of Alaska Fairbanks and was a Visiting Assistant Professor of English there when she wrote this essay. For two years, she taught English and music in the Yup'ik Eskimo village of Tununak on the coast of the Bering Sea. Her book, *Place of the Pretend People*, was inspired by her experiences there and is a narrative made of creative nonfiction and poetry. She likes to hike, cross-country ski, teach, and sit by fires.

Do you remember how you learned to sing? I do, and the story surprises me.

I can't remember the first time I held a pencil in my hand, but I remember the blue-lined newsprint Mrs. Krieger passed around the class in first grade, and what she said about the letters I printed on it.

"Look, children. Carolyn's a's and o's are as round as baseballs." Something inside me felt proud and embarrassed at the same time.

Learning to write—rather, sing—has always been contradictory for me. I can't remember how I began, the process has not been linear, and much of it has involved music, not writing. The more I think about this, the more I am intrigued. Nobody and everybody, nothing and everything, taught me to write. I mean sing. I could not have learned alone and yet, at the same time, I taught myself.

In second grade, we had to sharpen our own pencils. The walk from my desk to the windows was long and embarrassing, and when

I finally reached the sharpener and put my new pencil in, the monster always ground it up and jammed, breaking the pencil point just as I thought I was finished. This sharpener ate my new pencils, one after another, until one day the teacher noticed.

I was afraid to look up after Mrs. Santi saw me insert a brand-new green pencil and pull out a nub. She wore a red knit dress that day, the one that hugged her round hips as if she were a young woman. Mrs. Santi always wore high heels and thick red lipstick, and her dangling earrings shook when she got mad. Now she towered over me at the sharpener.

"PAY MORE ATTENTION, CAROLYN, AND STOP WASTING SCHOOL MONEY!"

Later, copying spelling word definitions from the dictionary, I thought I would never be able to get things right.

"Don't press so hard!" Mrs. Santi yelled, towering again. I could smell her perfume. "Look at the mess you're making!"

She was right. All the letters had smeared as my hand moved down the page. I decided I didn't like number two pencils, or maybe I didn't like writing.

In third grade, things got better. For one thing, I got appendicitis three days after having my tonsils out and I almost died. I had to miss two weeks of school, but Mrs. Smith didn't yell at me once. She let me make a diorama (that was a new word) of a simple machine and put it in the school display case one week late. I made a pulley inside a shoebox. I loved making things with my hands.

The class learned cursive that year, but I still pressed the pencil too hard and everything smeared. I liked making things with my hands, but not letters. My letters were neat and round, even in cursive, but they were too careful. Too pretty and slow. They couldn't keep up with my mind so, without me knowing, they slowed it down.

I wrote all my school assignments in cursive after third grade, but I never got the hang of it. In college, when teachers no longer cared, I was able to abandon cursive and go back to printing. But I didn't learn to write FAST—to transfer my thoughts onto paper in wild, messy lines and circles—until years after college.

Beginning in fourth grade, we got to have different teachers for different subjects, and I especially liked Mr. Berg. He taught spelling. Every Monday he peeled back the piece of butcher paper hanging from the easel at the front of the room and revealed a new one, with twenty-five words neatly printed in black felt pen. Then he lectured.

Mr. Berg told about homonyms and synonyms, prefixes and suffixes, silent k's and long o's, but he also told stories about the derivations of words: how prairie was French for meadowland; that detonate came from Latin *detonare*—to thunder; that diesel was named for Rudolf Diesel, a German inventor; and whirlwind had been spelled *hvirtilvindr* in Old Norse. Mr. Berg turned words into a labyrinth of history, linguistics, imagination, and musical sound, and we were only in fourth grade.

By fifth grade, I began to think that maybe I could have fun making things with written words after all. Nobody showed me this, I just noticed it. In science, when Mrs. Boyer told us to look in the encyclopedia and write a report about any animal, I chose the most unusual one I could think of: the praying mantis. I think Mrs. Boyer had in mind horses and elephants and dogs: farm animals and zoo animals, not insects. I wrote how the praying mantis devours a fly, pinning it with prickly front legs, and when the last morsel is gone, the mantis presses its empty legs together, as if praying. Using my father's colored pencils, I traced a picture on onion-skin paper. The hardest part was getting light to reflect off the transparent wings, like it did in the encyclopedia. Would Mrs. Boyer like my report? When she did, I began to realize that *what* I wrote about might be just as important as *how*, and maybe more interesting.

One day the following summer at Girl Scout camp, I wrote something under a ponderosa pine tree. I had been thinking about the sunset the night before: one of those spectacular Colorado summer sunsets, shot with receding thunderclouds and thick beams of pink and purple light. That sunset made me think of something else: berries. Raspberry, kinnikinnick, mountain ash, wild currant.

"Where did you learn to write like this?" the counselor asked, when I showed her my story. I didn't know. No one had told me how to write "creatively," or that I should write at all in summer. The sunset had reminded me of berries, and I had wanted to write it down. Wasn't that what people were always doing in books? Comparing one thing with another, playing with colors, painting pictures for others to see and taste and smell? And remember?

In sixth grade, I held a violin in my hands for the first time. A friend in Girl Scouts, Kathy, had borrowed it from school. I liked the smooth, slender maple neck, and the way the wood smelled when it got warm under my chin. And I liked guessing where to put my fingers to get different tones to come out. This was more fun than writing words. You could hear the results, and they were instant.

I experimented on Kathy's violin after Girl Scout meetings for a few weeks, figuring out "Mary Had a Little Lamb" and "Are You Sleeping?", and soon I was in the school orchestra, playing on a scratched-up, three-quarter-size instrument. The scraping and screeching must have been awful for my parents, but unlike Mrs. Santi in her red dress, they didn't say I was making a mess.

That year, I composed a musical, and my best friend, Nancy, wrote the words. I had fancied myself a composer since I was five, when I made up a tune on the black keys. I knew what a composer was, because I sang in the church choir and, every Wednesday afternoon, Mrs. Havekost began the rehearsal by reading. She read a story about Mozart or Haydn or Beethoven or some other little boy. By sixth grade, I had been taking piano lessons for three years and singing in church for six. I had heard several hundred stories about little boys who became composers, and I had learned how to write down music. This was more fun than writing down words. There were more symbols to manipulate, and some of them were really fun to make: like the treble clef, the double sharp, and the single sixteenth note. You got to move these symbols around, line them up, add and subtract numbers and notes, then test them on the piano to see how they sounded. Musical compositions were fun to invent, and other people liked to listen. So Nancy and I wrote a musical for our class to perform, and I also composed a farewell piano piece for my sixth-grade music teacher, Mrs. Marshall. The title still makes me laugh: "For Thee, Dorothy."

Now, you're probably wondering what all these stories about music have to do with writing. I think many people learn to write by studying, and loving, something else. In many respects, I learned to write by not writing. Often this was fun, but sometimes it wasn't.

Seventh grade was awful. I can't remember anything about writing. Mainly, I remember lying on the bottom bunk in our house on South Ash Street (my little sister always got the top bunk), crying, kicking my feet, and wailing, "I wish I was a boy!" Boys had so much fun. They could be whatever they wanted when they grew up, and they didn't have to wear dresses.

Eighth grade was better. We read science reports out loud to the class. We had to state our hypothesis, describe the experiment we had designed, and explain whether the results supported the hypothesis. Mr. Holmes was my favorite teacher that year—perhaps because he was the only African-American teacher in the school, he was funny, and he called me "Miss Kremers"—but more likely because he was very good at what he did, which is how I wanted to be someday.

Also in eighth grade, we started doing exercises in Warriner's grammar book. The book's cover was a different color every year, but the stuff inside seemed always the same: parts of speech, punctuation, sentence combining, diagramming sentences, and so on and on. Whenever the weather was nice, I escaped to the backyard and did these boring exercises under a tree.

In ninth grade, we had a student teacher from Princeton or Harvard or one of those other Ivy League schools out East. He was young and good looking, and he let us call him by his first name. He helped us write a slang dictionary. We brainstormed all the slang words we could think of, and Toby wrote them on the board without censoring any.

Then we each picked the words we wanted to work on for the dictionary, dividing them into syllables and writing pronunciation, parts of speech, definitions, and sentences for each. We designed a book with a blue cover and everybody in class got a copy. (By then, I had a crush on Toby.) And I was beginning to become interested in the *ideas* behind words—their social and psychological implications—not just where they came from and how they were spelled or what you had to do to them to get all 25 questions right on Warriner's grammar book tests.

Ninth grade was also when our papers were read by a lay reader, a person (usually a woman) who was not a certified teacher, but who was trained in writing and editing. We never saw her or even knew her name, but somehow our papers got given to her, and she read them carefully (so it seemed to me) and marked all the mistakes in red ink. She wrote *sp, awk, ww, //, run-on, frag, tense, mis mod—* whatever was wrong or whatever she didn't like.

This lay reader didn't correct things, though. We had to do that ourselves, by looking on a chart stapled to our writing folder, where we kept all our papers. In various columns on the chart, we checked off different kinds of mistakes and read an explanation of each (ww = wrong word, awk = awkward). Then we fixed each mistake on the paper. This seemed tedious to me—and I didn't always agree with this lay reader, whoever she was—but I didn't mind too much, because she always wrote a note at the end of my paper, and it was usually something nice. And sometimes this stranger used words I had never heard of, mystifying me and forcing me to use a dictionary for something other than spelling words. Like *metaphysical*: "Aren't you getting rather metaphysical here?"

In high school, lay readers disappeared. Writing assignments didn't, though, and I realize now that I learned many of the *skills* of writing in school, even though I didn't use them for much that was creative. Most of my writing in schools, until I entered graduate school, was transactional, structured, and dull, not expressive, intuitive, and interesting. But it was writing.

Talking helped. In competitive speech, I learned how to argue for and against. For and against compulsory service for 18-year olds (military? conservation corps? community service?), for and against legalization of marijuana, for and against nuclear weapons. I read the *Congressional Record* and the *Saturday Review*, besides *Time* and *Newsweek*, and I learned to choose credible sources, distinguish between fact and opinion, cull and organize evidence, construct thesis statements and logical arguments, make an outline, capture the audience's attention, and make a compelling conclusion.

In eleventh grade, Mr. Myers became my all-time favorite teacher. He had had polio and walked on an artificial leg, but we forgot about that because he forced us to concentrate on his face, not his legs. He always looked us right in the eyes and smiled or joked or pretended to be surprised. He kept us awake by asking questions like, "Tell us why you didn't like Whitman's poem, Mr. Grant," or "What might the heath symbolize in Wolf's novel, Miss Riley?"

One day Mr. Myers brought a Simon and Garfunkel record to class. He passed out freshly mimeographed copies of the lyrics (students near the front got the best sniffs), and he played "The Sounds of Silence." He talked about stanzas, chorus, rhymes, and other stuff. "Hello, darkness, my old friend / I've come to talk with you again. . . . " Then he said, "Okay. Now write a poem of your own. Go ahead. Just start writing and see what comes out."

Right. My poem was awful. It sounded sappy, with dumb rhymes, and it didn't sing. I was glad it was only words, not music, and no one could hear it as it travelled down the row to Mr. Myers. I handed it in because we had to, for a grade, but when I got it back, I tore it to shreds. I didn't know I was hooked.

That summer I checked out a tan book from the library and taught myself to type. Thequickgreenfoxjumpedoverthewilyfence. I was a piano player, so typing wasn't hard. Also that summer, my German class went to Europe for three weeks. My father gave me a small notebook with a black fake leather cover that said *TRIP DIARY*, and for the first time in my life, I kept an account of my daily activities. I was 16. The night I went to the Vienna Volksoper and ended up in a Hungarian restaurant, with the opera orchestra flutist buying me dinner and flowers, I knew something had changed. What? I wasn't sure.

That fall in Advanced Placement English, I turned in a story about Vienna, based on notes from my journal. The paper was fun to write: something about red and silver train lights and leaving Vienna and a tall blond man at night in the rain. Mr. Schanker made us turn in a composition every Monday, each in a different style: narrative, description, analysis, comparison and contrast, argument, persuasion. I wrote the Vienna story as a description. Mr. Schanker didn't write much at the bottom, just A and "Good Job," or something dull like that. His thing was theater, not writing, but at least he didn't embarrass me.

By the time I got to college, in the fall of 1969, the Vietnam War was in full swing, and I knew I wanted to be a musician. I wanted to compose music and play violin in a symphony orchestra. I liked ideas, and maybe I was good at writing about them, but I didn't want to talk. I wanted to sing.

By the end of my freshman year, though, I could no longer concentrate on the violin. The campus trembled with sit-ins, teach-ins, violent and nonviolent protests and demonstrations. Worse, the students in my music theory class seemed like snobs. They didn't know a war was going on or, if they did, they didn't care. I began to question my interest in classical music as a career. Wouldn't it be better to do something relevant? Teach in an inner city school, perhaps? I changed my major to English and Humanities, and I stopped playing the violin.

I started to write poems, and I wrote hundreds of letters: home, to friends, to old boyfriends and new ones. Many new ideas and experiences were coming at me in college—in California, in those times— so many that I could not sort them out without writing things down. I began to write to discover what I thought, and also what I felt.

After college, I did many kinds of writing, but something kept leading me back to music.

My first teaching job was in a "ghetto" high school in Chicago, where I taught music, not English. Most of my students were African-Americans from low-income families. Many could barely read or write, which seemed important, so we invented poems and stories to music and recited the lyrics to songs.

Later, I got a music degree, and occasionally I wrote music reviews for an arts newspaper in Boulder, Colorado. One day, the editor called and asked if I would review a Meg Christian concert in Denver. I didn't know Meg Christian was lesbian until I got there and saw the crowd and sat next to a female couple holding hands. I took notes, pages of them, and the next morning I wrote a personal narrative about my unexpected reactions to the music and the audience. The story was political, uncensored, and personal, and it ended with me and everyone else giving Meg Christian a standing ovation. It was not a conventional review. I thought it probably wasn't what the editor wanted—that I might never be asked to write for the paper again—but I submitted it anyway. It got printed.

It was after I moved to Alaska to teach music and English in a small Yup'ik Eskimo village on the coast of the Bering Sea, more than a hundred miles from the nearest tree or town, that I began to understand some important things. I kept a journal with my students and helped them translate elders' stories, illustrate bookmarks, and write and perform plays. They—and their elders and traditions and the beauty and power of the physical, spiritual place where they lived— helped me see that writing and music are related, actually intertwined, and that they do not have to be separated in the ways they have become, in my mind and in my world.

When I decided to get a Master of Fine Arts degree in Creative Writing—and to try to write about these ideas, in poems and creative nonfiction, still playing music—I had to break many habits. I had to stop trying to get everything right the first time; stop worrying about correctness too early in the drafting process; stop using clichés, vague descriptions, passive verbs, unnecessary adjectives, textbook jargon, and stilted phrasing that sounded like an English teacher.

I learned to draft an essay like I'm drafting this one now: by brainstorming ideas and then writing without stopping to fix anything, just writing my real thoughts, as close as I can get to them, in pencil, fast and illegibly, striking things out, not taking time to erase, just drawing arrows and inserting words, and scribbling in margins, until no one can read what I've written but myself. Capturing a *voice*. Then going back later, days later, and crossing things out—crossing out hundreds of dull and inaccurate and sappy and clichéd things— and adding other things. Then putting the essay on the computer and printing it and crossing out more lines and more lines, and adding more, and cutting and pasting big chunks and little ones, moving things around, expanding and contracting—like a musician breathing —until the overall structure feels right. Then fine-tuning, fine-tuning, going deeper and deeper into the meanings of individual words, the sense and sound of them, the rhythm: like writing a poem. Or like playing the violin or composing a musical piece.

The contradictions of this process called *writing* continue to intrigue me. I realize I learned to write because I wanted to: in order to express emotions, figure out ideas, share with others, write about things that mattered to me. And I learned to write because I had to, in order to jump academic hoops and get where I wanted to go: to Stanford; to Vienna, music school, Alaska, graduate school; to some of the depths of my mind and heart.

I learned to write when people criticized me: my second-grade teacher, my parents, the lay reader, rival debate teams, editors, professors. But I also learned to write when people praised me. One person who has praised me the most is also someone who has taught me the most. How can this be? My friend Rick Bass, a fiction and nonfiction writer, scribbles pictures all over my manuscripts—showing me things he likes and telling me why—and whenever he crosses something out, I listen. Closely.

"Carolyn! Trust us! We're dumb, but we're not that dumb. We can make the connection!" he writes. Or "Screech! We're not impaired!" or "Something about this bothers me . . . " or "This can be overdone—a little goes a long way" or "Cliché, and worse, inaccurate."

Criticism helps me see my writing in new ways and, as long as I can overcome my ego, I learn from it. But praise, especially from people I respect, gives me much needed courage and hope and inspires me to try to do even better.

There are other contradictions. I've learned to write by sharing my writing with others. Sometimes I share it before it's ready, which can be a good or a bad thing to do. Sometimes I share my writing when I think it's good and I want to see if anyone agrees. Other times I share it when I think it's terrible and I want help. Yet, I've also learned to write by not sharing: by keeping my deepest thoughts inside, listening to them, letting them float in silence, sharing them with no one until, bubbling and rising of their own accord, they spill onto the page, out of a dark, sparkling place, ready to brave the flood-lit scrutiny of others.

I've learned to write by writing, by doing it. But I've also learned to write by not writing—by skiing, running, daydreaming, night-dreaming, thinking, talking, drawing pictures, reading. Reading, reading, reading. And by loving music.

A very important thing I've learned is that good writing takes time. I've been learning to write since before I can remember—since first holding a crayon in my hand—yet I've only scratched the surface of what there is to learn and to write about. Some of my best writing has grown out of my journals, has come instantly, like magic. I didn't know what I was going to write, it just came out. Other writing has taken months to research, or years to simmer and season in my memory and my heart, before I could bear to write it down. I write better than I did, say, a year ago, but I still don't write as well as I want to, and I probably never will.

Sometimes I struggle with writing. I'd rather play music. I become tired of the tyranny of words, and I know that music is a more universal language than writing. People can't hear my writing unless they sit down and read it, and they can't understand it if they don't read English. Yet, I love to write. If I couldn't write, I'd feel all stopped up, like a violin stuffed with cotton.

You may not like to write at all, or maybe you do. What I'm wondering is, how did you learn? And do you feel like singing?

Sharing Ideas

- I'm interested in Carolyn's statement: "I think many people learn to write by studying, and loving, something else." It surprised me a little and made me think about my own writing past. What do you think? Has anything like that happened to you? How did you come to writing?

- How might composing music be similar to composing in words? Are there any other comparisons for composing that might help you understand your own process of developing written texts? For instance, I've read articles about "composing a life," and we all know artists talk about composing a painting. How do you define or see composing, and what does the term composing mean to you?

- Carolyn ends with a list of contradictions, explaining that she learns from sharing and from not sharing, from criticism and from praise, from writing and from not writing. Have you experienced some of these writer's contradictions? What do you make of them? Can you (or how can you, or—even—why should you) feel two or more ways about this activity called writing?

———————————

2

The History of My Struggle for a Clear Voice

Brad Usatch

Brad Usatch was a student at the University of Vermont when he wrote this essay.

One: Voice?

My Dad
and me like
to play baseball.
My Dad youstoo
play baseball.

This is the earliest recorded piece of my own creativity I could find. Punchy little fella, wasn't I? Kinda proud of my pop. When I was a kid there were things about my father that I thought were pretty neat. One was that he was recruited by the Brooklyn Dodgers, and the other was that he was Executive Vice President of M&T Bank. I probably wanted to write "My dad and me go to his offiss. My dad is the exekyootiv viseprezidint of MandT Bank."

My dad is no longer a baseball player. My dad is no longer Executive Vice President of M&T Bank. It's amazing that he always gets dragged into these conversations though.

Anyway, the point of looking at this writing is to notice how clear it is, even with its grammar and spelling imperfections. You can understand what I'm saying, and you can hear how it's being said.

13

And I think it's clear for a couple of reasons. First, it's a pretty simple idea. Second though, the effort I put into expressing the idea was focused only on stating it as clearly as possible. If suddenly you told me to write whatever's on my mind, the result would probably not be as clear or illuminating because, for some reason, I have a tendency now to try to be a writer, instead of trying just to write. I believe that most (probably all) good writers are conscious of their voice: they make a tool of it. But I also believe that for most good writers there can be no voice other than the one they use.

A writer's voice is what it is. It might change over time, slowly, but not in just any direction the writer chooses for it. It expresses who the writer is at that moment. Just as Ansel Adams would make a lousy paparazzi photographer, George Will could never write like Erma Bombeck, not that he'd want to.

So much of what I write now is schlocky because I write things the way I would write them if I were a writer. I try to be clever. Blech. I hate clever people. That's why I hate just about everything I write. And just because I'm aware of the problem, that doesn't mean I can reverse a lifelong trend and ignore all the subconscious devices I use to project who I want people to think I am, without divulging who I really am.

Wait, this gets worse: I think I am slowly becoming a better writer because I now realize that the person I want people to think I am is not the person that I see in my writing when I'm trying to project the person I think I want people to think I am.

This is relevant to a personal voice analysis because the only way I can imagine writing a personal voice analysis is to examine who I am in relationship to what I write.

Two: Neither Rhyme nor Reason

The Dancing Bear
Go to the circous and see dancing bear.
See one on a motercicle. See one hanging
in the air. See one dancing lighly see one
dancing free. I don't know about you but hope
he deosn't dance with me.

This poem is among the earliest pieces I could find of my own writing. It is a primitive attempt to instill meter into my voice, and as such, falls short of satisfying any notion of structural cohesion.

The title introduces the first component of what will be shown to be a recurring discontinuity, or at least uncertainty, in identifying the subject of the work. "The Dancing Bear" implies a certain, single dancing bear. The word "the" operates to select a specific example of *a* dancing bear. It is *the* dancing bear, *the* one I witness before me, *the* one I saw on TV last night, etcetera.

Then, in the first line of the poem, an ambiguity arises. The skeletal phrase "see dancing bear" leaves the reader hanging. Does the bear have a specific identity? Ambiguous? Yes. But the singular "bear" still implies strongly a particular bear, one witnessed at the circus, in fact. At this point we probably still feel confident in the particular bear assumption; we make a mental note of the oddity of the absent article and read on.

The next two sentences (one line plus one beat of the following) halt the reader in confusion. "One on a motercicle" (sic) opposed to "one hanging in the air" suggests at least two distinct bears. If I had been considering only one individual bear, why would I not have chosen to use it, or him, or her, or *the* bear riding on the motorcycle? This discontinuity must be the focus of further examination.

The following sentence is by far the weakest as a unit. There is an unfortunate misspelling of lightly, lacking the crucial "t" consonant. It is a bit of a run-on with no conjunction or punctuation separating the independent phrases. And finally, the content is insubstantial, lyrical, drivel—a shallow, unnecessary grasp for rhythm and melody does nothing to further the piece as a poetic study.

The concluding sentence brings us full circle in incongruity. "He" is a linguistic index finger pointing to a bear with an identity. I express that he, him, that one, that one that I have discussed, hope he doesn't dance with me. Thus the particular bear concept is solidly reintroduced to the poem. I'm afraid I've left some questions as to the scheme of my structure here.

The work is a fair, concise, and fresh attempt to enter the human versus nature genre. It accurately captures the irony of nature as harmless entertainment for the human, illusorily removed from nature, and nature as powerful manipulator of fate. Humans are mere components in a harmonious yet indifferent natural machine.

In all honesty, I believe that the sentences "See one dancing lightly. See one dancing free." are an omen of some of the problems that will arise in my later writing. Already, at age six or seven, I'm trying to be a poet. I'm not only setting up a twist; I'm going to make it rhyme.

I'm a victim of pop culture: MacArtist. If I played blues guitar, all my tunes would end up with one of those little guitar riffs that seem to end almost all blues songs. If I wrote a novel, it would begin "It was a dark and stormy night." And when I write a poem about a dancing bear, it ends "See one dancing lightly. See one dancing free. I don't know about you but hope he doesn't dance with me." I don't know about you, but I think I watched too much TV.

Believe it or not, the next piece of writing I kept was from here at the University of Vermont. I was a private kid, and I ripped up all my stuff before my parents posted it on the fridge. I kept my grades up in elementary school, so they let me get away with my little eccentricities. This shouldn't hinder my analysis since I'm sure that all my work between then and now would just show my attempts to sound like a writer at an increasing level of sophistication.

Three: Me, Wonderful Me

So, here's an early example of my adult voice. It's from Professor Howe's expository writing class. I got an A. Maybe you should talk to Prof Howe about his grading standards.

> On one of the more particularly lonely nights of my life I found myself climbing the ladder inside the housekeeping closet to the roof of Mason Hall. I had no purpose in mind. I wasn't trying to sort anything out, find any great answers or solve any great problems. But there I was on the roof. The logic of a lonely person isolating himself for comfort wasn't clear to me, but I knew that if I were downtown, swimming in people, I would still be alone.
>
> In the darkness I found my way to the edge of the roof and sat and dangled my feet over it. The wind was blowing hard from the Northeast. Although it was April, the air smelled like October. There's a certain kind of wind that always blows a cool Autumn scent. I wish I could find its source. Somewhere northeast of everywhere I've ever been I imagine there's a place that always smells like Fall. It's the odor of dry leaves, the first frost, the rekindling of dormant fireplaces, high school bonfires, and homecoming football games.

Yuck. See what I mean. My voice? It does not exist. This sounds like a soliloquy in a very important, made-for-TV-movie, about the traumas of young adulthood, starring Robbie Benson and Valerie Bertinelli. Perfect. Just what I wanted. It could be *Magnum P.I.*, or Walt Whitman or The Who, but it ain't me.

The direction of the wind, and the smell, and the reminiscences of better times—it's all cliché. I obviously tried to reinvent the most abused literary icons. "Although it was April, the air smelled like October." I guess that's not so horrible, but I should have left it alone. Instead, I felt inclined to embellish the thought with the ostensibly meaningful meditations of me, wonderful me, just to show what a deep, literary guy I am. My voice here is the voice of some cheesy freshman trying real hard to be Robert Penn Warren and failing miserably. Next.

Next is an example of a paper that is actually about something other than just what's on my mind at the time. This paper also is from my freshman year, Spring semester. It was written for an American literature class with Professor Cochran.

> Since industrialization began in the United States, authors have been exploring the possibilities of how the "American dream" can conflict with the personal dreams of the people caught up in it. In "Death of a Travelling Salesman" by Eudora Welty, and *Death of a Salesman* by Arthur Miller, the respective authors have chosen to use a travelling salesman to represent a good, honest American whom we can all sympathize with and who is overtaken by his own concept of success and the American dream. In both stories, the tragedy lies not in the fact that both men die without having realized their goals, but instead in that the very goals they surrendered themselves to accomplishing misguided them into death.

I actually like this. Grammatically and structurally it's very clumsy. But I could edit this without changing the ideas or their order, and it could be a pretty good opening paragraph.

I'll speculate that the reason it is uncharacteristically free of schlock is that for me, it was just another academic paper. If I had any sense that this would some day be evaluated on its artistic merit, I would have injected it with some of the instant art that I use in all my consciously creative endeavors.

The paper is unpolished and on onionskin, so I'm sure I wrote it the night before it was due. (Incidentally, I got an A on this one too. Maybe I should have been an English major.) The point is that I viewed the assignment not as Writing, but as writing. "Oh shit, is that stupid English paper due tomorrow? I guess I better get it done." So with that in mind, I did it, and I tried only to state my case as clearly and concisely as possible. The result is much more agreeable than my nonacademic voice, or it could have been with a revision anyway.

The problem here is that I would like to be able to write in a voice other than my academic one. I don't hear me talking in this paper. *But at least I don't hear me talking about me.* I guess what I like least of all in my present voice is that it sounds egoistic to me. My writing seems more focused on itself (whatever that means) than on what I'm writing about. My favorite paragraphs are the ones where I don't use "I."

Four: The More Things Change, The More They Stay The Same

It's funny that I stumbled across the piece for Professor Cochran that begins, "Since industrialization began in the United States. . . ."

because just last week I wrote a rough draft for a political science paper that begins, "Since the end of the era when philosophers and intellectuals undertook to support despotic rule. . . . " I wonder how many times I've used that opening construction. It's my prefab "since" intro. It's served me well. It allows me to get to the heart of the matter quickly, and my introduction isn't as obviously introductory, although it is more self-consciously so.

I don't think my academic voice has changed since Junior High. For assignments that I really don't care about, I can crank out a paper in a form so standard to me that I'm not even conscious of its components. I just do it.

As for my creative (if you will) voice, I'm constantly trying to analyze and change it, but I keep making the same mistakes. Does this sound familiar?

> It is frightening to hear the endless consequences of global warming. This is especially true when one considers that even the most forward-looking scientists will admit they can only imagine a few obvious effects of a warmer planet. It is frightening to realize that the warming trend has begun. It is frightening to consider the complexities involved in reversing the trend. It is frightening to see how far the human race is from undertaking the necessary measures as a matter of absolute urgency. It is depressing to see so clearly that we humans just don't care. We have finally lost touch with our world; so much so that people will mock me for sounding sentimental about it.

I knew when I wrote this that the repetition of "frightening" was a cheap device—me trying to sound stormy, I guess—but I left it in anyway. It really doesn't work, and I'm actually embarrassed that I used it. I suppose, in a way, the paragraph still accurately represents my thoughts. But that silly little writer's game I employed is so apparent, and draws so much attention to itself, that my point is weakened. No reader wants to pay attention to it. They see the repetition and they think, Yeah, yeah, nice gimmick. It is frightening, it is frightening, it is frightening, I get it, and they blow right through the paragraph because they don't want to deal with that crap, and why should they?

My written voice does not read the way I want it to sound. I know because when I read over my writing out loud, I come to words phrases where I have to stop and think, "There is no way any reader will interpret this, or pronounce this, or emphasize this the way I meant to write it."

In that same paper, I ended a rather despondent paragraph with "Stop the planet, I wanna get off." When I wrote that I thought that people (readers) would understand that I was conscious of "stop the planet, I wanna get off" as a catch phrase—something you see on bumperstickers. When I read it out loud I realized that I sounded like Erma Bombeck circa 1978. I think people in the classroom actually felt sorry for me for having made such a poor, desperate attempt to be clever. In my mind, I stated the phrase in a dry monotone. But I couldn't write it in a dry monotone.

I think one of the reasons sarcasm is so difficult on paper is because the more the writer hints at the fact that he/she is being sarcastic, the less the irony of the statement bites. When I'm verbally sarcastic, I don't need to leave clues of my sarcasm in the language itself. It can be communicated through vocal inflections or rolling my eyes. When I write, all I've got is the paper and the words and the punctuation. It's difficult to express a sarcastic point without being a total ham.

My voice isn't exactly what I want it to be. When my writing is working for me, I'm clear and conversational:

> What kills me, what really kills me, is that I have seen the weather changes in my own short lifetime. That's how quickly we are killing the planet. When I was young, I guess I'm thinking around seven or eight years old, summer meant sunshine, not haze, sunshine. (These days we don't distinguish between the two. We've actually weakened our definition of sunshine to accommodate the increasingly prevalent haze.)

It's not a big deal, but it's pretty clear. I'd rather be deep and poignant, but I seem to try too hard, and it ends up being a real mess on paper.

Now I'm at the point where my voice is finally becoming less self-conscious, perhaps consciously less self-conscious. The talky stuff seems to work better for me than the attempts I made at being a high-brow artiste. So that's what I'm concentrating on—just talking.

Sharing Ideas

- Both Brad and Carolyn mention talking *and* writing. Carolyn found that competitive speech helped her to organize her arguments. But Brad is looking at talk in a very different way. He seems to feel his speech is more authentically "him" than his written words. What do you see as the connection between speech and writing?

- Have you ever noticed yourself talking differently to different people and writing in different voices to different people?

- If you do change your speaking voice, do you change your writing voice in similar ways?

- Do you have some written voices you like better than others (for Brad at the time he wrote this paper, "natural-speech" writing was better than "high-brow artiste" writing)?

- Why do you think Brad is so critical of his own writing and his own voice? Do you ever find yourself saying similar things about your writing? Carolyn has gone through many changes as a writer too but seems more pleased with her developing voice, what do you think she would say to Brad about his essay?

- Have you ever reread your childhood (elementary and junior high school) writings? Are you (do you think you would be) pleased, surprised, alarmed, interested, and/or amused by what you find? Do you remember how you learned to write? Who praised you? Who and what discouraged you? Who and what helped you? Were there particular moments when things clicked and you felt your writing start to blossom?

———————————————

3

Changing as a Writer

Audrey Brown

Audrey Brown was a student at the University of Vermont when she wrote this essay.

I don't like to write.
I never did.
It always takes me a long time to get done.

—age 9

Eleven years later and I still feel this way. So what am I doing? I don't like my writing. I'm mad right now. I'm irritable. I just bit my sister's head off because she came in my room with an essay she wanted me to proofread. I always liked math. Maybe I should have been a math major. Math is good because it's straightforward and always either right or wrong. There's no emotional involvement with math. Writing, any kind of writing, drains me.

When writing, I have always felt that I am struggling with myself. The only reason I have continued to write is that once in a while I like what comes out. But I really don't want to write this paper that is supposed to trace the development of my voice. I've been sitting here for hours. Struggling. My brain is so jammed with all the possible ways to write this that I'm having trouble producing anything at all. Well, I have to write something, and analytical writing is a safe way to go, so. . . . I wrote my first descriptive piece when I was eight.

21

September 14, 1976
I like flowers. They smell nice. They are pretty.

I didn't take advantage of my youth and inexperience to write something off the wall here like "flowers are ugly" or something fantastic and imaginary like "the flowers are dancing." Although at the time, I'm sure I didn't even realize I had that option. I described flowers the way I saw them and the way I still see them. They *are* pretty and they *are* nice. Basic words for a basic subject.

Much of my writing actually reminds me a little of math. Don't take any chances, because if you take chances, you get the answer wrong. Just like math. Subject + verb + object = a sentence. $2 + 2 + 2 = 6$. Sometimes this strategy works well, as in the flower piece. Other times, this mathematical prose makes me sound very emotionless.

When I was nine my family had a dog named Tan. He was a great dog, and we all loved him a lot and were really upset when he disappeared during hunting season one year. But this is how I relayed the event in a school journal:

February 18, 1977
Last year my mother found a dog with no collar. We called some of our friends. The dog didn't belong to any of them. We had it on the radio but we couldn't find the owner. We kept him for a little while. One day in winter he didn't come home. We didn't see him the next day we didn't see him either. We never saw him again.

I never even mention being sad in this, but this lack of expressed emotion is typical of a lot of my writing.

Even when I was excited about something, I didn't express it well on paper. Having school cancelled because of bad weather was always a highlight of the school year. That fact is completely obscured by the following bit of writing:

January 1977
Yesterday morning about six-o-clock my father came in to see me before he went to work. He told me school was canceled. He said my mom was going to work but she wasn't. When I got up my friend called and I went to her house for a little while. We went outside for a little while and the snow was past my knees.

Believe it or not, I was very excited about that day, although there is not much evidence of that in my words. There's a sense of distance here between me and the reader. In all of my early writing I was very conscious of writing for some sort of audience. I can't quite identify who that audience was, but I know it never varied much, regardless of whether I was writing an analytical paper or a school journal or even a personal diary entry.

This mystery audience never knew me too well. I felt the need to identify the people I wrote about, to justify my beliefs or emotions, and to tie up any loose ends in my life's events. I think sometimes, mostly in the diary entries, the audience was myself. Not me as I was then, but as I would be in the future. I assumed, when writing, that in the future I wouldn't remember much of my past so I was careful to clearly explain everything. In the above passage, I was sure to say "my mom" and "my friend" instead of just "mom" and "Celina." I am careful not to confuse my audience by using a name without any explanation. This adds a touch of formality, of distance, to my writing.

In my final year of high school, I took a course in expository writing. I had intentionally put off taking this class, which I usually called the "dreaded Expo," until my senior year because I was terrified to take a class that was all about writing.

It turned out that the dreaded Expo wasn't really too bad. I actually liked the class, and I learned that writing is not *always* dreadful. I wrote some really good papers in that class and some really bad ones, too. But my absolute worst piece was the essay I wrote for my University of Vermont application.

One of our assignments for Expo was to write a practice essay for a college application. Since I had already sent in my UVM application, I just handed in a copy of the essay I had written. My teacher, not knowing I had actually sent in this essay, ripped it apart in front of the class, as an example of what *not* to write for a college essay. I was in tears the minute I left the classroom, convinced I would never get into college. Here's why:

> My main reason for wanting to attend this college is to expand my education and therefore develop a satisfying career.
>
> At this time, I have many interests, but no single outstanding interest. I would like to attend this college because of its wide range of areas that interest me both academically and socially. I hope that by attending this college I will be able to use its wide range of curriculum to develop a single strong interest . . . .

The subject of the essay was "why you want to go to this college and why you should be accepted." My teacher wrote four comments on my paper: "This is awfully *vague*," "vague," "such as?," and "repetitive and vague."

I think the reason I wrote such a "vague" essay was that I was uncomfortable writing about myself. There is a sense of discomfort in much of my writing. Even in my diary (I call it "the book" because I hate the word diary) where I write my most personal things, my words often sound stiff and contrived. My writing there is always controlled. Whenever I was mad or excited I would always express it in the size of my letters or with exclamation marks. In my life too, I tend to control my emotions, to hold a lot of my feelings inside: especially negative feelings. I don't express sadness very openly, and if I'm angry, the object of my anger rarely knows it, and I just hold it in until the feeling blows away.

Here is what I wrote in the book at age 11 about the traumatic death of a kitten. Don't laugh. People always laugh when they hear about this, but it's not funny, it's very sad.

> August 9, 1979
> Last night Wellington got killed. He was in the dryer when mom turned it on. At least he died fast and we can keep Mish.

When first considering what I would write about in this paper, I thought I might be able to get some good information from the book. I sat down and read the thing from cover to cover, entries from 1978 until 1989, although the entries in the last several years are few and far between. After all that reading, I felt I owed an entry. So this is what I wrote:

> November, 1989
> I have to write a paper on my personal voice—an analysis of it. So I just read this whole book hoping to get some good material but the whole thing is mostly the ravings of a lunatic.

And it is too. I really thought that the book would be the best place to see my true voice. But I'm having a hard time with that because in most of the book I am a stranger. Now I want to say that what I wrote was not my true voice, but how could it not be? I have mentally divided the book up into three categories: the obligation entries (including the death of the cat entry), the hate entries, and the high school entries. The obligation entries evolved somehow into hate entries like this one:

> February 23, 1979
> Today was terrible. I went to the Wheelers. I hate Dawn and Dawn hates me. There were these dumb girls there named Heather + Holly. Now my parents won't let us see "Hulk" on TV. My mom gets to see "Roots." Why can't we see "Hulk"? My braces don't hurt any more.

This series of unfortunate entries are probably the most emotional things I ever wrote. Even here though, it still sounds as if I am writing for someone other than myself. I say "*my* mom" rather than just "mom," and I'm careful in my attempt to define "Hulk" and

"Roots" as television shows with the use of quotation marks. Pretty academic considering the writing was completely personal.

The high school entries are unmentionable, and if I wasn't such a pack rat, I'd throw them out. I refuse to quote any of these entries, but this is what I wrote about them in May of 1989:

> I wonder if it's normal for almost this entire book to revolve around the male sex?. . . . Why not write about my friends or my family or school or my apartment or the sunset or my car or exercising or any other thing that is important to me. Writing might just not be for me—seems like pictures are better. . . .

My voice starts to change slightly during my senior year in high school. I became a little more present in my writing and started to relax a little. The following passage was written in a journal for an American Writers class:

Nov. 5, 1985
I really admire Thoreau for what he did about his taxes. . . . I respect and agree with Thoreau that he shouldn't pay his taxes when he doesn't agree with what they are for. I also know that if I was in the same situation, I wouldn't be able to do what he did. I would pay my taxes so that I wouldn't have to face the difficulties that not paying the tax would present. I'm not proud of that but I know that's what I would do.

The best paper that I wrote my senior year was called Oceanside. It was the first piece of writing that I actually remember feeling good about. The description was of a house on the Outer Banks of North Carolina that my family stayed in for two weeks one summer.

> The white and gold tiles on the kitchen floor are cool to the feet. The cupboard shelves are full of plates, glasses, mugs, bowls, and cooking utensils. The dishes from breakfast are stacked in the sink while the supper dishes still sit, sparkling clean and untouched in the dishwasher. Sand, collecting in the corners of the room, is hardly noticed and the broom and dustpan are left stationary in the corner. A note to all late sleepers says, "Gone to the beach. It's beautiful out!" The radio plays soft music from "Beach 95, F." A few smilie-faced magnets gaze cheerfully from the refrigerator door.

It's interesting that I do not physically exist in this paper even though the place I described was very special to me. I said that the tiles were cool to "the" feet, but they were really cool to *my* feet. It's as if this robotic eye is viewing the surroundings and putting the data down on paper. A note has been written but who is the author? Who is the reader? I suppose the reader must be the same person who is listening to the radio and I suppose that person is me, but the magnets in this are more alive than I am.

Just last spring I wrote another memory description of a favorite place: Montmartre, in Paris. This is how I began my paper:

> I smile uncomfortably, shake my head and try to blend into the crowd, but I am stopped by a persistent hand on my elbow. I had made the mistake of looking a little too interested in this particular artist's charcoal portraits. "Come, sit. Let me draw you," he insists in a heavy French accent. I ask how much. Three hundred francs. I do some quick mental arithmetic; 300 francs equals 30 pounds, which equals about 40 or 45 dollars. I shake my head, more emphatically this time, and start to back away. "Okay, 200 francs. Just for you, 200 francs." But I really want to look around first, at the other artists. "No good," he says, "now 200 francs, if you leave, you have to pay 300. I am good. If you don't like it, you don't pay . . . huh? Where are you from? America! Ah, rich American, come . . . come on," he beckons. I look to my friend for help, but she just smiles and shrugs.
>
> I am tempted. Perhaps because I would like my portrait done, but it's more likely that I'm flattered because he is the first Parisian who had treated me with anything better than annoyed indifference.

This was scary for me to put myself so fully into that paper, but since then I've done it more and more. I'm realizing that it's OK to be expressive and emotional in writing. And in person too. If I could write poems I would. Lots of times when something really strikes me, I want to write a poem or draw something to convey how I feel. But if I ever start doing that, some more rational part of me springs out, and I tear up the paper.

Last weekend I did something weird. On Saturday morning I went with Nancy to Swanton to see a fortuneteller. The fortune-teller is an elderly Abenake Indian woman. She is very poor and living in a run-down house behind a block of warehouses, with nothing but trailers for neighboring houses. We each paid $15 for her to read us through a regular deck of cards. Don't conjure up an image of her as a gypsy-type with a crystal ball in front of her; she's very normal looking, and we sat at her kitchen table with the breakfast leftovers still on it.

Nancy went first and got a pretty accurate reading. Then I went. Now, I don't necessarily believe in everything she said to me, but I don't not believe it either. You see, she's not really a fortune-teller, but more of a present-teller. Either way, it was pretty amazing. This woman told me things about my life that there is no way she could have known because she didn't even know my name when I went in to see her. She started my reading by talking about—of all things—

men. She described my relationship with my old boyfriend to a tee and told me that he was BAD for me (which I had already discovered), and I should send him to "you know where" (which I have already done), but reinforcement is always good.

She described my brother as a devil but a good devil (which he is) and saw a lot of darkness around my sister (which there is). She asked me why I stopped playing the flute (which I did) and told me I should start again (something I have considered). She told me that whatever is bothering my mother is not my fault (it's not) and that I shouldn't be worried because everything will be OK.

What made me angry was coming home from Swanton and being very excited about what had happened and telling another roommate some of the things the woman said and having him say, scornfully—well of course she just made an easy guess—or something to that effect. Why can't people believe in things that are a little stranger than normal? Why does everything have to be so rational all the time? Life is interesting because of things that are magical and strange and unusual and really beautiful or really ugly, and it upsets me when people say That's stupid or That's weird and turn up their noses.

I think in this country, and in a lot of other places, people are often raised thinking it is bad to be emotional. If you feel something or write something or say something that veers away from the traditional, then you are making a big commitment to being "radical" like that and setting yourself up for criticism. The reason I struggle with my writing is because what I write is usually not exactly what I feel. Instead, it is what I feel is a proper presentation of what I feel. It's the same thing as smiling when someone asks you how you are and just saying Good, thanks, when you are actually feeling lousy or even when you are feeling really great.

I have done a lot of growing up in the past few years, and my writing has grown with me. I have become a much more outgoing and expressive person. I am happier and more comfortable with myself, and my writing shows this. In fact, just the other day, I wrote a poem. And I didn't tear it up.

Sharing Ideas

- Audrey talks about different attitudes she has toward numbers and words. Sometimes I hear individuals talking about themselves as number people or word people. Is that distinction meaningful to or necessary for you? What do you mean when you make it?

- Have you ever found yourself in Audrey's situation, keeping your emotions out of your paper? Why did you do that? Were you worried, as she was, about your audience? Did you use any of the same techniques—passive voice, avoidance of first person, the robotic, reporting eye? Did you use any other techniques?

- Brad and Audrey talk about their great struggles to achieve a personally satisfying writer's voice; still, I think their essays certainly sound like someone talking to someone else. Can you describe their voices? How do they strike you? Who do you think they imagined as the audience for their pieces? Why?

- In Audrey's essay, what do you think about her visit to the fortune-teller and her thoughts about emotion and writing?

- I noticed that Carolyn and Audrey mention the importance journal writing had for them as they traveled to other countries and experienced different cultures. Have you had similar experiences? Have you kept a journal? With what results?

- It seems to me that each of these three quite different writers has particular goals for his or her writing. By talking about those goals, as you see them, can you discover anything about your own writing goals?

———————————

Part II

Changing the Writing Classroom

Part of your life story as a writer will include stories of your previous writing classrooms. In the next four essays, Donald McAndrew, Eleanor Kutz, Kate Ronald, and Jim Strickland describe several new versions of college writing classrooms. These classes often feel different from your high school classrooms, and they are also often different from college writing classrooms of the past. For instance, Don McAndrew uses new writing theories and activities to develop a community where students are key players; they are expected to help construct their own knowledge through active participation.

Eleanor Kutz talks about what you already bring to the college writing classroom—your own fluency with language. She shows how one student, Dana, grew into the new language demands of his college writing community. Next, Kate Ronald helps you understand writing teachers—their beliefs and their practices—because teachers' motives can sometimes seem mixed or confusing to students. Kate discusses the history of the field of composition and rhetoric and explains how college writing classes came to be what they are today.

In his essay, Jim Strickland introduces you to computer writing classrooms. If you are already a computer composer, you'll find some insights and hints for computer use as you study writing. If you are just starting to use computers as you compose, Jim will tell you what you can and can't expect from this new medium, showing why you still need to rely on your peers in the computer classroom as it becomes a place for community meetings.

All four authors emphasize an important point: you and your classmates are essential because *you* make the new writing classroom work. Certainly, the writing you do at home is important and is tremendously powerful, but these essays describe the benefits of sharing your work with others. Classroom communities allow you to articulate and test your ideas and to explore and revise your thinking. Often you collaborate with peer writers, and sometimes you even co-author and develop texts together. We hope to show you that college writing classrooms these days can be very exciting places indeed.

4

That Isn't What We Did in High School: Big Changes in the Teaching of Writing

Donald A. McAndrew

Donald A. McAndrew spends his work days teaching college
and secondary teachers of English at Indiana University of
Pennsylvania, about an hour northeast of Pittsburgh. He
spends his play days bicycling, gardening, watching the Pirates
play baseball, listening to classical music and jazz, reading,
lifting weights, driving his little, red sports car through
the hills, enjoying his wife's cooking, and teasing his three
teenagers until they scream. On both work days and play days
he writes about improving the teaching of writing, literature,
and reading in secondary schools and colleges.

When I sat down to start playing with this essay, I decided to write it
directly to the students I have now—Diane, Shelley, and Lori; Eric
and Darin; Julie, Leigh, and Ed; Dwight and Will and Chuck—to see
them sitting there, me flopped in a student desk, sipping hot black
coffee, gabbing about writing and the teaching of writing. I guess it's
fair to say that this piece is dedicated to those students—they are the
ones who asked the questions that got me thinking about how our
class was different from their high school English classes. In fact, as

you'll see below, I quote directly from written answers and comments they gave to questions I asked about our class. So, this essay will be both to them and from them, a testament to their risking tough questions and to their insights in helping us all find answers.

On the first day of our writing class, I pass out a course overview sheet, which shows what we will do in terms of work and grades. It doesn't take long for my students to realize that this course is going to be really different from what they expect. They expect a rerun of Grade 12 English, just a little tougher; after all, this is college. Well, very quickly they realize they are wrong—this course isn't going to be much like high school English, or at least most high school English courses. Here they will choose their own topics to write about. They will draft and revise in class. They will work with other students who will read their drafts and try to help improve them, and they will meet one-to-one with me to talk about their developing drafts. They will read what they decide they need to read to help with their pieces of writing and with their growth as a writer. They will turn in only their best papers for grades, and they will have a say in that grade. Here there won't be tests, lectures, raising hands, desks in rows, and a teacher up front. But there will be portfolios, peer response, talk, movement, groups, conferences, and everybody, including the teacher, writing things that are important to them, sharing those pieces for feedback and revision. This is different from most high schools, oh, yeah.

In what follows, I show you some of the differences you might see in a writing class that is taught like ours, taught as current theory and research on teaching writing would tell teachers to teach. I do this by letting you hear the voices of my students reporting on life in our class. After that, I also explain why our class is taught as it is—the theory and research that is the basis for the new writing class that many of you will experience. So, let me start by showing you some of the things my students saw as different from English classes in high school.

Differences from Previous English Classes

Atmosphere of the Class

Students frequently told me that the biggest difference they saw between their high school classes and our class was that the atmosphere was more "relaxed and comfortable" and "wasn't as tense." As a couple of students said, "it's not a sit-down-and-shut-up class" or a "sit, listen and take notes class." Many also reported that there was "a ton more interaction between the students" than there had been in their high school classes.

Class Activities

Students characterized the activities of their high school English classes as centered on analyzing literature, test taking, and grammar. Most often they mentioned literature, saying that they "read plays, learned about the different ages in history, and read certain works from these ages." After reading, the teacher "stood in front of the class telling us the acceptable interpretations." Next most often they mentioned studying "pieces of English like vocabulary, grammar, and punctuation" and "taking objective tests on trivial facts that I memorized and repeated on the test." Finally, they mentioned doing some writing, but explained that "the teacher was more concerned with grammar, fragments, commas, etc., rather than really what was in the paper."

In our class, whatever reading was done, whether literature or anything else, was decided on by each individual writer because of a need they felt based on a piece of writing they were working on. In our class, we never study the pieces of English, only the wholes, like pieces of student writing or pieces written by professionals or previous students. And in our class, I'm concerned mostly with what is in the paper, its ideas and content, not fragments and commas.

Writing Assignments

In high school, students told me that "the teacher controlled the topic" and that "you had to write about what the teacher wanted which was usually about a book we had to read" or "something you didn't know much about." Even the topics concerning the book were "very regimented." In our class, students told me they felt that they "could write about what you feel like writing about and this is good because it forces you to really know what you are talking about." One student explained it this way: "I have to write about topics of known interest to me because, if I'm not interested in the topic, my paper usually isn't my best work." Other students reported that writing about topics that they chose helped them to "expand on your own individual ideas" and "to be able to explore my own writing more."

Students also reported that their high school teachers controlled the form of their pieces of writing by requiring papers "always in the same style and always five paragraphs." In our class, the form of the writing and its length are decided by the writer. Also, students reported that in our class they just flat out did more writing, lots more. In high school they "didn't do much writing at all" except for "maybe a few stories and poems and essays about literature." In our class, they "get *a lot* of practice writing and revising everyday."

Response and Revision

My students reported that in high school they "wrote and revised by myself and turned it in to the teacher for her feedback." They also reported that "it was rare that students read and responded to each other's papers; only the teacher did that." They found this system of response to be inadequate, complaining that "there was no second chance to revise or rewrite a paper; so you couldn't learn from your mistakes." In our class, as you've probably already guessed, we did things differently. While writers were working on pieces, they could ask me or peers for a response. They found the one-to-one conferences with me valuable; they gave them "help when it was needed" during the process of writing the piece, helping the writers see "ways to better their work" and "what we could do to improve them." Students found response from peers equally valuable, stating that it was "beneficial to have your peers read and criticize your paper" because writers are "simply too involved to realize an error or another route to take" and because "being able to read other students' writings is a good way to see and compare the way they write with the way you write."

Outcomes and Improvements

Students reported that they felt "more comfortable to express themselves" and that comfort "helped you become more of an individual" and that "by writing freely on topics of our own choice, we are learning about ourselves." Students also thought that the frequent interaction between peers "taught me a lot about other people" and gave them "respect for the opinions of others and showed me how to handle them in a mature and respectable way." Others reported that the peer interaction taught them "to be a little more outgoing," "helped us make friends," and "gave me a sense of belonging."

In addition to these personal effects, students also reported that our course had effects on their growth as writers. They reported that writing "was not so intimidating"; so they "became more interested in it" and "put more effort into it." They realized that "it's what goes in the paper, thoughts and feelings, that are most important" and that they can "set aside worries about grammar and spelling and get my ideas on paper instead." They realized "the importance of receiving feedback and revising more than once or twice."

Theory and Research Behind Our Writing Class

One of the most important things for you to realize about our class is that it is well grounded in the latest understandings about how teachers *can best teach students to be better writers*. I like to think of our class as our construction of a state-of-the-art writing class. Your college writing class will not be exactly like our class, but you will see many parallels because your class and our class are grounded in the same body of theory and research, state-of-the-art theory and research, if you will. In what follows, I give you an overview of that theory and research so you'll see that we have powerful reasons for the things we do in our class. Then I close by tying that theory and research back to specific features of our class, showing you the theory and research behind a couple of activities that are at the heart of teaching and learning writing.

Social Constructionists

When I think of the theorists and researchers who support our writing class, I think of three groups, each with a fancy name and all overlapping each other a bit. The first group of theorists and researchers are called "social constructionists." These people are probably at the center of current understandings about how writing works and about how people learn to use it. As their name suggests, they are concerned about two issues—society and construction.

With "social" they hope to emphasize the fact that language is a phenomenon of societies, created by them and serving them. Language exists at a social level as speakers/listeners and writers/readers communicate. All language use occurs in a social world, among language users. Even when we sit alone writing at our desk, we are constantly thinking of the people we are writing to, the people whose previous writing we have read, and the people we have talked to. We are always in society.

By "constructionist" this group hopes to stress that language, and society itself for that matter, are constructed by humans. This constructionist belief also extends to what society does with its constructed language—it constructs communication, meaning, knowledge. We make our own personal understanding in language, either speech or writing, and share it with others as they listen or read. From this sharing of our individual understandings, we construct still more complex knowledge, both as individuals and as groups. Social constructionists believe we are simultaneously both individual and social, individuals-in-society, and that we build our knowledge and beliefs as a result of our lives and language as individuals-in-society. Knowledge is something we build, we create; knowledge is a social construction. That means that there is no knowledge "out there"; it is only "in here"—in the mind of social beings constructing it through language, not in textbooks, not in libraries. When you learn, you are not taking something from "out there" and stuffing it "in here." Rather you are building, creating, constructing it as an individual-in-society.

Participationists.

The second group of theorists and researchers behind the new writing class is the one I call "participationists." This group stresses that to know something, to have knowledge, means to participate in its making, constructing through language, reading, writing, and talking to others who are also participating in making knowledge. Participation is the key—being active, doing it, joining in history, accounting, nursing, sociology as a language user. For example, a discipline like biology is not in the biology textbook, something objective and outside people; rather biology is what participating biologists say it is as they use language in a community of other biologists to construct their discipline of biology. The biology textbook is just one person's construction of her understanding of the field of biology in written language. Others will read it, talk about it, and write about it. She will read, talk, and write about what they say. And it is this participation in the language interaction of these individuals-in-society that creates biology as a field of study.

Think about schools and classrooms. Participationists say that teachers can't give you knowledge; you have to make it by participating in language activities. Just as biologists have to make biology by reading, writing, and talking, by participating in the discipline of biology, so too you must participate in the language of your classes. Your General Psychology class is just that—yours; you construct it by reading, discussing, writing, in a group of others who are also making their General Psychology. It is the "-ing" on "making" that is important—the process and activity of making. Knowledge is an action—in this case a participation in the languaging of a certain subject. During language participation in psych class, all members, students and teacher, create General Psychology—it is a social construction made through participation in language.

Socio-psycholinguists.

The third group of theorists and researchers who support our writing class are the "socio-psycholinguists." Where the social constructionists look at our world generally—society, knowledge, language—and participationists look at knowledge and language, socio-psycholinguists look specifically at language, trying to form the big picture of how language works. Many have studied reading/writing, and it is these people who give us a lot of support for what we do in our class. Socio-psycholinguists have demonstrated that reading and writing are processes by which we make meaning—writers construct their own meaning and readers construct their own meaning, both actively building the meaning we commonly think of as "in the print" when, in reality, meaning is in writers and readers, in people not ink on the page. Writers and readers bring their prior knowledge of the world and language to bear on the new language event as they make their meaning based on this prior knowledge.

Socio-psycholinguists also remind us that reading and writing are a social action, always involving others. Here they echo the social constructionists and participationists I described above. They also emphasize the significance of context, the environment in which language use occurs, showing us that all language is inextricably tied to its context. The word STOP is a lot different on a road sign than it is in a magazine advertisement; the context in which the word occurs really gives much of its meaning. They demonstrate that real writing and reading only exist in real contexts, the natural and complex events of whole language at work among a group of languagers.

And finally, socio-psycholinguists emphasize how important risk-taking and ownership are in improving reading and writing. They argue that learners must feel comfortable enough to risk making a mistake because this is the only way to learn; without risk there is little important learning. They also argue how important ownership is in improving writing and reading. Writers and readers must feel as if they own the meanings they make; they should not feel that they are forced to make a meaning someone else wants. The class focus should always be their piece of writing, written their way, and their response to reading, constructed as their prior knowledge tells them.

A Final Look at Our Class

Above I showed you two things about our class: first, a portrait of our class based on how my students reported it was different from the classes they had in high school and, second, some of the theory and research that supports our class. Now let me try to draw these two together by explaining how the theory and research specifically supports two activities at the heart of our class.

In our class peers frequently respond to each other's drafts. Why is this a good thing to do based on our state-of-the-art theory and research? Peer response creates a mini-social constructionist world. Writing is social because you share it with other students and you may even have them in mind while you write. You, in turn, read their writing. All of this is done with much talk about your construction of ideas as peers have constructed it while reading your piece. Everyone is participating in making meaning while they write and while they read the writing of others. You and your peer responder make your meanings based on your previous experience of life and language. The class becomes a group of writers and responders, all writing and responding to the meanings constructed. The teacher also joins in the process of writing and responding, focusing on meaning as the highest priority and creating a comfortable atmosphere where risk-taking is easy. I hope you hear the echoes of the theory and research I described above: "mini-social constructionist world," "participating in the construction of meaning as the highest priority," and "comfortable atmosphere for risk-taking."

Let me show you another example. In our class, students write mostly about self-selected topics. How is this grounded in state-of-the-art theory and research? Since prior knowledge of the world and language is the starting place for all language and learning, as socio-psycholinguists explain, then choosing your own topics, forms, and lengths seems like the perfect place to begin improving your writing. Your prior knowledge is at the center. This creates a context for class writing that is more like real, authentic writing—you write about what you know and value. From the outset of each piece you have almost total ownership of ideas, form, and the processes of your writing. Since the atmosphere is relaxed and comfortable making risk-taking easy, and since you are writing about topics and in forms that you know about and are interested in, participation in the life of the class happens naturally. You become an active participant in the construction of your improvement as a writer, something that participationists tell us is essential to knowledge, to knowing how to write well. Again, listen to the echoes of theory and research: "prior knowledge of language and the world," "participation in natural context," and "ownership of ideas, forms, and processes."

I hope that the two examples of peer groups and self-selected topics show you that our class is firmly grounded in state-of-the-art theory and research. Remember this, especially when your writing class is doing things that seem different from many of the things you did in high school. When your writing class shows some of the features I've talked about, be glad because you're getting your money's worth for your tuition. Be glad also because you have a great chance to improve your writing ability, and that's what a first-year college writing course is all about.

Sharing Ideas

- What did you read and write about in high school? Do you agree with Don's students that your classes focused more on the form than the content of your writing?

- Did you ever have two writing teachers who took very different approaches? Tell the stories of those two classes.

- Do you agree with Don that reading in a writing class should be done *for* the writer's own purposes and that a writer should pick his or her own topics? Why or why not? What does that mean for you as a writer? How do you go about finding your own readings and topics?

- Before your current writing class, did you ever share your work with peers? How did that work? List some ways you could have made the sharing more successful.

- When you're sitting by yourself writing, what are the influences you feel? Do you agree with the social constructionists that you aren't writing alone? To what degree are you remembering other writers and teachers or things you've read and friends you've talked to about your writing?

- Try writing two descriptive scenes. In one, you're composing alone (what does the place look like, what are you doing, what in particular are you eating, listening to, feeling, thinking, etc.). In one, you're composing—or talking about composing—with others (who is there, what is each person saying and doing? How do you feel, what do you see, notice, or need?). Rereading each descriptive scene, how are you a different (more or less successful) writer in each scene?

- If you've never before thought of yourself as a participationist, what does that mean for how you act in the classroom, particularly the writing classroom? If you're shy, what might you do? If you're confused, what might you do? If you're not shy at all, how as a class member can you help those who are shy or confused?

- Now that you've thought about this new type of classroom, think of your strengths as a writer and as a class member. Explain what you contribute.

5

Must I Watch My Language?
Linguistic Knowledge
and the Writer

Eleanor Kutz

An English professor at the University of Massachusetts/
Boston, Eleanor Kutz teaches courses in composition and linguistics. She is especially interested in the ways schools
shape people's attitudes toward language and literacy and in
the ways these attitudes reinforce relationships of power and
social class in American society. She works with teachers, and
with students preparing to teach, to develop new approaches to
studying literature, writing and language that show how all
aspects of literacy are connected. She and Hephzibah Roskelley
have written a book about teaching English, *An Unquiet Pedagogy*. And she has written a book about composition, *The
Discovery of Competence*, with two other colleagues, Suzy Gro-
den and Vivian Zamel.

Now you're in a college composition class—perhaps a little apprehen-
sive, perhaps confident about your writing. You've done some writing
in high school—book reports, research papers, essays about literature.
You've probably studied a handbook or grammar book that guided you
through topics like subject–verb agreement and rules for using semicolons. When you've broken these rules in a paper, your error has been
marked by the teacher, most often in red, and sometimes with a note

40

giving the pages in your grammar book that explain that type of error. It's likely that you've come to see good writing, at least in part, as linked to a knowledge of those grammar book rules.

Your college composition class will focus on new concerns. In other essays in this book you're reading about the composing process, about how to become fluent and imaginative as a writer, about how to communicate effectively and respond to the needs of different audiences, about when to invent and when to edit. But there may still be a voice in your head that makes you hesitate before you put that first word on the page, that leaves you overly concerned about getting each sentence, each paragraph, each word right, with making sure you don't break any rules—the grammar book voice that keeps warning you to watch your language, to watch out for errors like split infinitives or dangling modifiers.

The knowledge about language that you need as a writer, however, isn't just the rules of the grammar book, and it is very difficult to gain that knowledge by memorizing or doing exercises or watching out for errors. You have been acquiring grammatical knowledge and a knowledge of how to adapt to different styles of language use in different settings unconsciously, since childhood. Writing seems different enough from speaking to demand a new attention to rules (and certain rules like those for spelling and punctuation are needed only for writing). But most of the linguistic knowledge you will need in the writing classroom is really an understanding of the ways in which people in this particular community use language— a kind of knowledge that's best acquired by participating in the community.

To help you silence the grammar book voice, at least until you're ready to edit what you've written, let me describe for you the kinds of linguistic knowledge that you already have and that you can rely on as you enter this new community. I use as an example the work of one of my own freshman students, Dana, from the first session of our composition class.

Like most of the other students, Dana enters the classroom talking to those who walk in with him, questioning other students who take seats near him to find out what they know about the teacher and the course, and perhaps joking a bit about the cafeteria food or the crowded commuter bus. He comes with some expectations about the course—perhaps that it will be hard, that it will help him to do the kind of writing that will be expected in his college classes, that it will review grammar, so that he can finally learn to get things right, or perhaps that it won't really teach him much of anything that he doesn't already know. He also comes with some knowledge of himself as a writer—how he writes (he knows that he procrastinates and does most of his writing in a rush just before a paper is due) and what others, particularly former teachers, have thought of his writing. Whatever he is thinking about the course and about himself in relation to it, his style changes when the class starts and I call on him directly. Suddenly he becomes self-conscious about how he speaks, conscious of the constructions he uses. He too hears the grammar book voice and thinks: This is an English class—I'd better watch my language.

But the class seems peculiar, different from what he expected. Instead of being told to write, the students are asked to talk to each other, to introduce themselves, to find out about each other's interests, and to think about the stories that they tell with their families and friends, the stories that help define who they are and what they think. They'll tell one of these stories to the class in the next meeting.

Dana tells a story about the time his brother smashed up his father's truck. As Dana talks, his classmates nod knowingly or laugh. They ask questions about whether his brother was punished, and they respond with driving mistakes of their own. As they go on sharing stories and responses, they begin to build a community, in the classroom, of people who can share common references "like Dana's brother and the truck," and a common vocabulary, repeating a term Dana uses: "the ultimate hard ass." They develop a sense of how long a turn they can take and keep their listeners' attention, of when it's OK to interrupt the speaker, of how to let the others know when they've just paused to think, or that their story has ended. They do the things people always do when they enter a new discourse community, a community that is held together by the things its members talk about and the ways they talk—their conventions of style, their patterns for taking turns. When they go on to a new discourse community—a more formal classroom where the teacher isn't "Ellie" but "Professor Walsh," who determines the length of turns by asking questions and calling on students for responses, they will acquire the style of that community, just as they'll shift again when they're out with their friends Friday night.

Some discourse communities are small and rather temporary, like this class. Others are more permanent and retain common characteristics over a long time—churches, families, the advertising world, the legal profession, the academic world of colleges and universities. Dana comes into this classroom, and into the larger "academic discourse community" that the college classroom is part of, with a large repertoire of ways of using language that he has learned from other discourse communities—beginning with his family. Like all children, he grew up as a competent language user in his own community, simply by being around other language users and being spoken to, without any conscious knowledge of rules of language or grammar. If he feels hesitant and uncertain as he enters his freshman classroom, it is not because he lacks grammar. But gaining a conscious, as well as unconscious, understanding of what he knows might help him to define the task of becoming a college writer.

The Acquisition of Language

There are two sets of rules that Dana acquired unconsciously with his native language: those governing structure and those governing use. The first refers to formal grammar of the language, like the fact that questions can be formed in English by inverting the subject and verb ("Are you going?") or that one way of forming a past tense is to add "-ed" to the stem of a verb ("She walked"). The grammatical structure of English is usually described in terms of its sounds (phonology), its words and components of words (morphology), and the ways these words are put together in sentences (syntax). Native speakers of a language learn its grammar unconsciously as children, and adult native speakers of a language can make accurate judgments of whether virtually any sentence they hear is grammatical. (Without any formal study of grammar, speakers of English know that "The old man was wearing a hat" is grammatical and that "wearing was man old hat the" is not.)

So all language is governed by grammatical rules. However, the speakers of a language are largely unconscious of the rules, and even linguists have difficulty describing many of them. Dana has learned some of these rules in school, and when he and his classmates begin to transcribe tape recordings of their stories, they are dismayed to discover that they don't speak in complete grammar book sentences with no "errors." They comment that "while telling a story a lot of the sentences are improper, and if you were to write them down they would be incorrect" or that "the grammar in my tape was not too good, and it probably wasn't good in anybody's."

Of course, some of what Dana finds wrong here comes from his transferring expectations about written language to spoken language. But a lot of what we teach as school grammar, derived from the rules of Latin and somewhat wrongly applied to English, just doesn't offer a very accurate description of the language and how it works. To describe English or any language as it actually functions, and to locate some of the rules of a language, linguists try out sentences on native speakers. If the sentence makes sense to the speaker, the linguist sees it as grammatical—an acceptable sentence in the grammar of the language. In fact, if native speakers of a language use a construction and it makes sense to listeners, it cannot be ungrammatical. Dana may have been taught by his mother not to say "ain't" or have learned the street chant: Don't say ain't or your mother will faint and your father will fall in a bucket of paint. But to the linguist, the fact that "ain't" is used and understood in ordinary communication makes it grammatical. All language as it is used for communication is grammatical; that is, it is governed by regular rules that allow speakers to generate acceptable, understandable sentences.

But not all constructions are acceptable in all social circumstances. While "ain't," as a construction used frequently by native speakers of English and understood by their listeners, is entirely grammatical, it is considered unacceptable in some social contexts. And so there is a second set of rules that learners acquire about language—rules for how language is used in varying social contexts—like what sort of greeting to give to a stranger versus a family member or what words one shouldn't say in front of Grandma, and these rules are learned by using language in those contexts. The term "language acquisition" is used to describe the process by which a child like Dana develops competence in his native language, competence in the grammatical structures of the language, and also in knowing how to use the language in particular situations.

The linguist Noam Chomsky believes that our brains are structured with much language competence built in, waiting to be activated through use in communication. But while much of our potential linguistic competence may be innate, this potential isn't realized unless we are actually involved, through our early years, in communication with those around us. A well-known movie by Francois Truffaut, *The Wild Child*, tells the story of one documented case of a feral child who had somehow survived in the woods without human contact—perhaps nurtured by wolves or other animals. This child, like others deprived of any contact with human language during the critical early childhood years, could learn vocabulary but did not develop a full repertoire of syntactic structures and could not speak in fully formed sentences.

It seems then, that we are born with an innate grammatical potential but that the potential is activated and expanded by actual use. Those structures that are part of the child's native language are activated and confirmed as others talk to the child, and they become part of the child's underlying language competence. Of course all of this happens without any formal learning of rules, and Dana learned most of the rules for the grammatical structures of English before he started school.

All the while, because he was hearing real speech in ordinary family and community and school contexts, Dana also inferred the rules for how to actually use this language in these contexts. He came quickly to understand that his teacher must be addressed formally (as

"Mrs. Brown") in the classroom, but if the teacher happened also to be a family friend, Dana probably called her "Teresa" or even "Aunt Teresa" on the street. He knew that if "Aunt Teresa" was talking to his younger brother, he could get her attention by jumping right into the conversation, but if she was talking to his parents he would have to wait for a pause, not interrupt, and insert himself politely if he wanted to be heard. So Dana, like all children, gained communicative competence—the ability to use language effectively in his real world, along with grammatical competence—naturally and unconsciously.

In Dana's family, several things would most likely have happened to support his linguistic development: (1) Conversations would have taken place in a familiar context and would draw on Dana's knowledge of the world around him—on the characters of Sesame Street or the foods in the refrigerator. (2) Adults or older siblings would have facilitated Dana's entrance into this language community, often by asking questions: "Is that Kermit?" or interpreting meanings: "Dana said he doesn't like Grover." (3) Conversations would have focused on the subject, not on the rules of language or the forms that Dana was using. If he said, "Me want juice," his father wouldn't have said, "Wrong. *I* is the pronoun to use for the subject of a sentence," but would simply have poured some juice or added "Do you want juice in your Grover cup?" Dana's parents probably responded with praise and delight to their child's expanding linguistic ability, focusing always on meaningful communication.

Language Acquisition and the Freshman Composition Classroom

What does his childhood experience have to do with Dana as a freshman writer? Two things. Like the child who learned when to say "Mrs. Brown" and when to say "Aunt Teresa," Dana as an adult entering a new language community will perceive patterns in the language as it is used there, make generalizations about them, and try them out, until gradually he approximates the forms of language used by this community. He'll do this mostly without a conscious awareness of specific rules. His attention, like the child's, will be focused first on actually communicating within this community. This means that he will concentrate on getting his meaning across, but that he'll also infer the rules for being heard in this community and will quickly acquire the patterns that will get others to treat him as a member. He'll shift from the rules of one language community to those of another as he moves in and out of different settings. (A lot of this is like style of dress. Dana wears jeans to class, but he may wear a suit to an interview for a student internship at the local newspaper.)

As Dana tells his story to the freshman composition class, he is
supported in his movement into the community by the same things
that supported his earlier language acquisition—talk within a familiar
context where people come to share knowledge and extend each others'
ideas about particular subjects. Even in these early classes, Dana and
his classmates begin intuitively to build a common store of knowledge
and to ask questions and extend the talk around his story, focusing
always on the meaning of his words rather than on grammatical rules.

Let's see what we can tell from Dana's story. (I've presented it
with sequences of dots to show where he pauses, since there are no
punctuation marks in speaking.)

> The thing is you gotta know my father . . . he's the ultimate . . .
> ah . . . perfectionist . . . he . . . the person that like . . . ah . . . I heard
> you talking before that has a schedule of events of everything and
> wears like a tie to bed . . . he and . . . a . . . on the other hand my
> brother . . . if I may . . . ah . . . be so coarse . . . as to say . . . is the
> ultimate hard ass . . . and the thing is that I . . . I think is hilari-
> ous . . . no one else does . . . what my father did was he bought a
> brand new truck . . . one of those short Isuzu . . . ah . . . pick-ups
> and . . . ah . . . it was nice . . . it was shiny . . . and the thing is you
> got . . . you have to earn . . . you have to earn the respect from my
> father . . . I shouldn't say points or anything . . . but to be able to use
> it . . . and he was . . . and he used the truck . . . and he took it up
> a . . . ah . . . up a . . . one of those parking garages . . . yes . . . and
> how it went was . . . it goes up a ramp and curves around . . . like
> where it's gonna . . . and you park it and . . . ah . . . a funny thing
> was he didn't put the emergency brake on and it was in neutral
> and . . . ironic . . . it's funny because the truck rolled down the hill
> missing like . . . Jaguars . . . Mercedes . . . you know . . . it's coming
> down and it's missing everything . . . and it slams into like . . . a gate
> thing . . . ah . . . concrete fixture somewhat like . . . you know . . .
> that over there . . . to only come home . . . yah . . . to come home and
> I . . . and I did . . . I wasn't there so I wasn't able to see my father's
> face but to see . . . you know . . . the look in his eyes as my brother
> was . . . ah . . . you know . . . who was . . . it would've been hilari-
> ous . . . nn ah . . . to this day my brother contends that its not that
> bad . . . I look at the truck and like there's no rear quarter and
> it's . . . it's totally . . . ah . . . disheveled and I . . . I think . . . I . . . it's
> kinda weird of me to think that that's a good thing that happened to
> him . . . but . . . ah . . . I think it's kinda funny.

The first thing that strikes me when I see Dana's spoken story
written out is how full of stops and starts and pauses and place holders
it is. It doesn't read at all the way we think that coherent sentences

should. Yet in the classroom the other students and I had no trouble following the story. We paid attention only to the meaning and didn't even notice interruptions in the syntax of his sentences (and when we edit out those interruptions, the sentences are perfectly grammatical, with no violations of the expectations of those of us who are native speakers of this language). In fact, Dana's telling of the story has been quite effective. We've all understood and laughed and sympathized with his feelings. He has demonstrated his communicative as well as his grammatical competence.

Dana's basic communicative competence can be seen in his response to a new situation. Dana doesn't really know this community, so he pays a lot of attention to whether his listeners can follow what he's saying, using "you know" frequently, partly to fill in while he thinks of what he wants to say next, but also to see whether his listeners do know—whether they've had experiences that make what he's telling them familiar. He explicitly ties his story to the others that have been told ("I heard you talking before") so that he can build on the shared knowledge that this community is developing. But there are other kinds of shared knowledge that he does assume in this community— "Isuzus," "Mercedes," "Jaguars,"—he effectively exploits the differences in these kinds of cars, in who is likely to own them and in how costly it's likely to be to smash into them, to build the drama of the pick-up's run down the ramp.

Although he's stepping into a new community, Dana also has a sense of some of the rules for what can be said here, or he's checking them out, based on his past school experience. "If I may be so coarse as to say" shows his uncertainty about whether terms like "the ultimate hard ass" are really appropriate to this new context, and his description of the smashed-up truck as "disheveled" probably reflects his attempt to find a word that will feel right in this relatively formal context.

So Dana, the speaker, enters this freshman composition class with many kinds of knowledge—about the world, about what a particular group of people are likely to know, about linguistic structures and styles, about strategies for communication, and about when and how to test out what will work and what won't in this new context. But Dana is also entering a community of writers. And he will communicate most effectively as a writer if he relies on the fundamental understandings that he has drawn on naturally as a speaker.

Language Acquisition and Writing

For writers, then, as well as speakers, the following principles hold true.

First Principle

The acquisition of new structures and forms comes about through the use of language for meaningful communication in a community (of speakers and listeners or writers and readers), not through memorizing rules, and acquisition depends upon experimentation and risk taking. In fact, even where a learner makes errors with reference to the usual forms used by speakers and writers in this community, the errors fit the learner's developing linguistic system and show how much knowledge is present. In many ways, language learning is like other learning. People learn a new language or dialect and (unconsciously) generate hypotheses about what that new language is like, about what its rules are, based on the data of what they hear and read. Speakers test these hypotheses, try out new constructions, and gradually the constructions they create approximate more and more closely the correct (which generally means the most used) forms of the new language.

During this process, speakers and writers are bound to make some errors. In fact, they could not learn anything new about the language unless they did make some errors. The errors are likely to be in some way logical or consistent because the learner is searching for patterns, like the student who, having learned that a noun could be formed by adding "tion" to a verb, then added it to every verb he encountered and produced words like "conflictions," or like the writer who tests out different possibilities for using a colon. In these cases, error is an important sign of active learning, for the error shows how speakers and writers are making predictions and trying out solutions, and of taking risks with the language they are using, the way Dana tries out the word "disheveled" to see if it is the right way to describe his father's smashed-up truck to this audience (and we can see that he has paused to think before choosing this word).

Second Principle

Writers, like speakers, are participating in a particular discourse community with its own rules for using language. If Dana were writing for the school paper, he'd be following some common journalistic conventions—putting the key information of who, what, where, and when into his first sentence: "Last night at about 10 p.m. an Isuzu pick-up truck, parked by a young man who had forgotten to set the emergency brake, rolled down the ramp of the Downtown Parking Garage, narrowly missing a number of vehicles before crashing into a wall."

One important convention of the academic discourse community is that the point of any written text is made explicitly. (This accounts for the emphasis on the thesis statement in writing instruction.) The convention holds true even for narratives. While a fiction writer or a street-corner storyteller is more likely to let the reader or listener infer the point of the story from the events and descriptions it contains, the writer who uses narrative in an academic essay is likely to make her point explicitly, several times, beginning with the title and ending with the final statement.

Dana's written version of this story was entitled "Perfectly Imperfect."

> My father is a very meticulous person: always pointing out details, doing things by the book and, if it is possible, showing no imperfections. My brother, although nothing of the sort, likes to think he is just like him.
>
> It all happened a year ago when my father bought a brand new small bed pick-up truck, and my brother finally got a chance to drive it. Apparently what had happened when my brother Don took the truck out was that he did not pull the emergency brake on all the way when he parked it. It would not have been so bad if the truck was not parked at the top of a curvy hill in a parking garage. Needless to say, the truck rolled down the hill only to smash into a cement wall structure at the bottom of the garage.
>
> I guess the only luck to come out of this adventure was the fact that the truck did not hit any parked cars on the way down the hill. It would have been a personal thrill for me to see the look on my father's face as my brother brought the truck in the driveway. My brother finally realized he did a stupid thing and that he was not that perfect anymore.

In this version of his story, revised after several sessions in writing groups, Dana has met the academic convention of giving an explicit statement of the meaning of his story. As he spends more time in this community, he will begin to see that the rules are not so rigid, and he'll begin to experiment with these conventions, perhaps drawing on some of what he knows about effective oral storytelling.

Third Principle

Writers too depend on shared knowledge with their readers, both of the world and of forms. Dana has eliminated, in his written version, some of the specific information that appeared in his oral story—like the kinds of cars parked in the garage (although such detail would have helped to create a shared world with his readers, as it did with his listeners). But he still assumes, as all writers must, some common knowledge, at least of a parking garage, and perhaps of sibling relationships. In his written story, though, Dana is depending on an understanding of other, formal, conventions—a title, paragraphs, definite statements of introduction, and conclusion. (Look back at his spoken version, where he eases into and out of the story, which begins "The thing is you gotta know my father" and ends "I think it's kinda funny.")

Written discourse for school purposes also tends to be formal in diction, and Dana eliminates phrases like "you gotta" as well as "the ultimate hard ass." In speaking, Dana was clearly addressing an audience of peers (and one teacher). In writing, we usually assume that anyone, not just friends or peers, might read what we've written. And since we now rarely use writing for informal communication, we tend to see all writing as formal. But all speakers and writers develop a repertoire of styles, and shift their style as they speak and write to different audiences, for different purposes. Dana's ability to shift style reflects his linguistic knowledge.

Another important convention of written text, one that's again tied to more formal communication, is the need to make all references clear and explicit. Dana, the speaker, can point to something in the room and say "It slams into . . . a concrete fixture somewhat like, you know, that over there." But Dana the writer can't just point over there, so he names "a cement wall structure," even if he doesn't have precise words to describe it.

Fourth Principle

Writers, like speakers, are addressing real audiences in real communities. Dana's classmates will provide an audience for some of his writing. (He'll later exchange letters with upperlevel students who choose to research the same subject he chooses.) It is important for him to know that most writing shares the characteristics of meaningful conversation. People write to those with whom they have some shared knowledge and interests, their readers respond with questions and new ideas, and the focus is on the communication of meanings. (Many readers will have read these essays by the time they appear in this book—colleagues, students, friends, my 17-year-old son, as well as various editors at the publishing house. All of these readers will be part of a supportive community, like the young child's parents, focusing on meaning, asking questions, trying to help us writers work out our ideas and communicate them clearly.)

So Dana will become a member of a community of writers not by holding back and watching his language but by being an active and engaged participant. By doing a lot of reading he will unconsciously acquire a vast repertoire of styles and forms, of words and structures, that he can draw on as a writer. By doing a lot of writing, he can experiment and try out different ways of shaping his ideas, and discovering those ideas, and teasing out meanings. By sharing his writing with real readers, he can discover how to communicate effectively to different people, for different purposes. And by listening to other writers, both to what they've written and to what they are thinking about how to write it, he can hear the voices in what he reads and learn to hear the voice in what he writes as well. It is by practicing and taking risks and by being wholly involved with others in the community (not by worrying about error and trying too hard to get things right)— through actual experience, rather than trying to apply any rules of academic discourse this essay might suggest, that he will be a writer in a community of writers. Writing is not only a process—it is a process of communication. And in that process, Dana and the others entering this community will shape and influence it, bringing a rich repertoire of linguistic resources from their communities to the college classroom, and shaping and enriching its discourse, even as they acquire it.

Annotated Bibliography

For writers who want to read more about language acquisition, discourse communities, and the ways in which people learn to shift styles as they move into different contexts, I recommend several readings.

Peter Farb. *Word Play: What Happens When People Talk*. New York: Knopf, 1974. Farb provides an easy-to read and accessible overview of how people acquire language and how they learn to play by their community's rules of what he describes as a language game.

Shirley Brice Heath. *Ways with Words: Language, Life and Work in Communities and Classrooms*. Cambridge, UK: Cambridge University Press, 1983. Heath describes the ways language is used in three communities, a rural white community, a rural black community, and the community of people in the town these smaller communities surround. She follows children as they shift from the patterns of their homes to the expected patterns of language use in their schools and suggests ways that schools can help them connect their two linguistic worlds.

William Labov. *Language in the Inner City. Studies in the Black English Vernacular*. Philadelphia: University of Pennsylvania Press, l972. Labov presents a series of more technically complex studies of linguistic styles in urban settings, particularly among peer groups of black urban teenagers. He shows that these teenagers use a syntactically complex style, that they can shift through a wide range of styles, but that those who don't want to be considered "lames" by their friends will avoid standard school style.

Mike Rose. *Lives on the Boundary*. New York: Penguin, 1989. Rose, a teacher of writing, offers an account of students' experiences, including his own, as they move from families and communities that don't have a lot of experience with academic styles and values into college classrooms.

————— .*Writer's Block. The Cognitive Dimension*. Carbondale, IL: Southern Illinois University Press, 1984. In this formal study, Rose looks at the writing processes of a number of student writers to discover the causes of writer's block. One cause he discovers is a writer's tendency to worry about rules from earlier instruction, like "Avoid the passive!" instead of focusing on her ideas and what she wants to say.

Sharing Ideas

- What was your definition of good writing as you started your current class? Trace the influences that shaped your definition.

- If you tell the story of the history of your school life with grammar instruction, what do you learn?

- As Ellie puts it, do you have "a voice in your head that makes you hesitate before you put that first word on the page, that leaves you overly concerned . . . with making sure you don't break any rules"? Now that you've read her essay, what do you think about that voice?

- If you've ever had the chance to watch a younger brother or sister learn to speak, then to read and write, share your observations about children's language acquisition with your class. Ellie says: "You have been acquiring grammatical knowledge and a knowledge of how to adapt to different styles of language use in different settings unconsciously, since childhood." Did you see this happen for your brother or sister (or remember how it happened for you, yourself)?

- In what way is your "story" similar to and/or different from Dana's?

- Does Ellie's classroom seem to be based on one or more of the three models Don described in his essay—social constructionist, participationist, and/or socio-psycholinguist? Explain how Don's definitions might connect with Ellie's discussions.

- As a class, you may want to make the rules you're working by more explicit: What are the rules for sharing stories in groups, for responding to peers' drafts, for writing informal class papers? How do you know when a writer is breaking or pushing those rules? How do rules help us and how do they hurt us as writers?

6

Style: The Hidden Agenda in Composition Classes or One Reader's Confession

Kate Ronald

Kate Ronald is an associate professor at the University of
Nebraska-Lincoln, where she is Co-Coordinator of Composition Courses. She teaches writing and rhetoric at all levels
from first-year to graduate courses. Besides teaching, she tries
every day to write, to swim, to play one game of Nintendo,
and to read. She has not yet won Mario Brothers 3, but her
nephews offer her long-distance coaching from Kentucky,
where she was born. Her favorite authors are Plato, Ralph
Waldo Emerson, and Stephen King.

In some ways I see this essay as a confession. I have been teaching
writing and theorizing about how it should be taught for almost 15
years now. During those 15 years, you, the students reading this
essay, have been in school, taking English classes and writing compositions. I have been teaching those classes and reading those compositions; plus I've been teaching some of your teachers for the past 10
years, and so I feel responsible to you even though I've never had you
in one of my classes. Now I'm going to tell you something you might
already know. Since you started school in the first grade, there's been
a revolution in the way you've been "taught" to write. It used to be
that teachers focused on and evaluated your writing according to two

main things: its structure and its correctness. Those were the days of diagramming sentences and imitating types of organization. In the 1960s and 70s, however, many people who studied writing began to talk about teaching the "process" of writing rather than the "products" of writing. In other words, the focus has shifted in the 1980s from organization and correctness to generating ideas, appealing to audiences, and developing a "voice" in writing.

Composition, or "rhetoric" as it used to be called, is an ancient discipline, going all the way back at least to Plato and Aristotle in the third century BCE. You are the most recent in a long, long line of students sitting in classes where teachers assign writing tasks and evaluate your ability. In ancient times, the art of writing was divided into five steps: invention (coming up with ideas), arrangement (organizing them), style (making them sound right), memory (remembering speeches), and delivery (oratorical ability). One way to think about the history of writing instruction is to look at the different emphases that different eras have put on these five steps. Today, with computers and photocopy machines, we don't worry much anymore about memory, for example, but it was terribly important in the time before the printing press. And we don't "deliver" what we write orally very much anymore, although the kind of font you choose from your word-processing program might be considered a matter of delivery. Of course all writers have to think about invention, arrangement, and style, no matter what age they work in. However, different eras have emphasized different parts of composition. Plato and Aristotle were upset by what they saw as an enchantment with style; they worried that writers could dazzle audiences without caring much about telling them the truth. And so they focused on invention, on figuring out issues by thinking and writing. By the sixteenth and seventeenth centuries, the focus had shifted back to style, going so far as giving students manuals that provided hundreds of ways to say "I enjoyed your letter very much." How a person sounded was more important than what a person had to say.

I see the shift from "product" to "process" while you've been in school as a reaction to that overemphasis on style. Once again, the focus has changed back to make *invention* the most important step in composition. Writing teachers who are up-to-date these days (including me) tell you (our students) not to worry, for example, about grammar or spelling or organization as you write your early drafts. We invite you to choose your own topics for writing and to get feedback from responsive small groups in your classes. We don't grade individual papers, but instead ask you to write multiple drafts and submit for final evaluation the ones you think best represent you as a writer. We don't lecture on punctuation or topic sentences. It's what you say, not how you say it, that counts. No doubt you all are familiar with this kind of teaching—I doubt you'd be reading this essay right now if you weren't in a class with a thoroughly "new rhetoric" teacher. Obviously this whole collection is focused on the *processes* of writing, the main theme of writing instruction in the 1980s.

But here comes my confession. Your teacher, and I, and all the others who were part of this latest revolution in rhetoric, haven't been exactly honest with you about the matter of style. We say we aren't overly interested in style, that your ideas and your growth as writers is uppermost in our minds, but we are still influenced by your writing style more than we admit, or perhaps know. In other words, despite all the research and writing I've done in the past 10 years about composing, revising, responding, contexts for writing, personal voice, and all I know about the new rhetoric, I'm still rewarding and punishing my students for their writing styles. And here's the worst part of my confession: I'm not sure that I'm teaching them style. Of course any teacher quickly realizes that she can't teach everything in one semester, but I worry that I'm responding to something in my students' writing that I'm not telling them about—their style, the sound of their voices on paper. This essay is my attempt to atone for that omission in my own teaching. Despite that selfish motive, I also want to suggest to you ways in which you might become aware of your own writing styles and your teachers' agendas about style, as well as show you some strategies for studying and improving your own style in writing.

Let me stop to define what I mean and what I don't mean by "style." I don't mean spelling, grammar, punctuation, or usage, although if I'm going to be completely honest, I'd have to tell you that mistakes along those lines do get in my way when I'm reading. But those can be fixed, easily, by editing and copyreading. By style, I mean what my student, Margaret, said last semester after another student, Paul, had read a paper out loud for the whole class. She got this longing look on her face and cried, "I want to write the way Paul does!" You know students like Paul. He's clever, he surprises with his different perspectives on his topics, and he has a distinctive voice. I call this "writing where somebody's home," as opposed to writing that's technically correct but where there's "nobody home," no life, no voice. Let me give you some examples of these two kinds of voices:

Much Too Young to Be So Old

The neighborhood itself was odd. Larger than most side streets, 31st Street had huge cracks that ran continuously from one end to the other of this gray track that led nowhere special. Of the large, lonely looking houses, there were only six left whose original structures hadn't been tampered with in order to make way for inexpensive apartments. Why would a real family continue to live in this place was a question we often asked and none of us could answer. Each stretch of the run-down rickety houses had an alley behind them. These alleys became homes, playgrounds, and learning areas for us children. We treasured these places. They were overgrown with weeds and filled with years of garbage, but we didn't seem to care. Then again, we didn't seem to care about much. (Amy)

The Dog

In 1980 I lived in a green split level house. It was a really ugly green but that is beside the point. The neighborhood was really rather pretty, with trees all over the place and not just little trees. They were huge. My friends and I played football in my backyard right after school every day. The neighbors had a white toy poodle that barked forever. You would walk by the fence and it would bark at you. I had no idea whatsoever that the dog was mean. (Corey)

Even though both these writers begin these essays by describing the settings of their stories, and both end with a suggestion of what's coming next, Amy's opening paragraph appeals to me much more than Corey's. I could point out "flaws" in both openings: I think Corey's suffers from lack of concrete detail, and he takes a pretty long time telling us only that the trees were "huge." Amy uses too much passive voice ("hadn't been tampered with"). However, I'm much more drawn into the world of 31st Street than I am to the neighborhood with huge trees. And I think that's because I know more about Amy from this opening—her words and her rhythm evoke a bittersweet expectation in me—whereas I'm not sure what Corey's up to. In other words, I get the distinct feeling that Amy really wants to tell her readers about her childhood. I don't see that kind of commitment in Corey. I know Corey's going to write a dog story, and usually those are my favorites, but somehow I don't very much want to read on.

But teachers have to read on, and on and on, through hundreds and hundreds of drafts a semester. So I can't just say to Corey, "This is boring." And, being a believer in the "new rhetoric," I'm interested in the process that leads to these two different styles. How does Amy come up with this voice? Was she born clever? And why does Corey make the decision to take himself out of his writing? I can think of many reasons why he would choose to be safe; in fact, he admitted to me later in that course that he had "copped out," choosing to write in what he called his "safe, public style" rather than take chances with what he thought was a more risky, personal style. That makes sense, if you consider the history of writing instruction up until the last 15 to 20 years. Certainly it's been better to get it right, to avoid mistakes, than to get it good, to try for a voice. And it makes sense that Corey wouldn't want to expose his personal style—writing classrooms traditionally have not been places where students have felt safe. Writing and then showing that writing to someone else for evaluation and response is risky, a lot like asking "Am I OK? Am I a person you want to listen to?"

And so, to play it safe in a risky environment, it's tempting to take on a voice that isn't yours, to try to sound like you know what you're talking about, to sound "collegiate," to be acceptable and accepted. There's also a sort of mystique about "college writing," both in composition courses and in other disciplines. To write in college, this thinking goes, means to be "objective," to take your own opinions, your own stake in the subject, completely out of your writing. That's why people write, "It is to be hoped that" rather than, "I hope" or, "There are many aspects involved" rather than, "This is complicated." And then there's also a real fear of writing badly, of being thought stupid, and so it's tempting simply to be bland and safe and not call too much attention to yourself.

And teachers have encouraged you, I think, to remain hidden behind your own prose. Remember when you got a "split grade" like this: "C+/B"? One grade for content and another for style. That sends a clear message, I think, that what you say and how you say it can be separated and analyzed differently. That's crazy—we can't split form and content. But teachers tend to encourage you to do that when they ask you to read an essay by Virginia Woolf or E. B. White from an anthology and then tell you to "write like that." Or, we teachers have been so concerned with form that we've discouraged you from real communication with another person. One of my students just yesterday described her English classes this way: "I wanted to learn how to write and they were trying to teach me what my writing should look like." Preoccupation with correctness, with organization, and with format (margins, typing, neatness, etc.), all get in the way of style and voice. So, too, do prearranged assignments, where each student in the class writes the same essay on the same subject ("Compare high school to college," "Discuss the narrator's attitude in this short story," "My most embarrassing moment"). Such assignments become exercises in competition, in one sense, because you've got somehow to set yourself apart from the rest of the essays your teacher will be reading. But they are also exercises in becoming invisible, for while you want to be noticed, you don't want to be too terribly different, to stick out like a sore thumb. And so you write safely, not revealing too much or taking many chances.

I used to teach that way, giving assignments, comparing one student with another and everyone with the "ideal" paper I imagined in my head (although I never tried writing with my students in those days) correcting mistakes and arriving at a grade for each paper. The new rhetoric classes I teach now have eliminated many of these traps for students, but I've also opened up new ones, I'm afraid. Now my students choose their own topics, writing whatever they want to write. And sometimes I'm simply not interested in their choices. In the old days, when I gave the assignment, naturally I was interested in the topic—it was, after all, *my* idea. Now I read about all sorts of things every week—my students' families, their cars, the joys and sorrows in their love lives, their athletic victories and defeats, their opinions on the latest upcoming election, their thoughts about the future, etc. Frankly, I don't approach each of these topics in the same way. For example, a dog story almost always interests me, while a car story might not. Or, a liberal reading of the latest campus debate on women's issues will grab my attention much more quickly than a fundamentalist interpretation. That's simply the truth. But, as a teacher of "process," I try my best to get interested in whatever my students are writing. And, I'm usually delighted by how much my students can move me with their ideas. So what makes me interested? I'm convinced it has to do with their style. And here I'm defining style not simply as word choice or sentence structure, but as a kind of "presence" on the page, the feeling I get as a reader that, indeed, somebody's home in this paper, somebody wants to say something—to me, to herself, to the class, to the community.

Mine is not the only response students receive in this kind of classroom. Each day, students bring copies of their work-in-progress to their small groups. They read their papers out loud to each other, and we practice ways of responding to each writer that will keep him or her writing, for starts, and that will help the writer see what needs to be added, changed, or cut from the draft. This can get pretty tricky. It's been my experience that showing your writing to another student, to a peer, can be much more risky than showing it to a teacher. We've all had the experience of handing in something we knew was terrible to a teacher, and it's not so painful. People will give writing to teachers that they'd never show to someone whose opinion they valued. But sitting down in a small group with three or four classmates and saying, "I wrote this. What do you think?" is, again, like asking "Do you like me? Am I an interesting person?" And so my classes practice ways of responding to one another's writing without being overly critical, without taking control of the writing out of the writer's hands, and without damaging egos. And they become quite sophisticated as the semester goes along. Still, one of the worst moments in a small group comes when someone reads a draft and the rest of the group responds like this: "It's OK. I don't see anything wrong with it. It seems pretty good." And then silence. In other words, the writer hasn't grabbed their attention, hasn't engaged the readers, hasn't communicated in any meaningful way. What's the difference between this scenario and one where the group comes back with responses like "Where did you get that idea? I really like the way you describe the old man. This reminds me of my grandfather. I think you're right to notice his hands"? I think the difference is in *style*, in the presence of a writer in the group who is honestly trying to communicate to his or her readers.

But I know I still haven't been exactly clear about what I mean by style. That's part of my dilemma, my reason for wanting to write this essay. All of us, teachers and students, recognize good style when we hear it, but I don't know what we do to foster it. And so for the rest of this essay I want to talk to you about how to work on your own writing styles, to recognize and develop your own individual voice in writing, and how to listen for your teachers' agendas in style. Because, despite our very natural desires to remain invisible in academic setting, you *want* to be noticed; you want to be the voice that your teacher becomes interested in. I think I'm telling you that your style ultimately makes the difference. And here I'm talking about not only your writing styles, but the reading styles of your audiences, the agendas operating in the contexts in which you write.

I'll start backward with agendas first. There are several main issues that I think influence English teachers when they are reading students' writing. First, we have a real bent for the literary element, the metaphor, the clever turn of phrase, the rhythm of prose that comes close to the rhythm of poetry. That's why I like sentences like these: "As the big night approached I could feel my stomach gradually easing its way up to my throat. I was as nervous as a young foal experiencing its first thunderstorm" (from an essay about barrel racing) and "Suddenly the University of Nebraska Cornhusker Marching Band takes the field for another exciting halftime performance, and the Sea of Red stands up *en masse* and goes to the concession stand" (from an essay about being in the band). I like the surprise in this last sentence, the unexpectedness of everyone leaving the performance, and I like the comparison to a young foal in the first one, especially since the essay is about horses. I tell my students to "take chances" in their writing. I think these two writers were trying to do just that. And I liked them for taking that chance.

But you don't want to take chances everywhere. Of course this kind of writing won't work in a biology lab report or a history exam, which brings me to another troublesome issue when we talk about style in college writing. You move among what composition researchers call "discourse communities" every day—from English to Biology to Sociology to Music to the dorm to family dinners to friends at bars—you don't talk or write the same way,or in the same voice to each of these groups. You adjust. And yet many professors still believe that you should be learning to write one certain kind of style in college, one that's objective, impersonal, formal, explicit, and organized around assertions, claims, and reasons that illustrate or defend those claims. You know this kind of writing. You produce it in response to questions like "Discuss the causes of the Civil War," or "Do you think that 'nature' or 'nurture' plays the most important role in a child's development?" Here's a student trying out this kind of "academic discourse" in an essay where he discusses what worries him:

> Another outlet for violence in our society is video games. They have renewed the popularity that they had earlier in the 1980's and have taken our country by storm. There is not one child in the country who doesn't know what a Nintendo is. So, instead of running around outside getting fresh air and exercise, most children are sitting in front of the television playing video games. This is affecting their minds and their bodies.

Why wouldn't Jeff just say "Video games are popular again" instead of saying that "they have renewed their popularity" or "Kids are getting fat and lazy" rather than "This is affecting their minds and bodies?" Besides using big words here, Jeff is also trying to sound absolutely knowledgeable: he states that every child in this country knows Nintendo, they are all playing it, when if he thought about that for a minute, he'd know it wasn't true. I don't like this kind of writing very much myself. Jeff is trying so hard to sound academic that "there's nobody home," no authentic voice left, no sense of a real human being trying to say something to somebody. I prefer discourse that "renders experience," as Peter Elbow (1991) puts it, rather than discourse that tries to explain it. He describes this kind of language (or style) as writing where a writer "conveys to others a sense of experience—or indeed, that mirrors back to themselves a sense of their own experience, from a little distance, once it's out there on paper" (p. 137). Here's an example of that kind of "rendering" from Paul's essay about a first date:

> Her mother answers the door. My brain says all kinds of witty and charming things which my larynx translates into a sort of amphibious croak. (Ribbitt. Ribbitt. I can't remember what it was I actually attempted to say.) She materializes at the top of the stairs, cast in a celestial glow. A choir of chubby cherubim, voices lifted in a heavenly chorus, drape her divine body with a thin film of gossamer. (No, not really. She did look pretty lovely, though. I tried to tell her as much. Ribbitt. Ribbitt.)

Now, perhaps Paul goes too far here, trying a little too hard to be clever, but I like this better than the discussion of video games. (And not just because I like the topic of dating better—since I've gotten married, I don't date anymore and I confess I'm addicted to Mario Brothers 3.) Paul here is conveying the *feeling* of the moment, the sense of the experience, and he's complicating the memory by moving back and forth between the moment and his interpretation of it. In other words, he's letting me into the story, not explaining something to me. Paul is involved in what he's writing while Jeff is detached. And Paul's funny. Besides dog stories, I like humor in my students' writing.

Now, this brings me to another issue in the matter of style. I prefer the rendering style over the explanatory style, perhaps because I'm an English major and an English teacher, and therefore I like the allusion over the direct reference, description over analysis, narrative over exposition. But perhaps there's another reason I like the more personal style: I'm a woman. There's a whole body of recent research which suggests that men and women have different writing styles, among all sorts of other differences. Theorists such as Pamela Annas and Elizabeth Flynn suggest that women writers in academic situations often are forced to translate their experiences into the foreign language of objectivity, detachment, and authority that the male-dominated school system values. Women strive for connection, this thinking argues, while men value individual power. Feminist theory values writing that "brings together the personal and the political, the private and the public, into writing which is committed and powerful because it takes risks, because it speaks up clearly in their own voices and from their own experiences" (Annas, 1985, p. 370; see also Flynn, 1988). Here's an example of that kind of writing, an excerpt from an essay titled, "Grandma, You're Not So Young Anymore":

> My grandma was always so particular about everything. Everything had to be just so. The walls and curtains had to be spotless, the garden couldn't have a weed, the kolaches had to be baked, and the car had to be washed. . . . Each spring she was always the first to have her flowers and garden planted. She could remember the littlest details about our family history and ancestors. . . . There were always kolaches in the oven and cookies in the refrigerator. . . .
>
> I really didn't notice the aging so much at first. . . . When I would come home from college Mom would always say, "Grandma's really lonely now. Grandpa was her company, and now he's gone. You should really go and visit her more often. She won't be around forever."
>
> I had to admit I didn't visit her all that often. . . . I didn't notice how much slower she'd gotten until Thanksgiving Day. Grandma

took us to Bonanza because she didn't want to cook that much. I noticed the slower, more crippled steps she took, the larger amount of wrinkles on her face, and most of all, her slowed mental abilities. She sometimes had trouble getting the words out as if she couldn't remember what she wanted to say. She couldn't decide what foods she wanted to eat, and when she did eat, she hardly touched a thing. I didn't think my grandma would ever get old. Now I don't think she will last forever anymore.

Here, Deanna uses her own experience and observations to go on and talk about how the elderly are treated in our culture. She could have written a statistical report on nursing homes or a more formal argument about how Americans don't value their old people. But she chose instead to draw from her own life and therefore she draws me into her argument about the "frustration" of getting old. I like old people, and I can identify this woman's deterioration with my own mother's several years ago. But I still think it's more than my personal history that draws me to this essay. I suspect it's Deanna's willingness to explore her own experience on paper. Deanna definitely needs to work on editing this draft to improve her style (something more specific, for example, than "larger amount of wrinkles" and "slowed mental abilities"). But she doesn't need to work to improve her style in the sense of her commitment to this topic, her presence on the page, or her desire to figure out and to explain her reaction to her grandmother's aging.

Each of these three issues might lead me to advise you that you should write metaphors for English teachers, formal explanations for male teachers in other disciplines, and personal narratives for your women professors. But you know that would be silly, simplistic advice about style. You have to maneuver every day through a complex set of expectations, some of which aren't made explicit, and the whole idea of teacher-as-audience is much more complex that simply psyching out a teacher's background or political agenda. "Style" in writing means different things to different people. I have to be honest and admit that my definition of style as presence on paper is simply my own definition. I hope this essay will lead you to your own thinking about what style means, in all contexts. But I am going to end by giving you some advice about your own style in writing anyway—the teacher in me can't resist. That advice is: Work on your style without thinking about school too much. Here are five suggestions to help you do this.

In school or out, write as if you're actually saying something to some-body. Even if you're not exactly sure who your audience is, try to imagine a real person who's interested in what you have to say. Probably the most important thing I can tell you about working on your style is:

Think of your writing as actually saying something to somebody real. Too often in academics we can imagine no audience at all, or at the most an audience with evaluation on its mind, not real interest or response. When I'm able to get interested in my students' writing, no matter what the topic, it's because I hear someone talking to me. My colleague Rick Evans calls this kind of writing "talking on paper," and if you keep that metaphor in mind, I think you'll more often avoid the kind of "academese" or formal language that signals you're hiding or you've disappeared.

I can illustrate the difference in style I'm talking about through two journals that Angie gave me at the beginning and the end of a composition and literature course last year. All through the course, I asked students to write about how the novels we were reading connected to their own lives:

> January 24: Well, I'm confused. I haven't written a paper for an English class that wasn't a formal literary analysis since 8th grade. Now, all of a sudden, the kind of writing my teachers always said would be of no use in college *is*, and what they said *would* be, *isn't*. Go figure. Now, if Kate had asked me to churn out a paper on some passage or symbol in *Beloved*—even one of my own choosing—I could get out 5–8 (handwritten) pages easy. But this life stuff? Who wants to know about that anyway?

> May 1: This portfolio represents the work closest to my guts. It's *my* story, not *Beloved*'s or Carlos Rueda's. I hasten to point out that this may not be my best work or even my favorite work, but it's the work that sings my song. My goal was to communicate a set of ideas, to spark a dialogue with *you*, as my reader, to inspire you to think about *what* I have written, not *how* I have written it. So here it is, bound in plastic, unified, in a manner, ready for reading. I hope you like what I have woven.

Notice how Angie's attitude toward me as her reader changed from January to May. At first she referred to "Kate" as if I wouldn't be reading what she had written, even though this was a journal handed in to me; later I become someone she wants to engage in a dialogue. (She had expected the kind of writing class I described at the beginning of this essay, but she found herself writing for a new rhetoric teacher.) Notice, too, how at first she talks about how she could write five to eight pages *even if she had to choose her own topic*. The implication is clear—that it's easier to write when someone else tells her what to do, what to write about. In other words, it's easier to perform rather than to communicate. Notice, finally, Angie's relationship to the literature we were reading in these two journals. At first she wants only to write about the symbols in Toni Morrison's (1983) novel, *Beloved*, focusing all her attention on the literary work and not on herself. At the end of the course, she subordinates the novels almost completely to her own stories. This is an engaged writer, one with a clear sense of her own style, her own presence.

Write outside of school. Play with writing outside of school. You'll need to write much more than just what's assigned in your classes to develop a beautiful writing style. (Sorry, but it's true.) One of the truisms about good writers is that they are good readers; in other words, they read a lot. (And they were probably read to as kids, but we can't go into that right now.) So, here's an exercise in style that I recommend to my students. Find an author whose writing you admire. Copy out a particular, favorite passage. Then imitate that style, word for word, part-of-speech for part-of-speech. Here's an example from one of my students last semester. We were reading *Beloved*, and Sarah used its opening passage to talk about the first day of class. I'll show you Morrison's passage and then Sarah's:

> 124 was spiteful. Full of a baby's venom. The women in the house knew it and so did the children. For years each put up with the spite in his own way, but by 1873, Sethe and her daughter Denver were its only victims. The grandmother, Baby Suggs, was dead, and the sons, Howard and Buglar, had run away by the time they were thir- teen years old—as soon as merely looking in a mirror shattered it (that was the signal for Buglar); as soon as two tiny hand prints appeared in the cake (that was it for Howard). Neither boy waited to see more. (p. 3)

> Andrews 33 was quiet. Full of a new semester's uneasiness. The students in the room knew it and so did the teacher. For a few min- utes, everyone took in the tension in their own way, but by 12:45 the roll call and Kate's lame jokes broke the ice a little bit. The course, a new program, was explained, and the syllabus, papers and papers, looked simple enough by the time Kate explained her marvelous approach—as soon as really deciding on a topic excited us (that was the reason for the authority list); as soon as four friendly voices read to each other (that was the reason for small groups). No students lingered to write more. (Sarah)

Sarah told me later that doing this imitation surprised her—she had never written with parentheses before, nor had she stopped sentences in the middle this way ("the syllabus, papers and papers"). She wasn't sure she liked this imitation, but it showed her she could write in different ways. And playing with different voices on paper will help you make choices about your own style in different situations.

Read your work-in-progress out loud, preferably to a real person. Looking back over this essay, I realize that so much of what I've said about style revolves around the sense of sound. Teachers have good ears, and so do you. Listen to your own voice as you read out loud. Do you sound like a person talking to someone? Or a student performing for a grade?

Practice cutting all the words you can out of your drafts and starting from there. This is one of the hardest things for any writer to do, and yet I think it's one of the most effective ways to make your writing more interesting. Most of the time there are simply too many words getting in the way of your meaning, making too much noise for you to be heard. Look closely at your drafts and be hard on yourself. Let me give you a few quick examples:

> The first thing that really upsets me is the destruction of our environment due to ignorance, capitalism, and blindness in the world. The attitude that most people take is that by ignoring the problem it will go away. An example of this attitude is the turnout for elections in America.
>
> Revision: Ignorance, capitalism, and blindness destroy our environment. Most people look the other way. Many don't even vote.

Once Jim revised this opening sentence from an essay on what worries him, he realized that he hadn't said much yet and that he was moving way too quickly. He learned that he had several ideas he felt strongly about, ideas worth slowing down to develop. Here are two more examples:

> I also think that we need to provide more opportunities for the homeless to receive an education so they can compete in today's job market. Another reason for educating these people is because the increasing numbers of unemployed persons is a factor that is contributing to homelessness in our country. There are declining employment opportunities for unskilled labor in todays job market, and since many homeless are unskilled laborers, they are not able to acquire a decent job. Therefore they cannot afford to buy a home. I think it is critical that these people be educated if the homeless problem in our country is going to be solved.
>
> Revision: We need to educate the homeless so they can compete in a market where jobs are becoming more scarce.
>
> There are so many things that a person can fill their mind with. I find that when talking with friends the majority of their thoughts are filled with worries. I don't really believe that it is all negative to

worry unless it becomes an obsession. So many people are worried about so many different things. Some of which are personal while others are more societal When I try to figure out what worries me most I find it to be on a more personal level.

Revision: I'm sort of worried that I worry so much about myself.

Each of these last two writers realized that they hadn't said much of anything yet in their initial drafts. Going back to cut words, asking themselves questions about what they meant to say to a reader, allowed them to start over with a different, clearer perspective. I know this isn't easy, especially in school, where you've been trained to "write 1000 words" and, by God, you'll write 1000 words whether you have 1 or 1000 words to say on the subject. Try to stop padding and counting words in the margins. Cut words. This is probably the most practical piece of advice I have.

Finally, write about your own writing style. Keep a record of your reactions to what you write, a list of your favorite sentences, and a reaction to the reactions you get from readers. Most of all, forgive yourself for writing badly from time to time. One of my professors in graduate school told me that I was capable of writing "awkward word piles," and here I am with the nerve to be writing an essay to you about style. I've tried to practice what I preach, and now I'm suggesting that you throw out more than you keep and to notice and remember what works for you. Writing about your own writing is another piece of practical advice.

This is really my last word: don't let *me* fool you here. Even though I understand what Angie meant in her last journal to me about my being more interested in what she has to say than *how* she says it, I'm still very in tune with the how, with her style. I'm happy that her focus has moved away from me as evaluator toward herself as a creator. But I'm still influenced by her style. Don't forget that. And I'm happy that the emphasis in composition has shifted from style back to invention. But I still reward and punish style in my reactions to students' writings. Yes, I try to be an interested reader, but my agendas also include listening for the sound of prose I like.

I suppose what I'm really confessing to you all in this essay is that I am not only a teacher, but I'm also a reader, with her own tastes, preferences, and phobias about what I like to read. And, as a reader, I look for style. There's a play that I love that I think can show you what I mean by style, by presence in writing. *The Real Thing*, by Tom Stoppard (1983) is about real love and real life, but it's also about real writing. At about the end of Act One, Henry, the playwright/hero, talks about good writing. He's picked up a cricket bat (could be a

Louisville slugger, but this play is set in London) to make his point. (Read this out loud and listen to the sound):

> This thing here, which looks like a wooden club, is actually several pieces of particular wood cunningly put together in a certain way so that the whole thing is sprung, like a dance floor. It's for hitting cricket balls with. If you get it right, the cricket ball will travel two hundred yards in four seconds, and all you've done is give it a knock like knocking the top off a bottle of stout, and it makes a noise like a trout taking a fly. What we're trying to do is write cricket bats, so that when we throw up an idea and give it a little knock, it might . . . *travel*. (p. 22)

This image has stayed with me for seven years, ever since I first saw and read Stoppard's play, and it's an idea that I think all writers and readers understand. "Ideas traveling"—surely that's what I want for myself as a writer and for my students. I love the image of the dance floor too—the idea of a piece of writing as an invitation to movement, a place to join with others, a site of communal passion and joy. But I don't think people in school always think of writing as something that travels, or as a dance floor, and I would like somehow to help you a little toward Henry's vision. Later in the same speech he picks up a badly written play that he's been asked to "fix" and describes it:

> Now, what we've got here is a lump of wood of roughly the same shape trying to be a cricket bat, and if you hit a ball with it, the ball will travel about ten feet and you will drop the bat and dance about shouting "Ouch!" with your hands stuck in your armpits (p. 23).

I've read writing, my own and my students' and professionals', that makes me want to do this different kind of dancing. Many of your textbooks read like "lumps of wood," yes? Henry tells us that no amount of simple editing will fix something that has no life or passion to begin with. But how to transform lumps of wood into cricket bats? It seems to me the key lies in this play's other theme—the "real thing," meaning real love and real passion. When I encourage you to develop your style in writing, I'm inviting you into the game, onto the dance floor, encouraging you to commit yourself to your ideas and to your readers. That's the essence of *style*, which, without knowledge and passion, amounts only to a performance that dazzles without touching its readers, and which, without practice, amounts to very little. In that sense, Plato and Aristotle were right to say that we shouldn't emphasize style over invention, ideas and voice. And in another sense, my last piece of advice would apply to students in ancient Greece as well as modern America: write about something you care about to someone you care about. Even if you are writing in school, try to have a presence—show them that somebody's home, working. Writers must know and love not only their subjects but their audiences as well, so that ideas will dance, so that ideas will travel.

Works Cited

Annas, Pamela. (1985). "Style as Politics." *College English, 4,* 370.

Elbow, Peter (1991). "Reflections on Academic Discourse," *College English, 2,* 137.

Flynn, Elizabeth. (1988). "Composing as Woman." *College Composition and Communication, 39,* 423–435.

Morrison, Toni (1987). *Beloved.* New York: Knopf.

Stoppard, Tom (1983). *The Real Thing.* London: Faber & Faber.

Sharing Ideas

- In different eras writers have been encouraged to pay more or less attention to style. In fact, style doesn't just manifest itself in our writing but in our living, also. We often talk about lifestyle and style of dress. Do you see any connections between your writing style (or the style you'd like to attain) and your lifestyle and style of dress?

- Don, Ellie, and Kate all talk about a shift from product to process. But Kate's article indicates such shifting can be problematic. She reminds you that "mistakes along those lines [spelling, grammar, punctuation, or usage] do get in my way when I'm reading" and then she suggests that writing teachers tend to listen for certain types of difficult-to-describe writing voices. What do you think of her discussion?

- Looking through some of your writing, find samples of pieces where you, the writer, are "not at home" and where you, the writer are clearly "at home." Do Kate's discussions of style and voice explain differences in voice in your own writing?

- Have you ever taken a piece of writing to class to share and had it flop? Why do you think that happened? Did you ever take a piece to share that you felt lukewarm about and it was a hit? Again, what do you think was going on, what were readers responding to in that piece of writing?

- Kate tells you that English teachers tend to like certain types of writing—writing that renders, writing that uses allusion, narrative, and (particularly for women teachers perhaps) personal style—do these attributes help you understand past teachers' responses to your writing? Explain by using examples of your own writing with the teacher's response if you still have them.

- Do you think it's silly to think that you might write "metaphors for English teachers, formal explanations for male teachers in other disciplines, and personal narratives for your women professors," or do you find yourself already making some of these shifts?

- How do you learn what type of writing a professor expects from you? How able or willing are you to deliver writing in that style? Are you comfortable or uncomfortable when meeting teachers' demands?

- Look at Kate's five writing suggestions, offered at the end of her essay. What in your own writing practices would you have to change to follow her advice?

7

The Computer Changes a Writing Classroom

James Strickland

James Strickland, Associate Professor of English at Slippery Rock University of Pennsylvania, has taught first-year composition courses, as well as other writing and literature courses, for over 20 years—using computer-assisted instruction for the last 10. He is the editor of the *English Leadership Quarterly* and has contributed the following chapters "Politics and Writing Programs" in *Evolving Perspectives on Computers and Composition Studies*, and "Prewriting and Computing" in *Writing On-Line*. He and his wife, Kathleen, have a son and daughter in college and two dogs at home.

Using a computer will change the way you write. I would like to be able to say that using word processing will transform your writing into prize-winning prose, or at least grade-A material. But I cannot. I can tell you that your writing will be different because my students tell me that the computer changed how they write. It didn't make them better writers; it made them different writers. Maybe that's not so bad. Changing old habits may allow us to examine the way we write, thereby prompting us to learn new strategies as we become different writers.

So, how might you expect to be changed? What will word processing do for you as a writer?

First, it does not matter what word processing program you use. Our university labs have several programs available to students for use through site licenses, a system allowing the programs to be used in the lab but not copied for individual use elsewhere (or pirated, the slang term for making an illegal copy). Some of your instructors may require that you purchase "student" versions, or stripped down versions of much more expensive software. They all work, and they will all do the job if you learn how to use them. In one sitting, you should be able to master the basics—creating a file, entering text, printing the paper—all you need to know to word process a paper. As you spend time with the computer you can learn the intricacies of its software on a need-to-know basis.

When I asked my students how the computer changed them as writers and the way they write, the answers I received were conflicting. Some said the computer lab was a quiet environment in which to work; others said that the computer lab was noisy, an aspect that they liked because they felt free to talk. Some said they talked less and stayed on-task more when using the computer; others said they were encouraged to talk and help each other in the computer room. Some said the computer made it easier to write the assignments because the ideas seemed to flow through their fingers; while others said the computer burdened them, especially those who could not type (or lacked keyboard skills). Some said their papers were better; others felt their papers were no better. See? I don't know how it will change you, but I know it will.

A student teacher, observing my class, asked me why I require my students to learn to use the computer. On the particular day she asked the question, my students had learned how to create paragraphs out of one large paragraph (a simple keystroke, striking the enter key) and how to add new sentences to the recently created paragraphs (another simple maneuver, positioning the cursor at point of insertion and typing). That day, my students learned what others had been trying for years to convince students of, students like yourselves: a large paragraph can be restructured as several smaller paragraphs, a decision that can only be arrived at after you have written the large paragraph. With typed or handwritten drafts, revision decisions such as that imply the reality of rewriting the entire paper. My students also learned another revision lesson others have been trying to convince you of: information and detail can be added to a draft at any point—within a draft, within a paragraph, even within a sentence. My students, like most, have a tendency to add to the end of their drafts, unless they are using word processing. The reason is obvious: adding details anywhere else necessitates rewriting the paper.

So, as teachers often do, I in turn asked this student teacher why she thought I required my students to learn to use the computer. She answered her own question very well. Students need to learn word processing because they will need to know it for advanced upper-level courses. They need to learn to use the computer because it makes their writing easier to read. And students need to learn to use the computer because it takes the drudgery out of rewriting a paper.

Expectations

The computer itself is not responsible for the changes you sense in the classroom; these differences are a result of your teacher's style, the writing activities, and the climate of your classroom. To clarify, let's think about your expectations for a "regular" classroom. Like most students, you should not be surprised to find a great deal of writing required of you in a college writing class. But what other expectations do you have for a writing class? For one thing, you might expect lectures about writing and grammar and reading assignments that are either concerned with writing or are to be the topics for writing assignments. Some students might expect to discuss the writings of their classmates, and others expect to do in-class writing on tests and exams. What students rarely expect in writing classes is to be given the opportunity to write. And yet, an important difference is that a computer writing class is a writing workshop, a class where time is allowed for writing.

Students in computer sections of writing classes expect help from their teacher and they expect to be able to ask for help, a relationship that rarely develops within a regular classroom. Students become comfortable with their teacher moving about the room, answering questions, offering advice, solving technical problems.

In most cases, your teachers will have to schedule a certain number of classes or assign outside work in the computer lab. My students tend to see the computer lab as separate from the rest of the class, divorced from the other activities—at least, initially. How extreme that separation is depends to a large degree on how well the computer activities fit with the other activities. As you come to anticipate that you will spend time writing in class, this will give you a sense of purpose and a sense of value to time spent in the computer lab.

The computer lab is a special workspace. The desks and rows of a traditional classroom are constructed to isolate you as a writer and focus your attention to the front of the room, the location where the teacher normally is found. Even if you arrange your desks in a circle, it is difficult to share your papers with more than one person and even that requires giving an actual copy to another person. In a computer lab, your classmates working at terminals are accessible and their work is shareable. Writing on a computer screen is so visually available that some people worry about privacy (a concern controlled by dimming the screen or angling the monitor to discourage uninvited reading). In the computer lab you can allow two or three people to sit around your screen and simultaneously read what you have written. If your lab is networked, you can send the writing to as many terminals in the room as you wish (or elsewhere for that matter), while retaining the original on your own screen. How successful you are as a writer in a computer writing class depends on how comfortable you become with the machine and its environment.

Worries with Computers

In your years of school, I am sure that you have been given conflicting information about what to do to create a good piece of writing. You've been told to find your thesis, told to develop an outline, told to write an introduction, told to write the body, told to write a conclusion, and told to remember to proofread. Now you're being sent to the computer lab and being told this machine will make you a writer. Oh no, it won't, you say, because unless you grew up using computers and machines, you're scared to death of them. Your fear may become a self-fulfilling prophecy. It's funny; I have students who mention in their journals being upset because they've lost a favorite pen, the pen they need to write. It's not that the pen makes them into writers, but it does make them comfortable when writing. How successful you will be writing with a computer will have a lot to do with how comfortable you feel with the machine.

First of all, you won't break the machine. Computers are built so that unless you drop them off the table, you won't hurt them. You may jam your disks in the disk drive; you may jam the paper in the printer, but both can be corrected. The only thing to worry about (if you insist upon worrying) is that you'll somehow lose your writing. Have you ever had a tape cassette eaten by a tape player or had your favorite video cassette taped over by a little sister, anxious to record her favorite cartoon on Saturday morning? Accidents happen. The disk is, after all, merely a device for the magnetic storage of information. Your writing, the information on the disk, can be erased or scrambled if you bring the disk near a magnet, experience a power outage, leave the disk in the backseat of the car on a sunny day, expose the surface protected by the metal covering to foreign materials, such as dust, cigarette smoke, cookie crumbs, or fingerprints. You cannot be too careful. With a second disk and the "save" sequence of keystrokes, my students make duplicates of their work, backup copies in case of accidents.

Students also worry about looking dumb. Consider the case of a man I work with, a professor with 25 years of teaching experience. I had been teaching word processing to him, and every day for three weeks, he would come into my office and say that he'd lost his file, everything he'd worked on the day before. Trying to recover it, I checked whether he'd named it something different or saved it on another disk. I checked that he'd put the disks in correctly, thinking he might have put them in backwards or upside down. I even gave him a new copy of the word processing program, thinking his copy had a bug, a defect in the program. Finally, I asked him to come and get me the next time he was finished working at the computer. He did, and when he sat back at the machine, I asked him if he was all finished. He replied, "Yes," and I asked him what he did next. To my astonishment, he reached around the side of the machine and turned it off. No wonder he couldn't find his file. He didn't save it; he didn't transfer what he'd been writing onto the disk. You probably won't do anything as foolish as that. In fact, many word processing programs have a feature that saves automatically every 5 or 10 minutes, transferring what you've been writing on the screen onto your disk, so that if the power goes out or you forget to save it before turning off the machine, little will be lost.

So if you're not forgetful or abusive to the disk, you have nothing to worry about. Unless of course, you worry that you'll have nothing to write. All writers have intermittent bouts with the same writing problems—getting ideas, writing introductions, working on organization, knowing what to change, judging whether a piece needs to be longer or shorter, and deciding how to interest a reader. Writers deal with each of these problems in different ways, but each of these can be addressed through a variety of computer strategies. I'd like to discuss some of the techniques that can be employed on the computer to help your writing, some of the things you should know about.

Computer Writing Strategies

Freewriting

A computer is great for freewriting, a strategy whereby you write as quickly as you can, allowing your mind to jump from one idea to the next as quickly as the connections are suggested. With freewriting, you never worry about grammar, punctuation, coherence, or a grade. You simply write. When you freewrite with a pencil or a pen, there is a temptation to erase errors and to be cautious of what is written in ink. When you freewrite with a computer, the words flow freely in electronic type—easily correctable at some later time, easily expendable if you don't think they are just right, easily rearranged if they are valuable but not in quite the right order.

Blindfolded Writing

Let's say you've tried freewriting but you don't feel free: you're the type of person who likes to go back and reread what you've written, checking for errors and thinking what to say next. Another trick that can be done with the computer, one that will help with your problem, is writing blindfolded. No, you don't really blindfold yourself or even close your eyes; you turn off the screen. Simply find the switch that controls the brightness of the monitor, turn it all the way until the screen is dark. Now begin typing. Keep writing for 5 minutes, 10 minutes, or until you can't stand it any longer and have to turn the brightness control back up. What you'll seen on the screen may look like this, "I kdon;t know what to write I think I;lll write about the problems of students are getting wripped off on the fees and tuition being changerd." It's not great: there are punctuation mistakes, misspelled words (typos), and grammatical errors, notably a fused sentence. Yet writing blindfolded on the computer generates content, text that can be easily corrected by deleting the excess and fixing the errors, allowing what appears on the screen to be changed to "students are getting ripped off by the fees and tuition being charged." Freewriting on paper would have necessitated a clean sheet and copying over the worthwhile stuff. Freewriting on the computer is more like sculpting: you take away what doesn't belong and you smooth out the lines of what is left.

Brainstorming

I'm sure you've heard of brainstorming, an idea-generating technique in which you call out or write down ideas as quickly as they come to you. These ideas usually come out looking like a grocery list, lots of things written down the sheet of paper but not in any particular order. If it were a grocery list, you would cross the items off as you find them on the shelf in the store. When brainstorming you might cross them off as you use them in your writing. Sometimes you reorganize the list before you begin to write the draft by employing a numbering sequence to represent the order in which you plan to deal with the ideas. When using paper and pen, brainstorming involves not only generating the ideas but a great deal of crossing out, drawing arrows, and adding sequencing numbers. The result is often a mess. When brainstorming on the computer, the ideas can be reorganized (using the copy/move sequence of keystrokes) and deleted (using the delete keys or a block erase). The result is the same: the brainstormed ideas that were judged useful are resequenced and the ideas that were judged inappropriate are removed. The writer is left with a clean, organized plan to follow in writing the draft. The notes from the brainstorming session can be placed in a window, a divided section of the computer screen, which I discuss shortly.

Outlining

At some point in your experience of writing in school, you have been taught or required to do an outline, a skeleton of the paper you plan to write, organized according to the hierarchy of ideas—the thesis subdivided according to major ideas, further subdivided according to points to be made under the major idea, in turn divided into subpoints. Although brainstorm lists provide the same sort of plan without the hierarchical emphasis, the creation of an outline makes the act of writing seem so logical and sequential. Outlines are often required for longer pieces of writing, such as term papers, where the failings of human memory would benefit from an organized plan. For years, I believed I was the only one who subverted the purpose of completing an outline by writing it after I had finished the term paper. It seemed so much easier to find the major ideas after I had written them. One interesting thing I noticed in doing my "cheater's outline" was that I could spot places where the ideas didn't really flow from one to the next. Textbooks call this testing for coherence. When writing on the computer, a variation of my cheater's outline can be used to check how well a piece of writing holds together. Once a draft has been written, I tell my students to create a second copy by renaming the file with an ".out" extension (for example, the file TERMPAPR.DOC would be renamed TERMPAPR.OUT). This second copy can then be reduced to outline form by identifying the sentence containing the statement of the major idea in each paragraph and stripping everything else from each paragraph (using the delete keys or a block erase), leaving just that one sentence. The sections that are left can be sequenced by capital and lowercase letters and Roman and Arabic numbers. Now the outline of the draft can be examined and evaluated for coherence (Does idea 2 lead into 3? Does there need to be a 2a to complete the connection?). Once the outline is made and adjusted it can be placed in a window and the original draft can be recalled in the bottom portion of the screen, the other window, and revised according to the insights gained from making the cheater's outline.

Windowing

When you write with paper, you have the implicit knowledge that, unless this copy is the final copy, you are always able to draw a line across the page marking out a separate section to carry out another task, whether it's drawing an illustration, scribbling notes for a later section, brainstorming ideas for another writing task, or even writing a reminder to videotape a movie on cable that night. The computer gives you the same capability on the screen; most word processing programs have a sequence of keystrokes that enable you to divide the screen into two sections. This can be useful for looking at two parts of a paper at the same time, giving you the effect of looking at page eight next to page two, for example. Windowing can also be useful for placing a different file in one window while working on text in the other window. The upper window might contain an outline or a brainstorming list, while the lower window has the actual text-in-progress. Windowing can allow you to compare two versions of a task, one written by a classmate with one that you wrote. Windowing can allow you to look at another paper you wrote to use as a model for the current task you are working on.

Sentence Separation and Rearrangement

Another computer writing strategy enables you to separate each sentence of your draft from the others by pressing the enter key twice after each period. This strategy lets you evaluate a sentence in isolation from what precedes it and what follows, to get a sense of how well each sentence functions on its own. Expand the detail in each sentence by adding phrases. Try reordering the sentences (using the copy/move sequence of keystrokes) to see if ideas in one sentence need to come before or after another sentence; sometimes a third sentence should come second, but as a writer, you can't see the wisdom of that until you try it out. Knowing or sensing what to try—and then taking the time needed for moving things around—takes imagination and patience. To look at something you have written and to try to imagine it in a different order is difficult to do. You are almost stuck with seeing it that way because of the fact that it exists that way; the physical existence is almost overwhelming. The computer however allows you to imagine the text as other-than-it-is and then gives you the chance to see it physically rearranged.

The computer gives you the chance to fiddle with your writing, not only with the style of your sentences but the chance to experiment with the arrangement of the sentences and paragraphs, the arrangement of the whole piece or the individual units. The computer, using the copy/move sequence for blocks of text, allows you to move things around and to fiddle with a purpose, not just shuffle for the sake of scrambling. I suggest that my students try moving their conclusions to the beginning as new introductions. When you are ready as writers to conclude your work, you have only just discovered what it is that a reader needs to know at the beginning of the piece of writing. I advise the same for paragraphs, reordering them to see if perhaps the fourth paragraph should come second, for example. In fact, the approach can be used to test out lexical choices of vocabulary—insert a new word, take out an old one. See how it reads. It sounds so simple. The machine allows you to compensate for not yet having a sense of language that more experienced writers have.

I know this evaluation of sentences in the outline strategy or the sentence separation strategy seems like a great deal of work to you and would certainly never be tried without a computer's ability to move and copy, but this exercise enables writers to look at their writing in a different light. These strategies are also ones that may be shared in community (in person or through a computer-hosted sharing of texts); writers can help each other by creating the outlines or the separations and by making suggestions.

Boldfacing

You will often want to share printout copies of your drafts with other writers or your teacher. A computer can generate a printed copy of each revised version of your paper, allowing you or someone else to assess the changes. A strategy for directing a reader's attention to particular sections of the revision is to use the boldfacing capability of the computer. Usually no more than one or two keystrokes are needed to mark the beginning and ending of sections in drafts that you wish to be printed in boldface, a darker typeface than the rest of the text. This strategy directs the reader to compare various versions of a paper at specific junctures. By noting the revisions and bringing them to a reader's attention, you begin to consider which changes are successful while developing a real understanding of what you're trying to say.

Copy Editing

When you begin to write with a computer, you will probably notice that you are becoming more and more concerned with getting things perfect. Often students who normally scribble early drafts of their writings, using sloppy handwriting to disguise words and grammatical questions they are unsure of, become overly concerned with spelling, grammar, and punctuation. I guess this happens because the computer's typeface makes every detail noticeable. If this happens to you, I'll wager that as you go back to fix a "typo" or make a correction you lose your train of thought. Once you return to what you were doing, you find yourself stopping to reread what you've written in the hopes of getting back to what you were thinking.

My advice is to hold off your premature concern with spelling, grammar, and punctuation—what we call the local concerns. Remember that the computer is capable of generating a perfect copy following each revision and alteration, so there is no need to worry about correctness until much later. By suspending the desire to have the grammar and punctuation perfect until the final draft, you are free to concentrate on more important matters, such as your ideas and your presentation—what we call the global concerns.

Community and Independent Learning

I admit that when I'm in the computer lab, I would rather ask someone how to do something than read the manual or look it up on-line. Although I can see why you, like me, would prefer to raise your hand for a quick answer rather than solve it yourself, it is frustrating when the teachers are the only ones in the lab who can answer those raised hands. It is important that you take responsibility for being able to operate successfully; you need to learn to be self-reliant. The presence of classmates who are more computer literate than you are helps to foster a learning environment where you are each learners in a community of learners and teachers of one another. Students in computer labs are great at asking technical questions but not at asking writing questions.

The two most difficult things to learn in a computer writing class are contradictory lessons: (1) you need to learn to be independent, able to operate the word processing program on your own and access strategies that will enable you to complete writing assignments, and (2) you need to learn the value of community for writing and learning. We need to reverse the perception that it is all right for you to ask for help with operating the machine while written work should be completed on your own. Perhaps when writing is the only activity you are engaged in while in the lab, you tend to become focused on getting the writing done, as if that were all the computer writing course were about. You need, as a computer writer, to take command technically and, as a writer on a computer, to ask for the help of the writing community.

I understand that many students are bothered by the community aspect of writing. You are aware of so many pressures to perform as an isolated individual. You get a grade at the end of every semester for every course you take, an evaluation of your individual performance. You feel in competition with those around you in class because, after all, not everyone can receive A's. Thus, helping someone else in this community of learners might cut you out of the A's. You are told to hand in work that is your own, and if someone else helps, significantly improving your work, you might be accused of plagiarism, as my sister was in her first-year college English class after her older brother, fresh out of graduate school, helped her with her assignment. Considering all these dangers, I cannot blame you for wanting to go solo and take your chances. Yet, I hope to convince you of the importance of inter-dependence within a community of writers.

You've probably realized that an important lesson about learning to become a writer, about thinking of yourself as a writer, is to assume authority over your writing, breaking free of the "write it/turn it in/see what it's worth" syndrome. Yet assuming authority does not imply that writers must work alone or that they are the only ones to evaluate the worth of their writing. While you are writing or after you have something written down, you can maintain authority and still get a critical view of the worth of your writing by receiving a second opinion. Writers need feedback from other writers. When I write something— no matter whether it's an interoffice memo or an article for a profes-sional journal—I ask someone else to read it. I'm not looking for praise or a grade; I'm looking for someone to suggest how I might make the writing better. All real writers do this. That is what I mean by being a part of a community of writers; it's sort of a support group.

Can computer software actually give advice about writing? Like other computer programmers, I tried to create software that would help a writer, asking questions in an attempt to mimic human inter-action. For example, my software makes the computer respond to your writing in this way: "Okay, JASON [inserting your name at the appropriate point]. I see that you have a great deal to say about GUN CONTROL LAWS [inserting your topic, the answer to an earlier question]. At this point, it might be helpful to compare the GUN CONTROL LAWS to a situation that you see as similar. Think of this as an argument by analogy. What could the issue of GUN CONTROL LAWS be compared to?"

Regardless of how computers behave in science-fiction movies, you can probably tell from that short example that a computer cannot understand the content of your writing, certainly not in the intuitive sense that another writer in your class, your dorm, or your social group could. To become a writer, you need to find your own commu-nity. To get a second opinion you need to find someone else to read what you've written and ask that person to react as to whether your writing makes sense, has interest, or contains errors (factual or grammatical). A good place to look is in your classroom because each of you shares an understanding of what sort of expectations and deadlines are in place. You could also look to classmates in the dorm, brothers/sisters of your fraternity or sorority, friends on a sport team. You might even consider your teacher as a fellow member of your writers' community.

To help you establish your interdependence within a community of writers, I suggest that you think of the computer lab as a place for the community meetings. Various lab configurations allow your fellow writers to revise a copy of your writing, add small, self-adhesive flags on the copy, and/or create a separate file with suggestions. While preserving your original text, the computer can generate a multitude of duplicate copies with a simple name change keystroke. For example, Laura might send a copy of her paper on Cryonics, a file named CRYONICS.DOC to her friend, Leah (physically or over a network). After reading Laura's original text, Leah can simply change the name to CRYONICS.TWO (or anything else) and begin to alter the original text, insert notes to Laura within the text, or write a letter to Laura giving her responses. Once finished, Leah returns the new file (CRYONICS.TWO) to Laura, providing her with the feedback all writers require while allowing Laura, since she still has her original (CRYONICS.DOC), to maintain responsibility for and authority over her writing.

The computer allows you a place for two or more people to hold writers' conferences, using the same screen or conversing over a network. If Leah were sitting as part of a group around the same screen, she could point to sections of the writing on the screen and make suggestions, trying them out in front of Laura and anyone else gathered around, a type of interactive feedback that is nearly impossible to achieve in a regular classroom setting.

Teaching you to word process is easy; it is much harder to teach you to see yourselves as part of a writing community, a community that is fostered by the computer lab. If you see writing as primarily a solitary activity, then there is no reason to spend class time in the lab. You can work on your own and turn in the writing when you're done. In this frame of mind, it is difficult for you to see that time spent in a collaborative effort—learning by interaction with other writers—is as valuable, maybe more valuable, than finishing your work, finishing the assignment, making an individual mark or effort. So, the purpose of a writing course includes helping you develop a sense of the way that writers and learners operate in a community where there is time in class to give and receive feedback from other writers, time to make immediate changes and risk trying new things, and time to ask advice of a teacher who is a writer by profession. Using a computer in this type of community will change the way you write and the way you think of yourself as a writer.

Bibliography

G. E. Hawisher & C. L. Selfe, (Eds.). *Evolving Perspectives Computers and Composition Studies: Questions for the 1990s.* Urbana, IL: National Council of Teachers of English, 1991.

J. L. Collins & E. A. Sommers (Eds.). *Writing On-Line: Using Computers in the Teaching of Writing.* Portsmouth, NH: Boynton/Cook, 1985.

Sharing Ideas

- Can you describe your experiences up to this point with computers and composing? Are you part of a new generation of college students who have always had computers available in their schools or are you just becoming familiar with a computer learning environment?

- Jim says his students had different experiences with the computer classroom—some felt it was quiet and some found it a noisy environment; some said they talked more in such classrooms, and some talked less; some felt their papers were better, and some felt their papers were no better. If you've had experiences in a computer classroom, explain how they match with the observations made by Jim's students.

- Jim claims that both teacher and student *roles* change in the computer classroom. Share your reasons for agreeing or not agreeing with his analysis.

- Which of the computer writing techniques reviewed in this essay do you already use (and with what results)? Which techniques are new to you and seem like they would aid your writing? Why?

- Are the types of writing communities described by Don, Ellie, and Kate possible in Jim's computer classroom? Additionally, what could a computer environment add to Don, Ellie, or Kate's classes?

- I know this book would not have come into existence without the help of a word processor nor would it have come into existence without the help of many readers and classroom communities. Can you envision writing classrooms of the future—ones that combine the strengths of human writers and their technological aids in even more exciting ways? Tell some stories.

Part III

Writing in Progress

In this section, nine essayists look at writing in progress. These authors examine up close the complex activity of composing written texts. The first three essays show how writing and reading are constructive processes. In different ways, Thia Wolf, Jeanette Harris, and Pat D'Arcy all assert that writing and reading are generative, lead to personal growth and self-discovery, and help us to explore and utilize our memories. They offer you visual representations of reading and writing and invention processes as well as advice aimed at enhancing your ability to think through writing.

Two authors, Susan Wyche-Smith and Stephany Loban, discuss in some detail professional and student writers' actual production of written texts. Susan uses her own writing history and a research study that she conducted of student writers to examine writers' productive (and sometimes unproductive) rituals. Then she offers some suggestions for exploring and extending the writing rituals you already have, although you may not have paid much attention to these rituals before. Stephany, on the other hand, took a careful look at a fellow student's composing habits in order to test the claims of composition researchers. Observing while a friend composed aloud gave Stephany a deeper understanding of her friend's writing strategies, confirming the complexity of the writing models (usually focusing on inventing, drafting, revising, and editing) that are available in composition research reports.

8

Writing as a Tool for Learning and Discovery

Thia Wolf

Thia Wolf is a professor of writing at California State University, Chico. She enjoys teaching courses in rhetoric and writing, in the tutoring of writing, and in writing program administration. Her home, which lies in a beautiful canyon overlooking a creek, sometimes serves as a writing workshop headquarters for writers who feel stuck or blocked on writing projects. In addition to her academic interests, she enjoys studying psychology and Eastern philosophy. But her favorite pastime is meeting with friends and sharing "wild mind" writing activities from Natalie Goldberg's excellent book *Wild Mind*.

This essay examines ways of using writing to improve memory, foster insights, and accelerate learning. Few of us stop to consider that writing can be more than a functional activity (something we do when we need to apply for a job or prepare for a trip to the grocery store) and different from mandatory assignments. Writing is a uniquely human tool, a means to stimulate memory, construct new knowledge, and explore both ourselves and our environment. Even people who don't like to write essays, letters, or research papers may find that they enjoy using writing to increase their learning potential. I want to introduce you to writing activities that can support you in learning and in living. You'll probably get the most out of this essay if you have paper and pencil handy. Rather than reading straight through, plan to sit down with the essay more than once. On each occasion of your reading, try one or two of the activities suggested here. They are scattered throughout the text.

Let's begin by looking at some ways that writing stimulates and enhances memory. Although researchers still have a long way to go before understanding all about the ways our brains work, they have created useful hypotheses, or theories, about brain function. Obviously, our brains store information over the entire course of our lives; this stored information forms the basic building blocks of our memories.

We'll try a simple writing activity that demonstrates how memory becomes activated through language. Start with a word that seems neutral, even uninteresting, and print it in the middle of a sheet of paper. (In my example, below, I started with the word "bread.") After you've printed this word, print other words or phrases that it reminds you of. (You'll see that I wrote names of breads, but pretty soon I found myself writing names of places where I'd eaten bread, people I know who like bread, childhood memories about bread, etc.) Keep track of the thoughts that go through your mind by noting as many words and phrases as you can around other words and phrases on the page that trigger a memory or association. You may be surprised at how many memories come back to you and how many associations you have for simple words such as "tree," "lamp," or "blanket."

The map below (Figure 8.1) is a visual representation of the ways my brain became stimulated when I thought of the word "bread." I began by categorizing breads: sourdough, French. And I suddenly remembered something I think of only rarely—the Helm's Bakery truck that used to visit our neighborhood when I was a child. The Helm's truck was like an ice cream truck, except that it was filled with shelves of breads, doughnuts, and other bakery goods. Although I didn't mention it in my map, remembering the Helm's truck brought back memories of some of the most delicious smells imaginable. When the Helm's man opened the large back doors to his truck and invited us up a step and into his bakery, my mother and I found ourselves enveloped in the thick, sweet smells of freshly baked treats.

Remembering what it felt like to enter the truck with my mother, I also remembered her favorite food: lemon jelly doughnuts. But my thinking didn't stop there. Coming back to my original word trigger, bread, I realized that sourdough bread reminds me both of my father, who loves it, and of San Francisco, a place renowned for its sourdough loaves. Thinking of San Francisco reminded me of my honeymoon, and of a film my husband and I saw while we were there. That film, a horror film, made me think of other horror films I've known.

Figure 8–1

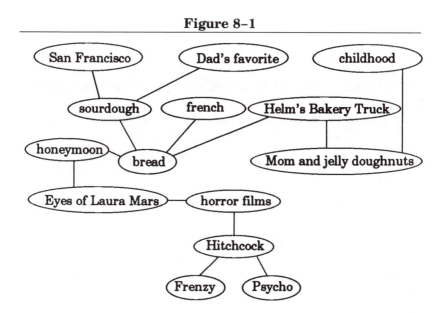

Create a map yourself and see what it shows you about how your memory works.

Activity

When I made my map and reviewed it, I realized how important the sense of smell is in my memory process: the smell of the Helm's Bakery Truck and the smell of the sourdough loaves on San Francisco's fisherman's wharf brought back the richest memories for me.

Writing researchers Linda Flower and John Hayes (1977) explain that we store memory in "rich bits," chemically encoded pieces of information that incorporate many experiences and associations. Flower and Hayes liken them to intuition and explain that without the intervention of language these bits never become useful to us. Although I have stored many complex bits of information about my family and my daily experience in my brain, I can only examine, enjoy, and use this information fully when I put it into words. Looking over my map I can also see that relationships occupy a central place in my memory process: most of my memories center on my relationships with my family members. The words in my map serve as memory triggers, allowing me to relive significant moments in my life and to make new connections between my past experience and my present situation. If you examine your cognitive map, what memory triggers seem to matter most to you? Did you remember any details when you did your map that surprised or pleased you? What were they?

Most people who use writing as a way of remembering the past find that many small details they had entirely forgotten resurface during the writing activity. This is not to say that all of these memories are accurate. Experiments on the working of memory reveal that many factors—including stress, distorted self-assessment, and elapsed time—alter the way we remember past events. Also, the way others remember or represent the past can influence our memories of it (Loftus, 1988).

To demonstrate how malleable memory really is, write a one-page description of something you remember from your childhood. Make sure that it's a memory that is fairly vivid for you and that someone in your family will probably also remember. After you've written your description down, talk to the family member who shared the experience with you. Ask for his or her description. What discrepancies did you find?

I've often found that my memory of a situation differs radically from others' memories. When I finished high school, I expected to be given my father's old Volkswagen Beetle; I clearly remembered that he had promised it to me when I was a freshman. My graduation day arrived at last, but my father had no memory of any such promise! He eventually traded the car in on a new car for himself. Because I know my father is an honest man, I know he really didn't remember having promised me his car. It's not impossible, in fact, that I made up the promise in my own mind and came to believe in it because I wanted it to be true.

The malleability of memory is one reason why some people like to keep daily journals: a written record of the highlights in one's life can help to keep memory more accurate. In business situations, many individuals like to create a "paper trail," a series of memos and notes that record each worker's responsibilities for a certain project. In these cases, writing becomes a way of preserving memory and creating a history of a business undertaking or a private life.

But writing has many more interesting uses than to preserve or explore memory. In and out of school settings, writing can help individuals synthesize new information with previously learned information and thus create new, complex structures of *understanding*. So let's move from the realm of memory and examine some writing activities that help us to think more clearly and create new ways of knowing what we need to know.

Activity

One writing activity my students and I both enjoy is the "teacher exercise," an activity passed on to me by a friend who took a workshop on creative diary keeping. The teacher exercise is an example of a dialogue activity, a way of externalizing some of the internal conversations that take place between different voices within yourself. To create a successful dialogue with one of your internal teaching voices, start by listing important teachers in your life. These may be people you have known and admired, people you've never met, characters in stories or film, places you've traveled, even objects. (For example, I learn a lot by watching the ways trees share ground and sky with one another; they're a cooperative group that live together peaceably unless dire necessity forces them to struggle for the same ground. From trees I've learned the importance of being as much as one can be wherever one stands.) I've included a partial list of my favorite teachers below:

My music teacher, Virginia Petersen

My dissertation director, Professor Don Daiker

My colleague, Elizabeth Renfro

My neighbor, Jean Graybeal

Trees

After you make a list that suits you, try writing a dialogue between yourself and one of your teachers about a problem you want to solve. Write as quickly as you can, allowing the dialogue to surprise you. Continue to write for several pages.

Written dialogue exercises like this one frequently allow writers to experience sudden insights about problems as diverse as family fights and difficult chemistry equations. Even if your internal teacher doesn't have an answer for your problem, he/she can often provide a strategy for approaching the problem so that you can think about it more calmly, analytically, and effectively.

Another useful dialogue exercise involves recreating an argument you've had with someone, but approaching the argument from the other person's point of view. Include not only the spoken part of the argument, but also the thoughts of the person you argued against. How does that person respond internally to the things you did and said during the argument? When you consider the argument from his/her viewpoint, can you better understand why he/she responded to you in the way he/she did? Try this dialogue exercise here, including the other person's internal thoughts in parentheses.

Being able to understand your opponent's point of view has long been a recommended technique for learning how to persuade others to see your side of an argument. Psychologist Carl Rogers (1965) has claimed that only through validating the viewpoint of another can we hope to have our own viewpoints validated. Analyzing and validating an opponent's view before opposing it may lead to better negotiations for a third, socially constructed viewpoint between all of the parties involved. And you may surprise yourself by finding that, after studying someone else's view, you agree with his/her opinion more than you'd realized.

I recall a turbulent time in my household when I was still in my teens. During an argument with my mother, I claimed that she always put her own needs and interests ahead of my own. She countered by telling me that most of her activities (cooking, cleaning, driving, shopping) revolved around my needs, and that if I didn't understand this, I had better start trying some of her responsibilities on for size. If I had stopped to think about the world from her point of view, I would have seen that she contributed a generous share of her time and energy to keeping me happy. Because I didn't stop to think about her perspective, I made her angry, had some of my privileges revoked, and took on a new household responsibility, that of family cook. She and I didn't have a conversation about our misunderstandings: we had a fight. And fighting, although it produces a satisfactory amount of adrenalin and a momentary surge of self-righteous indignation, rarely transforms the problems it seeks to address.

Now that you've warmed up your imagination by creating the voices of a teacher and an opponent, consider some of the other ways that imagination can intersect with writing to help you create connections and new insights. Below, I've described a few activities that students of mine have found useful. Read them over, then try one.

Activity

Letter from the Future.   Write yourself a letter from an older version of yourself. What will you be like in 25 years? Where will you live? What will you do for a living? What will matter to you most? Write to yourself from this older perspective. What advice should your older self give your present self to make sure you arrive at the future you most want?

Intersections.   List five subjects you've studied in school. Choose the two that seem most different from each other and write a paragraph describing all of their similarities and connections, even if you really have to stretch to find these.

Drawing into Writing.   Draw three pictures of a recurring problem in your life, whether it's studying mathematics or making satisfying friendships. Date one of these pictures from an earlier time in your life, one from the present, and one from the future. Write a paragraph or two that explores the connections between these pictures. What patterns can you start to detect by exploring the ways these pictures relate to each other. What alternative behaviors or approaches might help you solve the problem you've explored?

These activities work equally well for advancing your understanding of your private life and of your scholastic endeavors. You can just as easily ask a future version of yourself about the many reasons why studying writing or mathematics now might help you later in life as you can ask that self about the benefits of vigorous exercise over the course of many years. One important feature of activities like these is that they give you a chance to become more involved in your learning process. Research on cognition, our internal thought processes, indicates that personal involvement in any learning activity increases the chances that learning will be sophisticated rather than superficial, and memorable rather than easily forgotten (Mandler, 1984). With a little thought and creativity, you can see how activities such as these could help you in a variety of classes and situations. In a history course, you might write a journal entry from the point of view of a historical figure; in a chemistry course, you might write a conversation among the elements in an equation. You'll enjoy learning more and learn more effectively if you can construct approaches to learning that engage your attention and challenge your imagination.

One of the most powerful ways to challenge yourself through written language and to learn any lesson well is to develop a facility with metaphors and similes. Some researchers argue that metaphors— comparisons between unlike things—are the fundamental building blocks of all interpretive endeavors. This is because metaphors tap into our most basic ways of knowing about the world—through our senses and our bodily motions. Everything we understand, every new piece of knowledge we add to what we already know, connects with some physical experience of our environment. This is the critical function of metaphor: to provide us with linguistic links between abstract or unexamined thoughts and our physical understanding of the world in which we live.

That last sentence may be hard to understand without a concrete example of the way metaphors and similes work. Let me provide you with an example from my own life. As a freshman in college, I enrolled in an astronomy course, a class I nearly failed. I have hated astronomy ever since but never stopped to think about why. By constructing a simile, I can begin to examine my reasons for responding so negatively to this academic subject. To construct the simile, I'll use the abstract, unexamined problem ("I hate studying astronomy") and a physical experience to which I can compare it. For my physical experience, I use the technique of association, jotting down the first example that comes to mind of something else I hate: eating a rotten bing cherry. So here's my simile: Studying astronomy is like *eating a rotten bing cherry*.

What sense can I make of this comparison? I'll start with the physical side of the equation. Bing cherries are my favorite food. I look forward to cherry season every year and have been known to consume a whole bag of cherries for lunch or dinner. So when I get a rotten cherry, I'm disappointed and disagreeably surprised. My mouth is all set for one kind of taste sensation, but the cherry feels mealy and tastes moldy on my tongue.

Having sorted through these reactions to the rotten cherry, I can start thinking about ways the eating experience reminds me of the astronomy class I took. I remember now that before I enrolled in the course, I expected to like it. I've always been a science fiction fan, and I assumed an astronomy class would focus mostly on facts about distant planets (with some speculation about extraterrestrial life forms thrown in for good measure). In fact, the professor talked mostly about physics. He wanted us to learn a variety of mathematical calculations that would help us understand how scientists interpret the information they receive from telescopes. Because I expected one kind of experience in the course and got another (very much like expecting a good cherry but biting into a rotten one), I reacted to astronomy with distaste. Realizing this makes me wonder if I wouldn't be wise to give astronomy another try. After all, I may have caused my own problems in learning because of the expectations I carried with me into the class. Now that I'm older and a bit more open-minded, I might enjoy learning something about telescopes and the use of physics to understand the stars.

Writing theorist Peter Elbow (1981) suggests an interesting metaphor activity, which students in many of my writing classes tell me later is the single most useful discovery tool I taught them. This activity will help you make surprising, creative connections if you do the first half quickly and the second half thoughtfully. First, choose a problem (scholastic or personal) that you haven't yet solved. Quickly, without stopping to think about your response, write down its color, its shape, its size, its smell. Now take several minutes to explain, in writing, why you gave this problem each of these physical properties (for a whole series of metaphor activities, see Elbow, 1981). Were you able to discover what some of your metaphors meant?

Often, using metaphors to redefine a problem can give you an entirely new perspective on your situation. Developing skill with metaphors will also enhance your use of descriptive and poetic language in your more formal writing tasks.

Finally, you can also employ writing in classes across the disciplines to help strengthen your learning process. Most students take notes during lectures, even though many classroom lectures only repeat material that can be found in the course textbook. If you notice that the professors in some of your classes go over reading material in their lectures, consider using writing in their classes to do something other than take notes. Here are some suggestions: periodically summarize the key points the lecturer has just covered; decide what puzzles you about what you've heard, and write down questions that you'd like to ask in class or during the teacher's office hours; listen for and jot down discrepancies between what the lecturer says and what you thought you knew about the subject (discrepancies should be cleared up in a conversation with the teacher or by rereading the course's text). All of these writing strategies allow you to interact with your learning, to question the material actively instead of sitting like a porous lump in the lecture hall waiting to be filled with someone else's knowledge. Students who take an assertive, interested approach to learning get more out of the courses they take and enjoy their educational experiences far more than students who learn material by rote for exams.

The writing strategies mentioned above can help you during your assigned reading. Keep blank paper handy to copy out intriguing or confusing portions of the text. Select some of these passages for brief writing: what questions do the passages raise or what new ideas do they give you? A particularly rewarding technique for examining your assigned reading is to make connections between unrelated courses. Ask yourself hard questions, such as How does this rule in physics connect with what I learned about the law of supply and demand in my economics course? or Did the conquest of the New World by the Spanish that I'm studying in my history course contain any of the ethical dilemmas I'm studying in my philosophy class ? If you take a few minutes to note these questions and respond to them briefly in writing, you'll begin to see many opportunities for drawing on information from all of your classes in developing an educated world view. You'll probably come up with some interesting paper topics this way, too.

Above all, remember that writing for learning need not be correct, sophisticated, or polished. Writing for learning should serve you as a tool for analyzing and synthesizing many kinds of information in your life. This is writing for *you*, not a teacher, employer, or classmate. Although you may choose to share some of this writing or to develop ideas from this writing into more formal prose, writing for learning should be stress-free, exploratory, and mind-opening. Use it to enjoy and enhance your mind's activity as you study, reflect, and live.

Works Cited

Elbow, Peter (1981). *Writing with Power.* New York: Oxford Press.

Flower, Linda, & Hayes, John (1977). "Problem-Solving Strategies and the Writing Process." *College English, 39,* 456.

Loftus, Elisabeth (1988). *Mind and Body.* New York: Norton.

Mandler, G. (1984). *Mind and Body.* New York: Norton.

Rogers, Carl (1965). *Client-Centered Therapy.* Boston: Houghton Mifflin.

Sharing Ideas

- In a previous essay, Kate Ronald explained that "with computers and copier machines, we don't worry much anymore about memory." In Thia's essay, however, a writer's memories are very important, and writing is a way to "improve memory, foster insights, and accelerate learning." Are these essayists contradicting each other or are they discussing memory in different ways?

- Thia suggests that you can tap into your memories through writing in general and through particular writing strategies like mapping, setting up dialogues with internal voices, and drawing. What, then, is the importance of memory to writers?

- As you tried Thia's activities while you read, which proved most useful to you and why?

- You may have used memory maps before (the technique is sometimes called clustering) or you may freewrite or list to capture the vivid and important details of your past. Share your personal methods (listening to music, walking, etc.) for triggering memory.

- How have two different memories of the same event (yours and another family member's, for example) affected your life?

- Thia suggests that it can be very important for a writer to be able to understand the viewpoint(s) of others. Share a time in your life when that was true.

- Everyone knows that poets use similes and metaphors, and Thia claims they have a lot to offer to any writer. What do you think of her claim and her example (astronomy and rotten cherries)?

- Metaphors seem to come naturally to some people. Do you know anyone who regularly compares one thing to another? Write a sketch of that person, capturing his or her language, and the way he or she makes comparisons.

- If you don't normally make comparisons easily yourself, take a piece of your writing and try to consciously add some metaphors. What changes? How do you like the new version?

9

How Writers and Readers Construct Texts

Jeanette Harris

Jeannette Harris directs the Composition Program at the University of Southern Mississippi. Years of teaching writing courses, directing writing programs, and writing composition textbooks have convinced her that students write better and are more comfortable with themselves as writers if they understand the process they go through as they write.

In the past three decades writing has been taught in most composition courses, both in high school and college, as a process that consists of three parts: prewriting, writing, and rewriting. This model has, in general, worked very well, providing writing instructors with a simple, convenient structure for their courses and students with a simple, convenient guide for writing.

Once it emerged, the concept of writing as a process began to erode, slowly but surely, the notion that writing, especially good writing, results only from inspiration. To view writing as a process, something like changing a tire or putting on make-up, is to demystify it— to make it known and doable rather than mysterious and mystical. Providing students with a simple model of the writing process helped them understand what was going on when they wrote and gave them confidence that they could write, if not inspired, at least competent prose. Certainly, no one, or almost no one, wanted to go back to the idea that only those who are inspired can write.

But in time the simple three-part process began to seem too simple, and some people (mainly writing researchers) began to question this prewriting-writing-rewriting model. Oh, no one questioned the idea that a process was involved—just what kind of process. Does everyone go through the same three stages in exactly the same way? Is the process perhaps recursive (the result of backward as well as forward motion) rather than relentlessly and progressively linear (moving always forward)? Can the process consist of fewer or more than three stages? And do readers go through a similar process?

Attempts to answer these questions led to various theories of text construction. The idea of constructing a text may seem a little strange to you. A building perhaps, or a highway or bridge, but why speak of constructing texts? The term *construct* suggests that when we write we build or put together something that formerly did not exist in the same form. To construct is to act in a workmanlike or workwomanlike way. To construct is to be productive as well as creative. *Text* is a broad term that can be used to refer to any written document, whether it is carved in stone, inscribed on paper, or reflected on a computer monitor. It conveniently encompasses all forms of writing—book, essay, letter, note, story, memo, poem, and so on. All written documents can be referred to as texts.

What happens when writers construct texts? Clearly, a process is involved, but what is that process and how does it differ from the old three-stage model of prewriting-writing-rewriting? To be honest, no one really knows, but we can make some educated guesses. My own guess goes like this.

A text originates as an idea—usually in the form of an internal dialogue that a writer has with himself or herself. Although in some instances this dialogue may be so fleeting that the writer is hardly conscious of its existence, I believe all texts, however brief and inconsequential, initially assume this unwritten interior form, which I call a mental text. Even the most informal note or list originates as a mental text—a thought that both anticipates and shapes the completed text. The idea to jot down a note or to make a list in itself constitutes a mental text. However unformed and fragmentary this mental image of the text is, it is a very real and significant form of the text.

We might represent this process of text construction as follows:

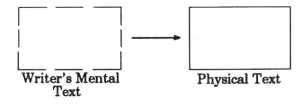

Writer's Mental Text   Physical Text

But the process is not as simple as this model suggests. Writers do not simply construct a mental text and then transfer that mental phenomenon onto a piece of paper or a computer screen. The construction of a written, physical text involves not just a single movement from mental to physical text but, depending on the complexity and length of the text, a series of recursive movements. It is, in fact, this recursive motion between the mental and physical texts that characterizes the process of constructing a text. The writer constructs a mental image of the text and then attempts to construct a physical text that reflects it.

Unfortunately, this model of text construction is not nearly as tidy and simple as the familiar three-stage process we have been using. Rather it is messy and indefinite. But I believe it is more accurate than the linear three-stage model. As anyone who has written at all knows, writing is not simple and tidy. It involves going backward as well as going forward as a writer attempts to reflect in writing what exists in his or her mind. Thus, although there are only two steps to this model of text construction, a writer repeats these two steps, shuttling back and forth from the mental to the physical text and back again, until a deadline or lack of energy or interest terminates the process.

But the process is even more complicated than this explanation suggests because the writer's mental text keeps changing. Once a writer generates something tangible, a physical text of some sort (even though it may be fragmentary), the mental text is modified, often in significant ways. For example, suppose you are asked to identify a problem at your university and write an essay about it. Your initial idea is that you will simply describe the problems with the food served in the campus cafeteria. You write a rough draft of your essay describing how bad the food is and complaining that the cafeteria never serves anything you like. When you finish this draft, you feel pretty good about it. Then a few days later, you read over this first draft and notice that your essay seems rather shallow and subjective. After all, why would a reader want to know about your food preferences? What is the point? So, you try again. This time you decide to argue that the cafeteria should serve a greater variety of food because the students who eat there come from varied backgrounds. You change your introduction so that the focus is not exclusively on you and what you like.

But once more, when you reread what you have written, you are not satisfied with the results. Arguing for a greater variety of food to accommodate the varied tastes of the students who eat there is an improvement over your first subjective version but still seems trivial and perhaps impractical. How can any cafeteria consistently provide food that everyone will like? So you begin to think about criteria other than taste. You now become convinced that the cafeteria's main concern should be good nutrition. In looking back over your first draft, when you were complaining about the food, you realize that most of the dishes you mention are high in fat, salt, and sugar. Thus you decide to rewrite once more, this time emphasizing the need for more healthy food. You revise your essay drastically, arguing this time that students need to learn while they are in college to eat a nutritious, healthy diet. In this version, you go back to your original introduction, writing about what you like, but use this as a point of departure to point out that what you like is not good for you. You then launch your argument that a school cafeteria has a responsibility to introduce students to sensible, healthy eating habits.

Just as the mental text shapes the physical text, so the physical text shapes the mental text. Although the example I've given may be somewhat extreme, subtle modification occurs almost every time you revise something you have written. As you write, your ideas about what you want to write undergo both simple and dramatic changes. If we were to try to represent this modification process in a diagram, it might look something like this:

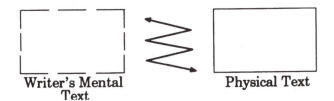

Writer's Mental
Text   Physical Text

However, the text construction process does not end here because readers as well as writers construct texts. Although readers do not construct a physical text as do writers, they do construct a mental text, which is their version of the physical text. Thus, a mental text exists not only in the mind of a writer but also, in a different but analogous way, in the mind of a reader.

Because the reader's experiences and information always differ somewhat from that of the writer, the reader's mental text always differs from that of the writer. For example, a person who lives in a large city in which innocent people are often shot would have very different assumptions about guns than those held by a writer who lives in a rural area and likes to hunt. However, the physical text that the writer constructs significantly shapes the reader's mental text.

The reader who fears being shot may not accept all of the arguments of a writer who likes to hunt, but may at least begin to appreciate the complexity of the issue.

Thus, to complete the process of text construction, we have to shift from writer to reader, for a text is completed in the mind of the reader. While a writer begins with a mental text and constructs a physical text, a reader begins with a physical text and constructs a mental text. But, like the writer, the reader moves back and forth between the two forms of the text, one modifying the other, until his or her mental text is constructed. Thus, in both writing and reading, a text is constructed by a process that involves a recursive movement between a mental and a physical text. A diagram of the complete process of text construction might look like this:

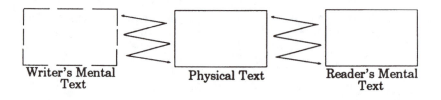

Writer's Mental Text   Physical Text   Reader's Mental Text

At this point you may well be wondering how all of this theory about reading and writing affects you. First, these theories about text construction will, I hope, make you more realistic about writing so that you will not expect to march through the process of constructing a text in a neat, sequential fashion. Although you may still want to follow the familiar guidelines of prewriting first, then writing, and finally rewriting, you should not expect a writing (or reading) project to be orderly. Your mental image of what you are writing will probably change as you write, and each time it changes, the physical text will also change as you attempt to accommodate both and reconcile one to the other. Thus, you may "revise" your mental text before you even begin to write, and may "prewrite"—make new discoveries about your subject and text—well into the project.

Second, understanding how writers and readers construct texts should provide you with a more accurate view of the relationship between readers and writers. As a writer, you are not writing in a vacuum but are rather constructing a text for a reader who will (re)construct that text in his or her own mind. Thus, as a writer, you do not control the reader's version of the text you write. But good writers, understanding the slipperiness of texts, keep the reader's possible responses in mind, trying to guide the reader's understanding. In writing some types of texts, especially fiction and poetry, you may want different readers to have different responses—to find in your words their own meanings. But here too you need to be aware of your readers and their purposes in reading as well as your purposes in writing.

Third, the concept that both writers and readers construct a mental image of the text should help you realize how important to both reading and writing are the mental, interior parts of the processes. Thus, the time you spend thinking about what you are going to write is not time wasted. Don't rush into actually putting words on paper or into the computer. Of course, this does not mean that you can put off constructing a physical text forever, but it does mean that what is going on in your mind before you write and as you write is an essential part of the process. Even more important, it means that you should allow enough time between drafts to accommodate this process of modification, to let what is in your head shape your physical text and to let that physical text, in turn, reshape what is in your head.

Finally, knowledge about how readers and writers work should give you increased control over both processes. What you understand you can usually control better. If you have a clear understanding of what is going on as people read and write, you will gradually learn to control your own versions of these processes. Writing is not a gift of the muse nor a mysterious process you cannot understand. Nor is it a simple one, two, three process. Writing involves mental as well as physical activity, involves readers as well as writers, and involves going backward—to the internal mental text—as well as going forward— to the external physical text. By understanding the process by which writers and readers construct texts, you will become a better writer and reader.

Sharing Ideas

- To construct your own text, you may, as Thia Wolf suggested in the last essay, tap your memory. But Jeanette Harris explains that we don't rely only on inspiration for composing. She suggests, instead, that composing is a complex activity and that writers begin with a mental text. Try to articulate some of the inner workings of your own mental text building processes.

- Some writers compose mainly in their heads and then write a fast and furious single draft. Is that you? Other writers do much more shuttling between mental text and physical text. Is that you?

- Explain how Jeanette's essay gives you insights into reading/ writing and writing/reading processes.

- How does your sense of audience expectations modify your drafting?

- Does Jeanette's essay illuminate your own history as a writer/reader? Does she add anything to the discussions by writers who were growing into writing in the first section: Carolyn, Brad, or Audrey?

- Many of us have become used to talking about writing process. It may be more unusual to consider how the act of reading is also a process. You have probably had an experience of bringing your own understanding (past reading, past life experiences, past school experiences, your travels, your love life, and so on) to a reading of a text. For instance, when a story is set in New York City, how important is it that you have a knowledge of large urban cityscapes? In understanding a written text, What is the reader's responsibility? What is the writer's responsibility?

- Describe a time when constructing a satisfying mental image of a text proved difficult for you. Does Jeanette's essay help you understand how you might have resolved those difficulties?

10

The Activity Is Thinking

Pat D'Arcy

Before her present post as the English Adviser for the County of Wiltshire, Pat D'Arcy taught 11-to-18-year-old students and worked with a couple of major research projects in the UK: *Reading for Meaning* and *Writing Across the Curriculum*. She worked part-time while her two children were in their early years. Her son is now an electronic engineer and her daughter a nurse. For the past 12 years Pat's job has been to work with primary and secondary teachers in their own classrooms and through in-service workshops. The challenge is how to help students of all ages and abilities to become more confident talkers, readers, and writers—and thereby more confident thinkers.

Visible Thinking

Learning how to write involves the following features:

- Learning the *CODE* of written language. The code converts the *sounds* of words into *signs* for words. The codes developed for written Chinese or Arabic are quite different from the codes developed for European languages. Learning to write code-wise, therefore, depends on whichever spoken language we are learning to spell out correctly in its written form.

- Learning how to handle the *MEDIUM* of written language. Like dance or music or art, writing is a powerful *mode of expression*. To write effectively, we have to learn how to work with written language just as an artist has to learn how to

103

work with paint or a musician with an instrument. This means that there is a *crafting* element to writing as we seek to give a shape to any written artifact, such as a story, poem, a short article, or a term paper.

- Most important of all, writing is a *MENTAL PROCESS*. The *act* of writing makes our own thinking visible for us; it simultaneously generates and reveals thoughts that would otherwise have remained shadowy and insubstantial. Where spoken thoughts vanish into thin air, written thoughts stay put (on page or screen), unless we choose to erase them.

High visibility can be a tremendous advantage if you value being able to think again, mulling your first thoughts over, teasing them out, using them as a trampoline for further thinking. But visibility can also be a real putoff, especially if you know that other readers are going to see your thoughts and maybe criticize or even dismiss them. Writers who feel that their writing is likely to be held in evidence against them understandably write as little as possible and often freeze up so that they write awkwardly with a strong desire to disown or disparage their own thinking.

Who For And Why

Writing for Yourself

Messages such as "dinner in fridge" or "remember to water the plants" are of course addressed directly to someone else, but with any extended writing where the *activity is thinking,* the most important audience has to be you, the writer. The thoughts about to become visible are your thoughts, to which you must give your full attention.

Often the most difficult moments for a writer are at the beginning of a new piece of writing. How to switch on, so that thoughts can start to flow. It may seem logical, but *it is not helpful* to assume that you have to begin at the beginning. You can get stuck trying for an opening paragraph or even an opening sentence if you haven't allowed for an exploratory stage first. There is a fair amount of data collection to do before you can decide how to start your draft.

With any predraft writing, you need to tell yourself firmly—and often—that when you are dipping into your own mind to pull up some of that huge store of data hidden inside the brain, you are somewhat like a scientist engaged in a pond study. You need to take note of everything that emerges from the depths.

There will be time for sorting out, selecting and rejecting later. Initially, whatever rises into consciousness deserves capturing in words. This exploratory writing is for your eyes alone, to help you arrive at some useful decisions before you embark on a continuous draft.

The trouble is most of us are so conditioned by that sense of another reader peering over our shoulder that we find it difficult to give our first thoughts an uninterrupted hearing. Instead, we often dam their natural flow because we have this nervous awareness of a critical audience. We even try to *become* that other person by imposing editorial constraints on words that are still reaching for their first uncertain formulations. Hence the white-out syndrome! DON'T DO IT!

What matters, when you first sit down to write, is that the *who* you are writing for is yourself and the *why* is to make that writing a process of discovery. It is the *act* of writing that makes the search for new meaning possible. You may decide to share this initial thinking with a fellow student or with your teacher, but hold on to the certainty that whether to share or not, at this predraft stage, is your decision.

Strategies for Thinking

To have confidence in your own thinking you have to have confidence that there is plenty stored away in your own head to think about! This is what makes writing about any *new* learning that you are doing particularly difficult (in math say, or science or literary studies), because your recently internalized knowledge is still bound to be fragmentary. However, don't despair, because as Frank Smith (1983) points out in *Writing and the Writer*, our brains are incredibly active organisms, continually absorbing, retaining, and *systematizing* our encounters with the world.

Every one of us has an enormous amount of human experience on which to draw. We can all think recollectively and, indeed, do so daily. For instance, what food we buy on the way home depends on our recollection of what is already sitting in the fridge or freezer. Fortunately, our brains can respond to whatever memory searches we set in train—sometimes with more success than others but usually with something! If we send the brain a mental request to recall the food in the fridge, it doesn't itemize for us the contents of the bathroom cabinet—although it may "forget" a jar of mayonnaise and a couple of tomatoes.

When more extensive memory searches are required, the simplest, most fundamental strategy for *recollecting, rediscovering,* what you already know, is to BRAINSTORM for it. Give your brain the topic to feed into your own memory bank and then write down whatever surfaces, as words rise in response.

The most basic form of brainstorm is a word list that has a particular focus, such as *names*: characters in a novel or play, parts of the body, chemical elements, rocks in geology, famous artists, musicians, and so on. Once you have such a basic list, you can do some more thinking about it, for instance:

1. Write down just as it comes (in single words, phrases, or sentences) whatever else you remember about each of the single words you have just listed.

2. If it's appropriate, picture each word in your mind's eye—if a picture forms, either sketch it or describe it. This way, you will discover which details you are *not* sure about as well as those you already have "fixed."

3. Write down any questions that could lead you to further information.

4. Freewrite for as long as it takes about whatever grabs your attention most in that first set of recollections that you have just made.

Remember, ALL this writing is *exploratory*. It is making your initial thoughts available to you so that you can do some further thinking about them, before you embark on your draft. The extent to which you need to take time, to read for further information or to talk to others, before you can move to a draft, will depend on the extent of your rediscovered knowledge. You may find that you know more than you realized—or less. Either way, you will have made a start.

Let me try out a brief example, which I hope will indicate how simple but at the same time resourceful this basic procedure is. I'll start by taking a couple of minutes to make a list of "water" words:

> river, stream, rippling, splashing, lake, mist, clouds, cumulus, nimbus, droplet, solution, suspension, rain, snow, ice, frost, crystals, pollution, fish, nutrients, nitrogen, water table, sea, waves, tides, floods . . .

That list took just over a minute to retrieve; I wrote every word down immediately as it came to mind. Five minutes brainstorming would have given me a longer list but as this has to be a short paper, one minute's recollections will do. Depending now on my intentions as a writer (for example, whether I'm setting out to write factually or poetically), I could begin a search for further *information* about water, by retrieving first as many facts from my own memory as I can for key words in my list, for example, *river:* small at source, widens as it moves toward the sea; lots of bends—oxbow (?) something to do with meanders . . . connection with water table—do all rivers start from springs? What causes a spring to spring? How long does it take for a river to form? Do some rivers never reach the sea?

As is now obvious—because I don't know very much with any precision about rivers, what I find welling up (note how our systematizing brains latch onto metaphors!) are all sorts of questions that could lead me to further information, if I now chose to spend an hour or two in my local library with a notebook and pen. The more questions I have listed, the more likely I am to spend that time profitably, for the simple reason that some of those questions are bound to turn up some relevant information.

Even if you already know a considerable amount about your topic having just, for instance, spent four or five weeks studying a particular module of work, and thus are at the let's-wrap-it-up point, in my experience it still helps to brainstorm freely first to allow what has been retained to flow out of your head, down your arm and through your finger tips onto page or screen. You can then *rearrange,* as you look for patterns or choose which patterns you will assemble your data into. With *your own* thoughts available as the data for an essay or an account, it is easier to find a focus than if you are swimming only in the huge seas of other people's thinking. You see how watery metaphors still insist on rising!

Now, if I go back to my original water words—supposing that my intention was to have a go at making a poem. In this case, I might switch into picture thinking to see what images come to mind for any of the words on my list. *Stream* as I wrote it immediately recalled a memory of clear water splashing over boulders, with children paddling in the shallows under the shade of overhanging trees—oak and birch. These further details cluster together readily as I realize that I am drawing on childhood recollections of a favorite picnicking spot.

River evokes a whole sequence of images. The immediate pictures that come to my mind are of the river Avon, which winds its way through the fields below our house. Memories are stored inside my head from all seasons of the year: the untidy nest that a pair of swans have built in the same spot now for two years running in late spring; the magical occasion one early summer morning when two kingfishers flashed brilliantly blue beneath the low arch of the town bridge one after the other; the fairy tale beauty of trees mantled in hoar frost by the water's edge. In this exploratory stage, I might just jot down a quick notation for each image, enough to work on more intensively when I come to make a first draft.

Alternatively, I could quickly list the wild flowers that grow beside or even on the river—water lilies, purple loosestrife, meadow sweet, cowslips, forget-me-nots, and so on. A different mental album waiting for its pictures to be contemplated.

Stages of Development

I still fail to understand the notion that thoughts can spring fully fledged out of anyone's head onto paper or screen. The growth of ideas needs time—and nurturing. The visibility that writing gives, doesn't mean that those first marks are unchangeable. On the contrary, writing offers you as many opportunities to revisit and to think again, as you wish. The feeling that once committed to paper, writing is immutable (unless all signs of change are whited out), only serves to straitjacket writers into a terror of the written word. No wonder so many students prefer talk!

Whether you are drawing upon personal experiences or upon knowledge passed on to you by others, any move toward fresh perceptions takes time. If you really believe that visible thinking is valuable because it helps you to think further, the idea of *changing* what you have written as you seek to clarify your thoughts, becomes a sign of success. Not changing anything could well be a sign of failure.

I would say that whenever a writer has the intention of achieving a finished piece, writing must move through the following stages: exploratory, draft, revision, and final presentation.

I described a few of the starting points you can use in the exploratory stage, because this stage tends to be either ignored or scurried through. Most students feel a compulsion to start drafting as soon as possible. HOLD ON! I am convinced that if more time is given to data collection and pattern finding, the draft will run more smoothly and be more sustainable.

At the *revision* stage (editing, proofreading), you are free to 'revisit' your draft once, twice or many times. Much of the pleasure of writing poetry comes at this stage of composition. A poet often returns again and again to that crafting and reworking of a poem, not as a chore but as a stimulating challenge. On the other hand an autobiographical piece may run easily from the start and require only minor retouching.

The whole point of editing is the *clarification of thinking,* and as you clarify your thinking, *the writing also is clarified.* As you reread your draft, there are three basic questions you can ask yourself:

Is there anything I can cut out?

Is there anything I can add?

Is there anything I can change?

Often it is useful to give yourself some space between finishing your draft and revisiting it. A time interval even of one night means that you can hear what you have written more clearly. Listen to that tone of voice—is it what you wanted? Are your thoughts still confused in places? Often another reader at this stage can help to point out confusing passages; talk to a partner to explain what you were aiming for; this will help you to write it more clearly. And overcome that reluctance to cut out chunks if necessary. Pruning often produces a more elegant shape.

I have little to say in this paper about proofreading and final presentation—only that *editing for meaning* should always precede that final spell check, because clarifying the *thinking* is, above all, what you are aiming for. As far as the punctuation is concerned, I take the view that we can usually agree about full stops, question marks and speech marks. BUT as far as commas, dashes, semicolons, and even exclamation marks are concerned, there are no clearly definable rules. These pauses and indications of pace and tone are tied closely to the writer's own voice and may be as individual as fingerprints. For this reason, I have asked Wendy Bishop, the editor of this book, not to change my punctuation to standard American. I can only hope this does not render my prose unreadable. . . .

Whether or not you are into desktop publishing, final presentation is always a pleasure. All the major thinking is done; now you can groom your finished piece to your heart's content, as you take pride in the structure you have achieved.

Writing to Reach for Understanding

I would like to put in a final word for the kind of writing that is variously referred to as think-writing, process-writing, learning logs or journals. As I hope this brief paper has indicated, *any* writing that renders thinking visible by definition comes into the first two categories. But there *is* a difference between writing that a writer intends to shape into a recognizable genre, and writing that is not product oriented.

In many respects, writing that enables a writer to gain a clearer grasp of relatively unfamiliar information is more central to effective learning than the production of a finished article. In other words, if writing *reflectively* (liberated from the additional demands that producing a finished piece imposes) can draw out further perceptions— and further questions—then the act of writing becomes a powerful *learning process*. I am still puzzled, therefore, that writing *to make sense* is still so underused in schools and colleges, by comparison with writing to produce a finished piece. Learning after all is open-ended. Nobody knows *everything* about *anything!* So why not come clean, especially if we are involved in the business of learning, and not only acknowledge, but *welcome* that fact? Why not encourage learners, whatever their age and experience, to write about their confusions and uncertainties, their tentative interpretations and speculations rather than struggling to make pseudodogmatic pronouncements as though they knew it all. If we really believe that the activity is thinking, then more opportunities to write *formlessly* could well turn out to be the most productive opportunities of all to write *thoughtfully*.

Works Cited

Smith, Frank (1983). *Writing and the Writer*. New York: Holt, Rinehart & Winston.

Sharing Ideas

- Pat advocates using images, metaphors, comparisons, and analogies to free your writing, to allow you to think on paper. Try listing some metaphors, analogies, images, and comparisons for your own writing and reading processes.

- What does it mean to you when Pat suggests that it would be useful to keep your paper fluid, not yet finished, and open to suggestions?

- When a reader in class responds to your writing, asking for or suggesting changes, how do you feel? Explore why you may be open to or resistant to suggestions for changing your writing. After doing this, you may want to skip ahead to Toby Fulwiler's chapter and look at different versions of students' drafts, writing in progress.

- Do you revise (Pat suggests this means at a minimum cutting out material, adding material, and/or changing material) or do you mainly edit (fix things up)? What is involved for you as a writer in both activities? Which are you best at and why?

- In what ways is writing a way of thinking for you? Where (how) do you do your best thinking? Reading this book, have you developed any new techniques for capturing that thinking on paper for yourself and your reader?

- Do you agree with Pat that we need more opportunities to write formlessly, without fear of evaluation? Decide if or how that could improve your thinking and/or your writing.

11

Time, Tools, and Talismans

Susan Wyche-Smith

Susan Wyche-Smith is an Assistant Professor of English at
Washington State University and Associate Director of the
writing program. She is currently completing a university-wide
research project on the subject of student writing rituals from
introductory to graduate levels. She has abandoned her
usual rituals to accommodate the remodeling of her nineteenth-
century farmhouse, and now shares writing space with her
husband's recording studio.

Famous writers have been known to do a lot of crazy things to help
them write: Dame Edith Sitwell sought inspiration by lying in a cof-
fin. George Sand wrote after making love. Friedrich Schiller sniffed
rotten apples stashed under the lid of his desk. A hotel room fur-
nished with a dictionary, a Bible, a deck of cards, and a bottle of
sherry suits Maya Angelou. Fugitive writer Salman Rushdie carries a
silver map of an unpartitioned India and Pakistan. Charles Dickens
traveled with ceramic frogs.

Writers also mention less bizarre practices. They describe eating,
drinking, pacing, rocking, sailing, driving a car or riding in a bus or
train, taking a hot bath or shower, burning incense, listening to
music, staring out windows, cleaning house, or wearing lucky clothes.
What do these rituals do for writers? The explanations are as varied
as the rituals themselves. Tolstoy believed that "the best thoughts
most often come in the morning after waking, while still in bed, or

111

during a walk." Sonia Sanchez says that she works at night because "at that time the house is quiet. The children are asleep. I've prepared for my classes . . . graded papers . . . answered letters. . . . [A]t a quarter to twelve all that stops . . . then my writing starts." Although interpretations differ, one need not read extensively in the journals, letters, essays, and interviews of writers to know that they consider rituals an essential component of their work.

Do these behaviors serve a purpose in the composing process? Are some practices more common than others? Do rituals make for better writers? Until recently, the answer was usually "No," but anthropologists and others who study the subject of consciousness now say that private rituals are used by individuals to selectively and temporarily shut out the daily world. Researchers in psychophysiology have observed that rhythmic activities that can be performed "mindlessly" alter brainwaves into a more relaxed, creative state. Walking, pacing, and some kinds of exercise have this effect. So does staring out windows, which some researchers now believe may actively trigger daydreaming rather than being a symptom of it. Although coffins and frogs are probably effective only in the personal psychology of a Sitwell or a Dickens, scientists at Yale have discovered that rotting apples produce a gas that suppresses panic—a reminder that we should be careful not to scoff too soon at writers' rituals.

I became interested in the subject of rituals after suffering through my master's thesis with a bad case of writer's block. When a counselor asked me to describe my work habits, I became aware of the conditions under which I had chosen to work: at school in the afternoon (my worst time of day) in an office where I was constantly interrupted or at home (also in the afternoon) while my husband's band practiced in the living room. I answered the phone, made coffee, and tried to shut out mentally what the walls could not. As Tillie Olsen points out, writing under such conditions produces a "craziness of endurance" that silences a writer. After awhile, even when I wasn't interrupted, I'd create my own distractions by calling friends, scrounging food in the kitchen, or escaping the house to run errands.

At the counselor's prompting, I began looking for a protected place to work—at first in the library and later at coffeeshops, where the conversational buzz and clatter of dishes provided consistent background noise. Somehow the interruptions in these places were less disruptive than those at home. I also began to pay attention to those moments when ideas bubbled up effortlessly, like on my walks to and from the university or while soaking in a hot bath late at night. I realized that ideas had always come in offbeat moments, but I had rarely been able to recapture them at "official" writing times. In the next three years, I gradually revamped my work habits and was able to face writing my doctoral dissertation, not with fear-producing blank pages, but pocketfuls of short passages scribbled in the heat of inspiration.

As a teacher of writing who works with unprepared students who are "at risk" in the university, I began to wonder what they did when they wrote. I knew there were times when they, too, became frustrated, blocked, and turned in work that did not represent their actual abilities. In Spring 1990, I conducted a project with two writing classes in the Academic Skills Department at San Diego State University. I wanted to know

> What rituals did students practice when they wrote for school?
>
> What explanations would they offer for their practices?
>
> Where did they get their best ideas?
>
> What did they do when they blocked?
>
> Were they aware of habits that sabotaged their composing processes?

Students filled out several pages of a questionnaire on their schedules, their rituals, and the amount of time they allocated for writing school assignments. Afterward, several met with me for follow-up interviews. In the following section, I present edited transcripts of three students who represented the range of responses I received.

Interviews

The first student, Adriana, provides a profile of work habits typical of other students in her class. She takes 5 classes, works 20 hours each week, and spends 6 to 10 hours per week on homework:

> I create a schedule for a day but if there's one particular thing I'm supposed to do, and I fall behind, I just throw it out. Sometimes I call my friends on the phone and tell them what I'm writing about in the essay, and they give me ideas.
>
> Everything has to be clean and neat because if I see my clothes hanging everywhere, I can't study; I can't concentrate. So I have to straighten it up—everything—before I start.
>
> I do most of my writing at night. Last night I stayed up till three o'clock. Before, I used to go to the public library, but it got too loud because of all these high school students jumping around. Now I work primarily at home.
>
> Pacing gives me time to relax and jot down what I'm doing. I can't stay in one place, like for five hours and write a paper. I have to stand up, walk around, watch a little bit of TV and then start again.

If my favorite program comes on I just have to watch it. Sometimes its hard to do both—writing and TV.

To relax, I breathe deeply, stuff like that. I lay in my bed, looking at the ceiling. Nothing special. I work sitting down or lying down. I stare out a window. That's how I get my thoughts all together. I guess it helps, I find myself doing it a lot. I also have this one cassette with all piano solos by George Winston.

At times I put off working on an assignment until it's too late to do my best work, because I work better under pressure. If I start maybe a month before, I won't really concentrate. If I start three days before, then I'll get on it. If I have a month to do a project, and I sit down the week before, I'm not even thinking about it the other three weeks. Sometimes I work when I'm too exhausted, because I have a deadline to make. I've got to do it or fail the class.

I get my ideas sometimes right away, but most of the time it takes an hour to sit and think about it. I also get ideas from reading essays or from the person next to me. I'd ask what they're writing about, and sometimes I get some ideas. When I do go blank, I get frustrated—don't even know what I do. I think I just sit there and and keep staring at my paper.

Adriana has difficulty creating and following through on self-made schedules. Her problems are further compounded by being unable to concentrate for extended periods of time; instead, she takes numerous breaks, including watching television. By her own account she begins drafts cold, using only the hour prior to drafting to give the paper serious thought.

Given all this, it is surprising to note how many beneficial rituals she practices. She cleans her workspace, paces, and breathes deeply to relax. She stares out windows to gather her thoughts, and focuses her attention by listening to instrumental music. However, she mitigates the effect of these practices by placing herself under the pressure of imminent deadlines. It's no wonder that she becomes frustrated when she blocks. She has little time left for delays, and her coping strategy—to sit staring at the blank page—is more likely to create stress than to relieve it. The conditions she chooses would torpedo even a stronger writer's chance for success.

The second student, Marcia, also has 5 classes, averages 18 hours each week at a job, and spends 16 to 20 hours each week (twice as much as Adriana) on homework.

Usually I study in the evening. I start at seven or eight, and lately I've been finishing about one or two. I talk my paper over with my friends. I ask if it's OK to write on this, or I ask them to read it when I'm finished, to see if it's OK. I usually work in my room, sometimes on my bed or in the living room on the floor. For some reason, I can't do my homework on my desk. When I'm in the family room, I just lie down on the couch, and do my homework with my legs up on the table. I play the radio, sometimes I'll watch TV. If it's an interesting show, I'll continue working during the commercials.

I guess I'm just a procrastinator. I always tend to do my writing assignments at the last minute. Like when they give it to you, and they say, this is due a month later, I'll start on it a week before it's due. Sometimes when I'm thinking about a paper, I think, oh, I could write that in my paper, but when I come to writing it, I forget. I get distracted when I watch TV, or when there's people there and I say, OK, I won't do this now, I'll do it later when I'm by myself. Sometimes I'm on the phone or I go out. Then I end up not doing it, or starting late. When I was doing one assignment, I wrote it in about an hour.

If I block, I put it down for awhile, or I ask somebody to read it, or do something else. Then I'll go back to it. When I block, I feel mad, yeah, frustrated. I don't cry. I just think, I hate writing, I hate writing. Why do I have to do this? That kind of stuff. Writing is not my subject.

Marcia writes in the evening, after a full day of work and school. Like Adriana, she describes herself as a procrastinator. She has no designated workspace and often seeks distraction in friends or television. Although Adriana describes using an hour to generate and organize her ideas, Marcia mentions no such practice. She doesn't write down ideas and often doesn't remember them when she is ready to draft the assignment. There are other clues to serious problems. Although help from peers can be useful, she seems overly reliant on her friends for ideas and approval. She looks to them to tell her whether her choice of subject is a good one, to help her when she blocks, and to tell her whether her draft is adequate. She spends very little time on the work and may not even finish if interrupted. Her frustration with writing is obvious; her rituals—what few she practices—sabotage her efforts.

The third student, Sam, represents a highly ritualistic writer. He is enrolled in 4 classes, works 25 hours, and spends 6 to 10 hours on homework:

I'm really into driving. When I drive I notice everything. Things like, Oh, that billboard wasn't like that yesterday. I notice if my car feels different. I'm constantly looking and thinking, What's going on? And so, when I have time to prepare for my paper, all the thought goes into that, from there.

In high school, my thoughts used to go down on microrecording. But I haven't used it since college. My batteries went dead. I do a little bit of performing stand-up comedy, so now I carry a little book for when I see something funny or some kind of story I want to keep. I've probably been through three of those books. I lose a lot of creative energy when I don't write things down.

My roommates and I lift weights every day. A lot of thoughts come from that. I don't like to sit. When I'm thinking, I pace. I do a lot of what you could call role playing. I think, if I come from here, then I gotta hit the next paragraph this way. I actually look this way, then turn the other way. I really get into my papers, I guess. I'm Italian, I talk with my hands. It's a way to release energy both physically and mentally.

Ideas come at different times. I've been known to write paragraphs on napkins at work. At home, I don't have a desk. I have my computer which just sits on top of my dresser. I usually sit on my bed. A lot of times I lie down; a lot of times I'll stand up, just depends. I write in the afternoon, I feel a lot better than I do when I write at night. I look out a window and just write. But, when it comes to the mid hours, six o'clock, seven o'clock, there's too many things going on. I'm too jumpy, too hyper to concentrate then.

I'm a very procrastination kind of guy. If I had a paper due in two weeks, there would be a lot of afternoon writing, a lot of jotting down. I'd probably end up pulling it all together late one evening. You never know, that last week, I might come up with something more. But at all times, I'm actively thinking about it.

I never keep working on a problem once I've blocked. I feel this is useless. So, I'll stop, and a half hour later, it'll hit me. If I block at night, I'll stop for the rest of the night. If it's in the day, I'll try to get it again at night. I prefer a sleep period in between. Everybody believes in a fresh new day. A new outlook.

Like Adriana and Marcia, Sam considers himself a procrastinator. But unlike either of them, he actively makes use of the interim between assignment, noting down ideas, even writing entire sections if they take shape in his mind. Because he works better in the afternoon than late at night after he's put in a full day, he tries to schedule his work periods early. He seems to be a kinetic thinker—getting ideas in motion—and he takes advantage of that by allowing himself to pace and act out ideas rather than work at a desk. His interest in stand-up comedy has taught him to pay attention to the world around him, and this has become a source of material for his school assignments. In a way, Sam is always preparing to write. The result? He spends less time on his homework than Marcia and rarely experiences, as Adriana does, the frustration of being blocked.

I appreciated the candor of these and other students in responding to my questions but, as a teacher of writing, I was disheartened by many of the things I learned. Over half of the students surveyed spent fewer than 10 hours per week on homework for a full schedule of classes, and three-quarters averaged twice as many hours on a job. The picture that emerged of their composing processes, from both statistics and interviews, was even bleaker. Few practiced rituals to help them write, most wrote under conditions hostile to concentration, and more than two-thirds admitted that procrastination regularly affected the quality of their work.

How Rituals Help

Rituals cannot create meaning where there is none—as anyone knows who has mumbled through prayers thinking of something else. But a knowledge of rituals can make a difference for students who want to make better use of the time they spend on writing. For one thing, rituals help writers pay attention to the conditions under which they choose to work. Some people think, for example, that 15 minutes spent writing during TV commercial breaks is the equivalent of 15 minutes of continuous, uninterrupted time. If they knew more about the nature of concentration—such as the destructive effect of interruptions on one's ability to retain and process information—they would recognize the difference. If they knew that language heard externally interferes with tasks requiring the production of inner speech, they would know that instrumental music or white noise (like the hum heard inside a car) might enhance their ability to write but that television or music with lyrics is likely to make work more difficult.

A knowledge of rituals can also encourage more effective use of the time spent on assignments. While many teachers consider two hours of homework a reasonable expectation for each hour in class, the students I talked to spent half that time and projects were typically written in one stressful sitting. Writing teacher Peter Elbow calls this "The Dangerous Method" and warns that it not only increases the pressure but depends for its success on a lack of any mishaps or mental blocks.

The problem with waiting until the last minute to write is that ideas rarely appear on demand. Instead, they come when listening to others, while reading or dreaming, or in the middle of other activities. Certain conditions stimulate their production, such as when a writer is relaxed and the mind is not strongly preoccupied with other matters. These moments may occur at particular periods of the day, for example, during "hypnagogic" states, the stage between waking and dreaming. Automatic, repetitious activity has a similar effect, which may be why writers often mention the benefits of walking, pacing, or exercising of some kind. They learn to make use of those times by noting down ideas or combining naturally productive times with their scheduled writing time.

Having some ideas to start with is an advantage to the writer, but not enough in itself. Ideas seldom occur as full-blown concepts, complete with all of the details, order, and connections that are required for formal writing. More often, they begin as an image, sensation, key word or phrase, or a sketchy sense of shape and structure. Transforming these bits into a full-fledged piece—whether poem, essay, or short story—usually requires one or more periods of concentration. The term concentration means "to bring together, to converge, to meet in one point" and in reference to thinking, it refers to keeping one's attention and activity fixed on a single problem, however complex. For the kind of writing required at the college level, concentration is crucial.

Most of us know that it is hard to concentrate when we are tired, when interrupted or preoccupied, ill or under stress—thus we recognize, experientially, that writing requires the concerted effort of mind *and* body. Some people can concentrate under adverse conditions— they could work unfazed in the middle of a hurricane if they wanted to—but most of us aren't like that. Concentration comes naturally to a few things that we like to do or are vitally interested in—music, perhaps, or sports. The rest of the time, we juggle several things at once, like jotting down a shopping list while we watch TV or organizing the day ahead while we take a shower. Switching from this kind of divided or scattered mental activity to a state of concentration often generates resistance, especially when the task is unpleasant or formidable.

Mihaly Csikszentmihalyi (1975), a psychologist at the University of Chicago, refers to this state of intense concentration as "flow," and from interviews with athletes, artists, and various professionals, theorizes that flow can only be achieved when a person is neither bored nor worried, but in control, possessing skills adequate to meet the challenge at hand. The key to achieving and maintaining flow is to balance one's skills against the challenge. "What counts," he says, "is the person's ability to restructure the environment so that it will allow flow to occur" (p. 53).

Although rituals can take a bewildering number of forms, they help writers restructure their environment in one or more ways: clears the deck of competing preoccupations, protects from interruptions, encourages relaxation, reduces anxiety, and provides a structure (through established limitations of time) for dividing projects into manageable increments. This last use is especially important as writing assignments increase in length and complexity. The transition from the shorter assignment that can be completed in the space of two or three hours to an assignment that requires weeks of reading, research, and multiple drafts can be devastating to those who have conditioned themselves to write in only one, high-pressured session. In such cases, the writer needs strategies to help him or her overcome mental resistance and make good use of scheduled worktime.

Using Rituals

Because no two writers are alike, no formula for effective rituals exists. Even the same writer may use different rituals for different projects, or for different stages of a project. One writer may need several rituals involving workspace, time, and repetitive activities; another may need only a favorite pen. Every writer must learn to pay attention to his or her own needs, the demands that must be juggled, the mental and biological rhythms of the day, and the spontaneous moments of inspiration. Here are some suggestions for establishing productive rituals:

1. Consider the times of day in which you are most and least alert. Most people have two or three cycles each day. Note the times that are your best.

2. Identify those times and activities in which ideas naturally occur. These may include certain times of day (when waking up, for example), during physical activities, or when engaged in repetitive or automatic behaviors (driving a car or washing dishes). Carry a tape recorder, small notebook, or some means of recording your ideas as they occur.

3. Draw up a schedule of a typical week. Mark those hours that are already scheduled. Note those times that are left open that correspond with the times identified in items 1 and 2. These are the most effective times to schedule writing. If possible, plan to do your writing during these times instead of "at the last minute." Each semester, once I know when my classes meet, I draw up such a schedule and post it on my refrigerator. Although I can't always use my writing time to work on writing, the schedule serves as a constant reminder of my priorities.

4. Consider the amount of time in which you are normally able to maintain concentration. Even experienced writers tend to

work for no more than 3 or 4 hours a day. They may spend additional time reading, making notes, or editing a text, but these activities can tolerate more interruptions and can be performed at less-than-peak times. Remember, too, it sometimes takes time to achieve a full state of concentration—an hour may provide only 15 to 20 minutes of productive time. Writing frequently for short periods of time may be best. Many writers advocate working a little bit every day because the frequency helps lessen the initial resistance to concentration.

5. Consider the conditions under which you work best. Do you need absolute silence or background noise? Does music help you to focus or does it distract you? Do you prefer to work alone or with other people around? Do you prefer certain kinds of pens, ink, or paper, or do you need access to a typewriter or computer? Do you work best when sitting, standing, or lying down? Does it help you to pace or rock in a rocking chair or prepare a pot of coffee? Do you prefer natural, incandescent, or fluorescent light? Is the temperature comfortable? Is this a place you can work without being interrupted? Identify these needs and assemble an environment in which you are most comfortable.

6. Cultivate rituals that help you focus. Many writers use meditational exercises, write personal letters, or read recreationally to relax and prime the inner voice with prose rhythms. Some writers eat and drink so as not to be bothered with physical distractions; others eat or drink while they work because the repetitive activity helps them stay focused. Some writers feel they are more mentally alert if they write when they are slightly hungry. Experiment with different rituals and choose what works best for you.

Once concentration is achieved, writers tend to lose awareness of their rituals, but when concentration lapses or writers becomes blocked, they may consciously use rituals to avoid frustration and regain concentration as quickly as possible. The rituals vary according to the writer, the situation, the task, and the cause of the interruption or block, but common practices suggest several options:

1. Take a short break from the work and return later. If pushed for time, a short break may be most efficient. The trick is to stay away long enough to let strong feelings that may sabotage the writing subside, without letting one's focus shift too far away from the project overall. This is time to get something to

drink, stretch out, or put the clothes in the dryer—activities that don't require one's full attention.

2. Shift attention to a different part of the same task and work on that. If you don't need to take a break, work on a section of the project with which you are not blocked. If you know, for example, that you plan to describe a personal experience later in the draft and you know what you want to say about it (even though you are not yet sure how that experience fits within the overall organization of the piece), go ahead and write it and set it aside for later.

3. Shift attention to a different task and return later. Other tasks can provide a break from the writing and, simultaneously, maintain the feeling of productivity; some professional writers juggle more than one writing project at a time for this very reason.

4. Switch to reading—notes or other texts—to stimulate new ideas and to help regain focus. If you are working from notes or research materials, sometimes browsing through them will remind you of things you wanted to say. If that doesn't work, try reading materials that are not related to your task. One student told me that he used articles in Rolling Stone to help him get into a "voice" that helped him write. If you are working on a computer and have lost your sense of direction ("What should I say next?"), printing out your work and reading that may also help you regain your flow of thoughts.

5. Talk to someone about the problem or, if no one is around, write about it. Writers frequently use a friend or family member to talk through their ideas aloud (notice how often family members are thanked in the acknowledgments of books); reading or talking to someone not only offers a respite, but may result in the needed breakthrough.

6. Take a longer break, one which involves physical activity, a full escape from the task, or a period of sleep. If the block seems impenetrable or if you are so angry and frustrated that a short break won't make any difference, then spend enough time away from the task that you can begin afresh. Get out of your workspace, go for a hike, see a movie, or spend an evening shooting pool. Intense physical workouts can burn off tension created by writing blocks. If you're tired, take a nap. Some people can work well when tired, and pulling an all nighter is possible for them, but others are far better off

sleeping first and working later, even if that means waking up at 3:00 a.m. to write.

Coda

Writing this article has reminded me that knowing about rituals and making use of them are not always the same thing. Parts of this developed easily; others had to be teased out line by line. Ideas came while walking the dog, stoking the woodstove, taking hot baths, and discussing my work with others. After reading the last draft, my husband asked me how I intended to conclude. By discussing X, Y, and Z, I answered. I knew exactly what I wanted to say.

That was several nights ago, and today, I can't for the life of me remember what I said. If only I had thought to write it down.

Annotated Bibliography

The writers' rituals described here were gathered from a variety of sources—interviews, published diaries and letters, biographical and autobiographical materials—but anecdotes about rituals appear almost anytime writers discuss their writing processes. For further reading, see the *Paris Review Interviews with Writers* series, Tillie Olsen's *Silences*, or *Working It Out: 23 Women Writers, Artists, Scientists, and Scholars Talk About Their Lives and Work*, edited by Sara Ruddick and Pamela Daniels.

For further reading on writing and altered states of consciousness, see Csikszentmihalyi's *Beyond Boredom and Anxiety*, Richard Restak's *The Brain* (based on the PBS Television Series "The Brain"), and Diane Ackerman's *A Natural History of the Senses*. For an older but excellent introduction to the subject of psychophysiology see *Altered States of Consciousness*, edited by Charles T. Tart.

Although the subject of rituals is not a common one for most teachers of composition, a few have discussed the personal and idiosyncratic needs of writers. See especially several of the self-reflective articles in *Learning by Teaching* by Donald M. Murray, Peter Elbow's *Writing With Power*, and James Moffett's essay, "Writing, Inner Speech, and Meditation," in *Coming On Center*.

Works Cited

Csikszentmihalyi, Mihaly (1975). *Beyond Boredom and Anxiety*. New York: Jossey-Bass.

Sharing Ideas

- Describe your best writing conditions and your most effective (even your most secret) writing rituals. For instance, as I write these questions, I have my two cats sleeping behind me, a quiet house, a desk with lots of pencils in a room that is just messy enough (my mess, no one else's), and a mug of coffee. Surely I could write without any one of these conditions, but I spent some time arranging the atmosphere I wanted for writing to you.

- You may want to read ahead to Marcia Dickson's essay. She describes her own writing rituals and habits. Do any of her habits, practices, confessions, or rituals match up with the behaviors that Susan reviews in this essay?

- Who do you sympathize with most or view as most like you as a writer: Adriana, Marcia, or Sam?

- What advice would you give each writer for improving his or her writing processes?

- Tell some stories of times when you achieved flow states (as a writer or during other activities, too).

- What would be involved for you in adopting some of Susan's advice for establishing productive rituals?

- Explore the connection between rituals and inspiration.

- Interview professional or amateur writers of your choice; describe and analyze their writing rituals.

- Use Susan's essay to help you read Stephany's report of Kevin Jackson's writing process in the next essay.

12

What Goes on in the Mind of a Writer

Stephany Loban,

with a response by Kevin Jackson

Stephany Loban likes pool, pedagogy, and piano. She and
Kevin Jackson were students at Florida State University when
they shared in this writing research project.

When a student receives a writing assignment, the heat is on. Deadlines are set, and research, planning, and preparation must begin.
Some writers procrastinate, and some start early. Either way, the
assignment is a result of an intense writing process that goes on
inside the writer's mind. I have decided to witness an actual process
taking place. I wanted to investigate how a writer thinks throughout
the complete composition of a paper.

I chose to study an entire process of composing through the mind
of a composer, Kevin, a senior at Florida State University who is ma-
joring in English with an emphasis in writing. Kevin has been writing
for eight years, and she has been writing seriously for the past four
years since she has decided on English as her major. Although there
has always been an interest in writing, Kevin admits that there have
been some major influences in her decision to write seriously.

It is evident that most writers were encouraged to write because
of one or more sources of motivation in their schooling years, as
Kevin was. At school, Kevin says her ninth-grade and third-year-
college teachers helped her a great deal. At home, her mother, also an

English major, played an important role in Kevin's interest in English. It was not getting "A's" that caused Kevin to appreciate these teachers any more than others; it was the teaching methods they chose. Kevin feels that the qualities of patience, objectivity, and guidance that the teachers had helped her the most. When Kevin had trouble focusing on her thesis, her teacher would not only be patient, but would make Kevin think through exactly what she was trying to say. This special attention is what guided Kevin through her writing process when she was learning.

It is evident that students are more open to learning when they are taught that writing is flexible. Jennifer Hicks (1987) explains this in her essay "A Writer Composes Aloud: Teaching Cognitive Processes in Writing": " . . . we would be wrong to teach the writing process as static. We must instead let the students understand that the entire writing process is flexible and malleable and can be adjusted by the writer to suit different types of writing . . . " (pp. 197–204). Unfortunately, even though writing became easier, the writing blocks that Kevin experienced were detrimental to her actual composing.

"Writer's apprehension," or "mental block," is extremely common in most writers. In "Writing Apprehension: A Review of Research," Donald A. McAndrew (1986) says, "A certain amount of creative tension is present and necessary in all writers, but for some the situation brings on a destructive amount of tension" (pp. 43-52). These blocks are a big problem for Kevin. When she revised a sentence over and over again, about four times, nothing she changed sounded logical. This caused her to become frustrated and to give up. It is at a time like this that Kevin admits that working with others is a great help.

Although Kevin has no problem composing on her own, she prefers composing with others. She feels that others help her mind to expand and to think of different techniques and styles of writing. There are times when Kevin narrows her focus so much, while writing, that she uses only one angle of approach. Other types of insights offered by others who use a different type of approach are what help Kevin to become enthusiastic rather than stuck in the middle of her pre-composing, thinking process. It is during this process that the environment must be the most comfortable for Kevin.

I was able to accompany Kevin through her process without distracting her because we sat together where she felt the most at ease. This was a definite advantage for me because she was also able to recall events in the past, of writing papers in this exact atmosphere, etc., and told me about them, in turn aiding my research.

Kevin writes her best when at home, in the morning, by a window, with a beverage (nonalcoholic), and when chewing gum. When she writes, she completes the entire piece in one sitting. The work usually consists of two rough drafts and one final draft. Unfortunately, one draft is eliminated when Kevin is under pressure. Like many others, Kevin procrastinates until about a day or so before her paper is due because she is intimidated by complex writing assignments. As a result, she does not write as well. This is another cause of writing apprehension among writers. Some research evidence shows that preplanning of a writing assignment is a key factor in lessening the writer's apprehension level (McAndrew, 1986).

When I asked Kevin why she writes, she told me that when she is not attending school, or when she does not have an assignment, she writes for pleasure, keeping a diary. Her style of writing is altered a little bit from her usual style in school. Although her writing style basically stays the same, Kevin does consider writing in school to be solely to earn a grade. During the composition of the paper she wrote in my presence, Kevin wrote with the intention of getting an "A."

Before I discuss my actual observations, I would like to discuss the "cognitive-process model of writing" developed by Linda S. Flower and John R. Hayes (Hicks, 1987), which describes the writing process as a set of mental processes. These aspects are divided into three parts: (1) The task environment, (2) the long-term memory, and (3) the writing processes. As I convey Kevin's approaches to her writing process, I look at each of the different parts of the cognitive-process model of writing:

1. "[T]he task environment . . . consists of everything outside the writer. The rhetorical problem, the task itself, and the text in the process of being produced are components of the task environment." (Hicks, p. 198)

   As I sat opposite Kevin with my notepad and my taperecorder ready to record, Kevin proceeded with her composition. Kevin spoke out loud, occasionally looking up to grasp a concept of what her thesis would/should sound like. Kevin reviewed all of her resources, reading passages and accumulated outlined material, deciding on what type of approach she should take. As she narrowed her focus, and finally decided on what she would argue, she opened a pack of gum and took a sip of water. We moved into the second part of the cognitive process.

2. "[T]he long-term memory . . . consisting of the author's stored knowledge, his or her awareness of writing structures, and the audience . . . . " (Hicks, p. 198).

   Kevin spoke each sentence out loud. As she spoke, she revised if she did not like the way it sounded. Sometimes,

Kevin rewrote a sentence four or five times. It was after intense thought processes such as these that Kevin referred, once again, to her resource materials where she found a quote that supported her findings. I also noted that Kevin seemed excited that she was being so productive. She cheered herself on when she wrote something that said exactly what she wanted to say, "Okay, Kevin, perfect! You're on the right track! That's exactly it!" (I smiled as I wrote down this quote). There were times however, when Kevin experienced mind blocks and said things that I would prefer not to write.

3. The third part of the cognitive process is the writing processes, which are divided into three parts: (1) planning: which generates and organizes ideas and sets goals, (2) translating: which translates abstract ideas into written words, and (3) reviewing; which is used during the evaluation and revision of the paper. These processes are governed by what Flower and Hayes call a *"monitor*, a sort of manager that determines at what points the writer progresses from one process to another" (Hicks, p. 198).

Moving from one idea to another proved to be no problem for Kevin, it was elaborating on these ideas that did cause a problem.

Kevin put down her writing utensil and picked up her draft. After taking a sip of water and refreshing her gum, Kevin reread what she had written. I tapped the table to remind her to think aloud. Kevin reread the draft three times, reviewed her resources, and began to sum up her composition. As she proceeded, she got stuck several times. Kevin reread the small amount a couple of times by trial and error, speaking out loud the different possible sentences that could follow her already-existing sentence. She slowly began again, revising as she wrote.

During the entire process, Kevin crossed and scratched out each sentence, revising and critiquing as she went along. Each revision consisted of saying the sentence about three times, until it sounded right to her.

Three hours later, Kevin put her pen aside, refreshed her gum and water, took a sip of water, and began to read, from the beginning, the entire draft. As Kevin read aloud, I noticed several nods of approval and several frowns of disapproval, followed by adjustments to the draft. Kevin fixed and trimmed minor errors, usually grammatical, which consisted of flaws in tenses, commas, or quotes. When she adjusted these flaws, Kevin smiled again and occasionally, drank her water. I felt relieved when I saw that she felt relieved. At the conclusion of her rereading–revision process, Kevin spoke to me with a sigh of relief, like a proud mother who had just given birth! "Well? I'm done. Now all I have to do is type it. Are there any questions you'd like to ask me?" I asked her to retrospect on how her writing/ composing process was affected by my presence.

My research shows that there is a lot more to the observing and interviewing process than one might expect. According to Barbara Tomlinson's (1984) article, "Talking about the composing process":

> Interviewers take writers down particular paths, through land-scapes more or less familiar, to destinations known or unantici-pated: Each interview is a distinct, special expedition. And each interview exhibits special problems.
>
> For instance, because of the cooperative social expectations characteristic of interviews, writers may attempt to answer extem-poraneously questions that they have not previously considered or that they have not been able to answer. (p. 429–433)

Kevin felt that my presence was good for her. She was able to be more productive, whereas, when alone, she gives up easily and pro-crastinates. My presence and my topic of research (her writing pro-cess) motivated her more. Thinking out loud also helped Kevin visu-alize her thoughts. She was able to say the sentences and ideas for me, before she wrote them down. Kevin also admits that during this way of composing, she discovered more about herself as a composer. When asked if my presence hurt her process, Kevin recalled a few instances, "When I had a mental block, I was extremely frustrated, and I felt the tape recorder staring at me. I wanted to give up and walk away but I knew that I couldn't. It also distracted me a bit to see you writing more than I was during times like these!" Kevin is not the only writer who becomes frustrated while experiencing mind blocks during her writing process. It is only when the writing has been completed that the author feels more relieved to have been able to overcome such obstacles.

When I shared my observations with Kevin, she laughed, not re-alizing until that moment that she had done such things during her composing process. She told me that she cheers herself on as a private motivating technique, which helps her feel good about her highly self-critical writing. She revises as she goes because she feels that she can-not continue on unless she feels that what she has just written is absolutely perfect. At times when Kevin wrote faster or stopped think-ing aloud, she was "brainstorming." She would feel a rush of things she wanted to say and could not write or say them fast enough before she lost the thought(s) altogether. This caused her to reread what she began to write in order to try and recall what she was trying to say. This was when she would completely forget that I and my tape recorder were there observing her. I have included a comment sheet that I asked Kevin to write summarizing how she felt about my project and her entire composing process. I also asked her to draw her writing process as a model of composing because I was interested in finding out what the writing process looks like to her. I feel very good about the project. I wanted to investigate the actual process of another writer besides myself. During my project, I found myself discovering a lot about my own process. I realized that much of what Kevin did/does, while writing, I also do while writing—and for the same reasons.

Basically, I have discovered that writers who enjoy writing and are willing to learn more about their writing process by introspection have been taught about writing in very developmental atmospheres where their creativity was not only encouraged, but also enhanced. "Teachers can also help students learn to take advantage of their own creativity in writing and initially ignore concerns for correctness, which tend to impede the creative processes" (Hicks, p. 204).

In conclusion, my case study has revealed that the writing process entails a great deal of thought processing. Each writer experiences procrastination, mental blocks, and relief upon finishing. I also conclude that this cognitive mental process of composing is always subject to conditioning. Every reader must realize that his/her process can always be perfected . . . I do!

Kevin Comments on the Project

I am not the type of writer who can sit down at one sitting and produce an organized, well-written paper. Unfortunately, I am not the efficient student I would like to be, either. I find myself procrastinating up until the last moment when I finally must sit down to produce a paper (see Figure 12–1). As I did this, with Stephany's presence, I found the job to be much easier.

Because her questions and entire focus were concentrated on me and my writing process, I was better able to center my attention. As she ran her tape recorder, I spoke my thoughts out loud, as I usually do, mostly unconscious that I was being recorded. I positioned myself in an environment familiar to me, in front of a window with my water and gum, and began to narrow my ideas into a thesis—a big step for me. The body of the paper was written fairly smoothly, and I found that Stephany's presence kept my attention from wandering.

After Stephany read her observations back to me, I became more aware of my actions while writing. For instance, when I am in a rut or when I am experiencing a mind block, I throw another piece of gum into my mouth. I also constantly edit and revise as I progress. I require that my paper be in its final-edition form before I continue on.

Figure 12–1

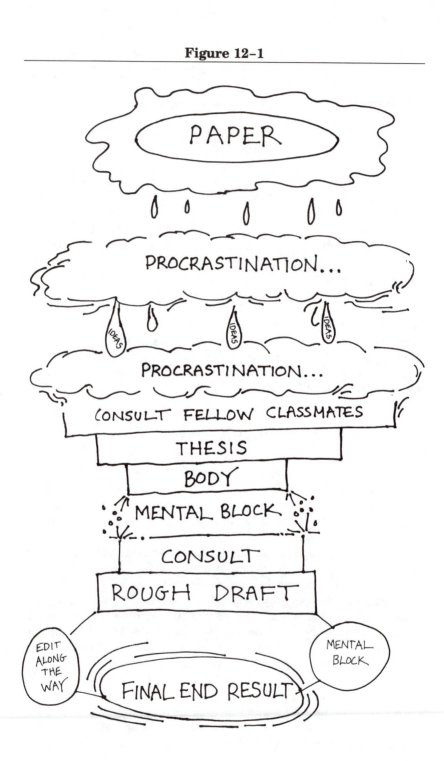

Stephany's presence really did not distract me from my normal writing process. If anything, it helped me to move through my writing process more fluidly.

Works Cited

Hicks, Jennifer (1987). "A Writer Composes Aloud: Teaching Cognitive Processes in Writing" in Glenda Bissex and Richard Bullock (Eds.), *Seeing for Ourselves: Case-Study Research by Teachers of Writing.* Portsmouth, NH: Heinemann.

Flower, Linda S., & Hayes, John R. (1981). "A Cognitive Process Theory of Writing." *College Composition and Communication, 32,* 365–387.

McAndrew, Donald A. (1986). "Writing Apprehension: A Review of Research." *Research and Teaching in Developmental Education,* **43–52.**

Tomlinson, Barbara (1984). "Talking about the Composing Process," *Written Comunication, 1.4,* 429–445.

Sharing Ideas

- Draw your writing process and compare it to Kevin's.

- Do you think, like Kevin, that you would actually compose more effectively and efficiently if someone were studying you? Why?

- Is Kevin using techniques discussed in the other chapters in this section?

- You can complete a project very similar to Stephany's. Use a journal and tape recorder to capture your own or a friend's entire composing process for a single paper.

- Kevin was writing for an English class. Explain how you might expect her composing process to change when writing for a class in another discipline? Do you find changes in your own writing?

13

A Lesson in Revision

Toby Fulwiler

Toby Fulwiler has directed the writing program at the University of Vermont since 1983. Before that he taught at Michigan Tech and the University of Wisconsin where, in 1973, he also received his Ph.D. in American Literature. He currently teaches classes in first-year composition as well as upper division courses with titles such as "Personal Voice" and "Writing *The New Yorker*." He is the author of *College Writing*, editor of *The Journal Book*, and a rider of a BMW motorcycle.

The real secret to good writing, for most writers, is rewriting. It's true that a few gifted writers compose, understand, and edit all in one draft—but neither I nor my students seem to do our best writing that way. Even when writers are pleased with their first drafts, those drafts don't usually tell the whole story that could be told—the one revealed only in second- and third-draft writing. In other words, it's the act of writing itself that explains the whole story to the writer. There are no shortcuts to full understanding, even for good writers.

There are no shortcuts, either, to careful writing. Just as first drafts seldom tell the whole story or make the best case, so too are first words and sentences seldom as polished, careful, and precise as they could be. What makes words and sentences more polished, careful, and precise is returning to them over and over again, each time with a little more distance, a little more clarity, and a little more rigor, and editing them until they create just the effect the writer hopes to achieve.

132

As result of teaching writing and writing professionally over the past two decades, I have come to believe that knowing when, where, and how to revise is the greatest difference between my own good and bad writing as well as between the practices of experienced and inexperienced writers. This essay will try to explain in some detail that difference.

The following story describes the effect of systematic revision on 26 first-year college students in a writing class at the University of Vermont. All were required by their various majors to take this course; none who entered claimed to enjoy writing. My job was to change this attitude and, in the bargain, help them become better writers.

Draft I

The first assignment, a common one for first-year writing classes, is to write about a recent personal experience of some importance to the writer—a good place to start a composition course because it starts with what writers already know best, their own experience. While I asked that these first drafts be typed, I specified no particular form or length. Students brought their papers to class, read them out loud in groups of four or five, and commented to each other about "what interested them" and "where more information would help." After class, I took copies home with me to read. Let me show you some of the first paragraphs of these first papers:

—This probably is the most heroic event of my childhood. Everyone has their moments, but I believe that this episode is indeed commendable.

—In everyday life there are so many things that frustrate us, annoy us or make us upset that when we find something that makes us truly happy we should take advantage of it at every opportunity. For me, that thing is chocolate. The experience that I had which helped me to form this philosophy was one that will remain forever in my mind as a beautiful memory.

—Life—it definitely has its ups and downs. Most people don't need to think about what to do with themselves for amusement during life's livelier moments, but have you ever considered the things people do when life seems to be getting quiet dull? Well, every so often I realize just what stupid, mindless things I've caught myself doing to fill time.

—Last summer my mother and I flew to Ireland. I've traveled there four times before. I thought it would be the normal three week

tedious venture of traveling the countries visiting relatives and seeing the sights. This action-packed vacation turned out to be more
than I could handle. From recalling old memories, to falling in love,
I helped discover a new side of myself.

Most of the 26 papers were variations of these four, where the
writers told us of forthcoming heroism, frustration, ups and downs,
and action. Nothing is really wrong with any of these beginnings,
except that they are slow, foreshadowing excitement to come and
summarizing the writer's point before the paper demonstrates it.
Would you rather have action promised or delivered? Would you like
to be told the meaning of a story before hearing it? While I can't
answer for you, I want the story to start fast, and I want to figure out
its meaning for myself.

Farther on in some of the same papers, however, I found both
fast and interesting writing. Here is a passage from Avey's paper,
exploring the story of a boarding-school friendship:

>—Let me draw a picture for you. My first day of boarding school, the
>first person I see was a girl with black, starchy hair and face was as
>white as a clown. She wore huge black combat boots (which I never
>knew existed until I went to the Cambridge School) and a dangling
>cross earring protruding from her nose.

Avey draws a picture with words, allowing us to see the girl she's
talking about "with black starchy hair," and "combat boots," and "a
dangling cross earring protruding from her nose." When I read this,
I can make my own judgment—that this girl is bold, fashionable,
weird, whatever. And the writer shows me the character, asking me
to evaluate it myself; I am drawn farther into the story and want to
see whether my judgment will be confirmed or not. (More on Avey's
story later.)

In a different paper, John writes about spending 11 months in
Equador and includes the following dialogue:

>"You mean in America people live together before marriage?" she
>asked me in a childish voice.
>
>"Well, yea, I guess so. Once in a while, it's a pretty common
>thing," I said back in a casual voice. I had to think alot before
>responding because I hadn't learned much of the Spanish language
>yet. She looked at me stunned as I looked at her and giggled.

I especially enjoy hearing John and his Ecuadorian friend talk
with each other—a conversation I imagine taking place in halting
Spanish. Hearing people speak, overhearing them actually, puts me in
the story and lets me make of the conversation what I will. In this case,
because the writer doesn't summarize for me, I infer the difference

between a liberal North American culture and a more conservative one in South America.

Look at one more sample from these first papers, this one written by Amanda, a student from Scotland attending college in the United States:

> For most of this summer I again worked on the farm where I removed rotten, diseased potato shaws from a field all day. But I was in the sun all the time with a good bunch of people so it was quite good fun. . . . Later on I signed up with an employment agency and got a waitressing job in Aberdeen, a city thirty-five miles north of our farm. It was only for one week, but I didn't mind—it was the first job I got myself and I felt totally independent.

Amanda cannot quite make up her mind what her story is about: the paper's title is "Waitressing," and we see here some of the details ("Aberdeen, a city thirty-five miles north of our farm") and importance of this first "job I got myself." In addition, however, she also describes in brief but wonderful detail the potato field "where I removed rotten, diseased potato shaws . . . in the sun . . . with a good bunch of people." In other words, she includes descriptive rather than summary detail about two possible directions her paper might take: she could focus on either her week as a waitress or her life picking potatoes on her father's farm.

It turns out that a lot of students were in the same situation as Amanda, trying to write one story that had embedded within it the seeds of several others, each of which, if told fully, would itself be substantial and complete. Remember Amanda, we will keep tabs on her throughout this essay.

For their second drafts, I suggested that each writer create (recreate) as much action, dialogue, and detail as possible, while keeping summary comments and judgments to a minimum. I concluded by telling the class: "If you want to switch topics, please do. Your topic needs to be interesting enough to endure several more weeks of attention and experimentation!"

Draft II

I asked the students to meet again in their same small groups to share the second drafts. This time each writer brought enough copies to share with his or her groupmates, read a draft aloud while the others followed along, received comments on it, then left a copy for me to take home and read. Please look at these two paragraphs from different parts of Amanda's second draft:

Waitressing

"Hey Muriel, how much are the chilli-burgers and chips?"

"Two pounds ten pence" came the reply.

"Okay. . . . . .oh heck, Muriel, I've done it AGAIN! I'm never going to get it right. Blimming tills!"

This was a common conversation between me and the cook with whom I worked in a small snack bar during the summer holidays this year. It was the first time I had worked outside a farm. Normally during my holidays—Easter, Summer or October I would work on neighboring farms or on our own in the North East of Scotland, which is a large agricultural area.

I have also worked on potato fields, where I either picked them in a squad of about fifty to sixty people. We would bend over collecting the "tatties" til there were none left on our "bit" only to have a tractor drive past and dig up some more. This job was always in October, so the weather was never very good. It either rained or was windy, often both. Some days it would be so cold that we would lie in between the drills of undug potatoes to protect ourselves from the wind.

Amanda still can't decide what to focus on; however, she now includes good lively dialogue about waitressing (first paragraph) and specific details of farming (second paragraph). Look especially at the details of the potato field, where Amanda describes herself as "[lying] in between the drills of undug potatoes to protect ourselves from the wind." Her concrete, specific language puts us with her in that freezing October potato field, all the while allowing us to be safely warm vicarious observers—which good writing does—and we want more. Lying between those potato rows to keep warm is the kind of detail that it's hard to fake or imagine—only the writer who's been there would think to include it, and so we believe her completely.

I also want you to see the second draft of a paper by a nursing major named Dawn who had spent the previous summer as a nurse's aide in a nursing home. Here are two paragraphs from her story, the first early in the paper, the second later on:

Well, I walked into the first room, expecting to see women, but no there were two men lying in their beds. My face turned red with embarrassment, I didn't expect that I would have to take care of men. So Charlene gave me a washclothe and towel and told me to wash them up and dress them. As I washed them I thought to myself, I can handle this, I mean these people don't know what is going on and I am just here to help them survive.

It was this year when I got my last surprise. It was on a Saturday when a dear patient of mine died. His name was Frank, he was my first death. I sat there and watched him go on his journey to heaven. The time was 12:45 p.m. when I heard his wife yell to me. I ran as fast as I could. I kept thinking, "Oh my god, what do I do?" When I got to his bed, Frank's eyes were rolled back and he was breathing with difficulty. I yelled to the nurse and stood by Frank, making him as comfortable as I could. The nurse ran to call the doctor and the rest of his family. As all this was going on, I just stood there applying cold compresses to his face and wondering what happened. Earlier that morning he was smiling and laughing, and now here he was dying. All of a sudden Frank stopped breathing, I felt for a pulse but couldn't get one.

Dawn now includes the reader with her on the hospital floor as she begins work. Her surprise at finding "men" in the room ("My face turned red with embarrassment") is another of those telling details; few writers who haven't worked in a nursing home would invent that anxious insight, which, like Amanda lying in the potato field, is entirely convincing. I now want to see even more details of the washing of the men: How did she get over her anxiety? How does she actually dress and shave them?

You might also notice in her second paragraph both some tense action ("I felt for a pulse and couldn't get one") and some fanciful summary ("I sat there and watched him go on his journey to heaven"—How does she know?). Note the difference between what a writer can authentically know (the data supplied by her senses) versus that she cannot (what goes on in someone else's mind). In recounting personal experiences, writers create the strongest belief when they record what they experience and know first hand, rather than their guesses, speculations, and judgments.

By now, in draft two, at least a dozen other papers also include rich and specific details that make the writing exciting to read. Many are shared in the small groups, and I read as many of these passages as I can to the whole class, knowing they will encourage still other students to reconsider their own next drafts. They do. I found the following entry about these second drafts in John's journal (Figure 13.1).

Then, a few days later, in another journal entry, John assesses his own second draft before beginning a third. The story he set out to tell covered one whole season when he coached an eighth grade basketball team. John, a business major, now understands that to recreate a truly believable narrative, he must write with careful detail—a kind of writing he has never done before (Figure 13.2).

Figure 13-1

9/12 Today in english Toby took
parts of some peoples papers to teach
us how to write better. I think I
am starting to feel my writing coming
together ~~Its very hard to tell a
story and not show.~~ You begin to
totally reshape the actual incident when
you want to get down to the littilest
detail to give the reader the feeling
you have. I really think the idea of
having all the diff't drafts really
helps. You totally can get to the root
of your topic. It makes you feel
like a surgeon. Tonights assignment is
to focus on a very short time span.
I think this one is going to be
the toughest.

Figure 13-2

I'm going to try to use more
dialogue in my paper. That is
what I really think I was
missing.

The second draft is very
dull. As I read it, it has
no life. I should have used
more detail.

I'll try more dialogue,
lot's more, in draft #3

I'll have it take place
at one of my practices. Goiving
a vivid description of what those
practices were like when
the kids showed up.

I have SO MUCH MATERIAL.
But I have a hard time deciding
what seems more interesting.

John's problem has changed from the novice writer's dilemma of filling enough pages to fulfill the assignment to the working writer's dilemma of selecting from among "SO MUCH MATERIAL." He now sees that he has stories within stories and must decide which one to tell and in how much detail.

Draft III

Many writers are now beginning to see that the more they write, the more their stories grow, develop, and evolve into tales they didn't at first intend to tell. However, most still need coaching about how to actually make this evolution happen and their stories continue to grow. In the spirit of play and experimentation, I placed two new limitations on draft three: (1) that the time covered in the narrative be limited to a single day or less and (2) that the setting be limited to one specific place. With this draft everybody's writing really took off. Students had more material than could be shared in one period. Look at what Dawn's paper has become, an internal monologue inside her head written in present tense with new specific details:

My Job As A Nursing Aide

Up the steps I go, through this big white door again. The fowl odor of urine strikes my nose. Sounds quiet. . . . for now anyway. Of course it is quiet, it's 6:30 a.m. in the morning. Got to get on this elevator that creeks when it moves. Time to punch in already! Seems like I just got out of here. Another eight hours for a small paycheck. I hope my feet stay under me.

It is my last day, YEAH, tomorrow is a day off. Oh no! I've got to listen to this report, it takes too long and what do I care about who gets what medications anyway.

"Dawn, you have assignment five!" yells Terry while laughing at me.

"Gee thanks, why do I get stuck with the mens end? Oh I get it, just because I am younger than all of you, so I have more time on my hands!"

Well, stuck with the men again. I kind of figured I would, but it would have been nice to get a different assignment. Report is finally over, now I have to hurry and get my bucket filled. . . . let's see powder, soap, gloves, bags for the laundry, shaving cream, after shave cologne, razors and medicines for my patients treatments. Yup, I've got everything. First I should do my rounds to make sure everyone is still breathing. Then I will start to get up at least two people.

"Dawn, breakfast trays are here!"

"Already, I only got up two people and nine more to go!"

Amanda, meanwhile, has dropped the waitress story and elected to go with the potatoes. Look at the first full page of her third draft:

Potatoes

Potatoes, mud, potatoes, mud, potatoes, that was all I saw in front of me. They moved from my right side to my left, at hip level. A conveyor belt never stopping. On and on and on.

I bounced and stumbled around as the potato harvester moved over the rough heath, digging the newly grown potatoes out of the ground, transporting them up a conveyor belt and pushing them out in front of me and three other ladies. Two on either side of the belt

The potatoes passed fast, a constant stream. My hands worked deftly, pulling out clods of dirt, rotten potatoes, old shaws and anything else I found that wasn't a potato. They were sore, rubbed raw with the constant pressure of holding dirt. They were numb, partly-from the work, and partly from the cold. It was October, the ground was nearly frozen, the mud was hard and solid. Cold. Dirt had gotten into my yellow and yet brown rubber gloves, had wedged under my nails, increasing my discomfort.

On and on the tractor pulled the harvester that I was standing in, looming high above the dark rich earth, high above the potatoes.

My back ached right at the bottom of my spine. A searing, nagging pain. I stooped over the belt unlike the other ladies who were short and able to lean their hip's and waist's on the side of the belt, resting their bodies as they worked. "Oh to be short."

A bump and a shuggle, all movements hurt as the harvester moved. My feet throbbed, tired from lack of support in welly boots and standing all day. My eyes blurred as they moved over the potatoes in front of me, guiding my hands to the dirt and noting the difference of a rotten or dirty potato.

My brain is dead, dormant. Boredom, tediousness and pain. I was tired, tired of thinking, looking at and picking at potatoes. My mind wandered to the old days, before I went to boarding school seven years ago. Where potato picking was with your friends, and families would turn up at the field early on the cold October mornings to labour all day and make some extra cash.

I was there, lines up, waiting for the tractors to start. A bunch of men passed, red baskets fell in front of me ready to be filled. The sky was still duskey, it was seven in the morning, the sun was beginning to rise. A hush is on the field. The squad are silent remembering the feel of their warm beds and the personalness of their dreams.

A whirr and clatter, an engine starts. A sigh escapes my body, I watch the pattern of the hot air condense in the cold. A buzz is felt on the field. The day has begun. It is work, but the fifty of us are experiencing it together, as a team.

Nobody in class had yet written like this, making the rhythms of sentences match the rhythms of the experience ("Potatoes, mud, potatoes, mud"). When Amanda read this draft out loud to the class, the students sat in awed silence. Here was their classmate, 18-year-old Amanda, to whom her Scottish teachers had said she could not write, demonstrating new and exciting techniques, writing an interior monologue complete with sentence fragments, flashbacks, made-up words, colloquial language, and compelling details. In the comments that followed I could hear the admiration for a classmate's work well done and an unspoken resolve to try still more experiments with next drafts: "I could really feel your work!" "Good job, Amanda!" "Nice going!" "Good writing!"

Draft IV

What next? Actually, more of the same. Revision, when taken seriously, is a process that generates ever more and deeper thought, telling the writer that "Yes, you're on the right track. It's getting better," or "No, I think I've exhausted what I have to say on this subject. Better start something else." I wanted to give my writers one more shot at discovering still more about the story they were trying to tell, so for draft four I suggested writing from still another perspective: "Change either your TENSE (from past to present), POINT OF VIEW (from 1st to 3rd), or FORM (from essay to drama, letters, or diary)—or all three."

Some students, especially those who were pleased with the shape of their writing, resisted "new" drafts, but only because their old ones were developing in pleasing directions. In a journal entry I find later, Dawn takes me to task (Figure 13.3).

At this point in the course, these student writers had been trying out new and different approaches to telling their personal stories. Now, with virtually everyone accepting the idea that good writing was the result of intensive exploration, frequent and frank feedback, risk taking, and seeing good models, I felt it was time to slow down and see what the whole might look like.

So, during the fifth week of the term, I scheduled conferences where we talked one-on-one about each writer's several drafts: What did the writer like best or least? What story was emerging? Where would the next draft lead? We concluded each conference with plans for a fifth more focused and comprehensive draft, which would give shape to each experience.

Figure 13-3

Write a new paper he says! I was
doing great with the one I was working
on. I really had a strong feeling
about it!
    I guess this draft, I will do
two different deaths but in a diary
form. That sounds interesting but
it will be tough. It only has to be 1-2
pgs good!

With these last drafts, virtually every one of the 26 students had arrived at a pleasing story of self. Dawn's story in the nursing home finally took the form of "a day in the life," where she invited readers to accompany her throughout her whole eight-hour shift. Had I space here, I would share with you Jon's recreated journal of 11 months in Ecuador as an exchange student—which is how he solved the problem of writing in detail yet still covering a long span of time. Or I would show you Avey's portrait of a deteriorating relationship with her boarding school best friend over a 4-year period, which she finally told as a series of telephone conversations each a few months later—and more distant—than the previous one. Or John's decision to capture his basketball coaching season by focusing on a three-minute talk with the rival coach sitting in the bleachers before one game began. As you can see, some writers, such as Dawn, found their stories early on and stayed close to it, while others, such as Amanda, kept moving their pieces outward, adding ever newer dimensions to what they started with, finding out ever more about their own stories.

Let me conclude this study of one writing class with excerpts from Amanda's last draft, for which she invented a narrative in three scenes, to tell the story of her work in the potato field. In Part One, Amanda described her most recent season (1988) working on the farm before coming to college, working in her father's newly purchased mechanical harvester so now only four people were needed to complete the entire season's harvest. As she explained in our conference: "The last year when I worked there, it was only four of us and the relentless machine." This was the experience she recounted in the "Potatoes, mud, potatoes, mud" draft.

In Part Two—separated by white space and a new date (1983)— Amanda flashed back to when she was younger and one of 60 local people who hand picked the potatoes—the origin of the passage about lying "down among drills of undug potatoes."

For Part Three Amanda wrote only a single paragraph, set off from the other sections by white space and dated in parallel fashion to the other parts (1989). Here is the whole of her third and last section:

1989. October 17th

This year the potato harvester is still working, the same women on board, with the same bored expressions on their faces. Soon this job will probably not need anyone to work or help the machinery. Labour is an expense farmers cannot afford. There are no tattie holidays anymore, no extra pocket money for the small children of the district. Change, technology, development is what they say it is, I say that it is a loss of a valuable experience in hard work, and a loss of good times.

Do you remember that I said at the start of this chapter that it is important for writers to hold off telling readers exactly what to think about their stories? That readers needed to be invited in and allowed to make meaning for themselves? Well, Amanda has done that right up until the end, showing us the two different versions of potato picking on her father's farm. In the beginning she didn't know which story to tell, waitressing or potatoes. In draft three she found the story behind her other stories, and that's what that last paragraph is about—but it only emerged in the sixth week of writing. By then, of course, I didn't need it, having understood her point by the way she ordered her detail, dialogues, and monologues. But I think Amanda needed that last paragraph, for herself. I would not have wanted it earlier, but it closes her paper well.

By now I think you understand the story I wanted to tell about revision. But just in case, let me do as Amanda did and suggest some ideas that might help you when you return to your own drafts—so long as you understand these to be suggestions and not commandments. Although writing gets better by rewriting, there are no guarantees. I know of no formula for revising that works every time or for everyone—or every time for anyone. Revision is a chancy process: Therein lies both the excitement and the frustration.

Ideas for Revision

The story I just told you involves personal experience writing. However, the premises about the generative power of writing and even many of the specific revision strategies apply, with some modifications, to reports, reviews, research papers, and arguments as well. In argumentative papers, for instance, try writing one draft from the opposite point of view, one as if you were a politician, and maybe one as a newspaper editorial. To that end, the following ideas are sound for virtually any substantial writing task you are called upon to undertake.

Attend to matters of conception first. Focus on what you want and need to say, try to get that out, and worry later about how it looks. Keep rereading and keep asking yourself: What is my story? What else should be included? What's no longer necessary? Worry about sentence-level matters, including correct spelling and punctuation, and precise word choice, only after these larger purposes are satisfying. (It's not an efficient use of your time to carefully edit a paragraph that you later delete because it's part of a story you no longer want to tell.)

Allow time. If a paper is due next week, start it this week, no matter if you have all your data and ideas or not, no matter if the big chem test is on the horizon. Beginning to write, even for 10 concerted minutes, will start the incubation process in your own mind, and you'll actually be working on the paper in your subconscious. Plan, at the outset, to do more than one draft—as many more as you need to find and tell your story.

Start over. Even when you return to a draft that you think just needs a conclusion, reread the whole thing all over, from start to finish, with an eye toward still other possible changes. Every time you read your own paper you create yet another dialogue with it, from which could emerge still a better idea. The conclusion may be all the old paper needed—when last you read it. But that was then and this is now, so don't stand pat; keep looking for what else could happen to the story you are telling.

Compose on a word processor. Computers make all the difference when it comes to making changes easy. Save early drafts by relabeling files so that you always have a paper trail to return to or old copy to restore in case you change your mind. If you don't have access to a computer, try to make at least one typed draft before the final one: typed words give you greater distance from your own ideas and invite more possibilities of change. (When Amanda entered my class, she had never typed a paper before and had to learn keyboarding while she learned to revise.) One more hint: For early drafts, start a new file each time and see what else your paper can become. The new file guarantees that you generate new language and, therefore, new thought. You can always merge files later on and synthesize your several insights.

Seek response. As soon as you have enough copy in reasonable shape, read it or show it to someone you trust and get their reaction. Another pair of eyes can always see what you cannot. Most good writers ask others to read and react to their work *before* the final copy is due. And, of course, you needn't feel obligated to take all the suggestions you're given.

Imagine a real audience. Keep your teacher or several skeptical classmates in mind as you write and especially as you reread. Of course whatever story, essay, or report you write is clear to you; it's your story, essay, or report. Ask What information do *they* need to know that I already take for granted? Then put it in because they'll understand you better.

Play with titles, introductions, and conclusions. These are emphatic, highly visible points in any paper. Provocative titles catch readers' attention. Good introductions keep readers going. Strong conclusions leave strong memories in readers' minds. But these same elements work on the writer as well as the reader, as a good title, introduction, or conclusion can suggest changes for what follows (or precedes). Sometimes these elements come first—as controlling ideas—sometimes later, but in any case they can capture (or recapture) the essence of your paper, telling you what to keep and what to cut.

Imagine other points of view. Whether the paper is based on experience, data, or opinion, try to see it from another point of view: your job as seen by your boss or a customer; the pro side of the gun control debate even though you are arguing con; how other reviewers have interpreted a movie, play, poem, etc. Seeing and acknowledging other points of view is especially helpful for anticipating questions and objections to your own and therefore allows your writing to present a more complete case.

Let form follow content. Be aware that writing can be and do anything you can make it do, that there are no real rules that all writers *must* follow. There are, however, conventions of genre (writing a 20-inch book review for the local paper) and discipline (the voice, form, and style of a laboratory report). To violate conventions is to risk not being taken as seriously as you might wish. But more often than not, so long as your content is substantial and your style clear, the actual form of your writing is more open than you may imagine. Is your paper best written as a report? As an essay? As an exchange of letters? As drama? The point is this: Changing form is not cosmetic; it causes you to see your subject differently.

My Students Respond

When time came to hand in the midterm portfolios, week seven, we (the class and I) agreed to call these personal experience papers done. Meanwhile, they had started on their second writing assignment, a collaborative research essay on a local issue or institution—which would also be a many-draft process, this time with both the research and the writing shared among group members. At this point, I asked my students to comment anonymously on the process of writing and rewriting this first assignment (see Figures 13.4, 13.5, and 13.6).

At the beginning of the term, I believed that people learned to write by some combination of provocation and nourishment. I set out, dutifully, to provoke these 26 students into as many experimental drafts as they would tolerate, reminding them often that the more they tried, the more they would grow. I allowed no one to stand pat and only write what he or she was already good at. Then when someone took a risk and tried something new, I, along with others in the class, would say "Wow! Good job." In fact, it was amazing how much improvement the word "Wow" seemed to engender. Of course, not everything worked, but everything counted, and the class understood that good writing meant, in the words of one, being "involved," but not being "attached." In the end, however, I learned something else: When students write well, they teach writing teachers to teach well. Thanks, class, for a wonderful lesson.

Figure 13–4

I have a lot different attitude towards writing now, than I did during the first class. At the beginning of the year, I was scared to write. I've written more papers in these first few weeks; than I did all of last year in English. As we have gone on this year, I feel the writing has gotten easier. It isn't taking me so long to start a paper and once I am started there is no stopping me. This early writing has also drastically improved my typing abilities as well.

I am hoping that this class will break me out of this writing shell and help me enjoy writing on my own. I don't want to just write when it is required.

Figure 13-5

writing has changed for me. I'm beginning to realize how much you can do with a single idea. I like the idea of writing 5 pages about a single hour, day or afternoon on the first day of class I wasn't really sure what to think it seemed like such an odd way to start class. Yet, maybe one of the best ways considering the type of class this is I still find writing very difficult I never seem able to get the way I feel down on paper My goals are to be able to do this by the end of the semester. I want there to be some of me in the paper also.

Sharing Ideas

- Describe the ways this essay influenced your thinking about revision.

- If the essayists in this book have convinced you that writing is thinking, take that idea one step farther and explore the ways writers *think* through revision.

- Have you ever felt the same way about your opening paragraphs as Toby felt about the opening paragraphs of the student papers he shared? You might want to look through your old work and see if you have any consistent strategies for starting out a paper.

- Toby pushed his students to undertake a demanding and organized drafting sequence. What would happen to your writing under similar drafting conditions?

Figure 13-6

Writing: I'm more involved in it.
But not as attached. I used
to really cling to my writing,
and didn't want it to change.
Now, I can see the usefulness
of it. I just really like my
3rd draft. But for the final
draft I am thinking of struggling
with it. I feel like I have to
let go of my third draft. but
that's not what it's all about.
I can still really enjoy my third
draft and create another exciting
paper.

Writing is more than just pen
to paper or hands to key board.
It is also reading, rereading and
getting some criticism on it. ~~It will~~
I have improved my papers so
much after getting feedback from ~~Kel~~
Kelley, ~~Dave~~ Dawn. ~~Gavin~~, Kelley, Lanc
Amy and Toby, and Amanda.

- What does it take to make you want to revise your writing?

- What environmental, physical, and/or mental conditions get in the way of revision for you? Make a list of ways to overcome those blocks.

- Go over Toby's ideas for revision and connect them to your own writing.

- You'll notice at the end of his essay that Toby quotes from students' journals. You might want to read ahead to Chris Anson and Richard Beach's essay on journaling in the writing class.

- If you've ever had teachers learn (write) with you in the writing class, tell stories about that experience. You'll notice that Toby, like other teachers in this book, thanks students for the journey they take together.

• As I mention in my introduction, all the essays in this book were reviewed by students in writing classes who then suggested new revision directions to these authors. Think of who reads your work, who helps you to revise. Describe your best actual reader and your best (imagined) ideal reader?

14

The Cupped Hand and the Open Palm

Hephzibah Roskelly

Hephzibah Roskelly teaches a variety of writing courses at
University of North Carolina–Greensboro, from freshman composition to graduate theory. She writes about composition and reading theory and has recently published a book
with Eleanor Kutz on the theory and practice of teaching
English, *An Unquiet Pedagogy*. She received her Ph.D. from
the University of Louisville in 1985 and remains an avid basketball fan.

When I was in first grade, I was a bluebird. Funny that I remember
that after so many years. Or maybe not so funny. I suspect you
remember your label too. I remember being proud of being in the
group I was in. Somehow everybody in Mrs. Cox's class knew it was
pretty awful to be a yellowbird, common to be a redbird, and therefore best to be a bluebird. One student of mine remembers her experience in first grade this way: "My first grade teacher waited for us to
make a mistake in our group and then she'd pounce. She always stood
behind our desks. That's because I wasn't in the fast reading group. I
was in the bears." She laughs. "To this day I think bears are stupid."
For Susan, like for many of us, the first grade reading group is our
first real experience with group work, and for many of us, like for
Susan, it's not remembered fondly. Especially if you happened to be a
yellowbird or a bear.

By third or fourth grade, though, your early memory may have dimmed a little as group work began to get less attention. You and your fellow students were "tracked" by this point, grouped into classes according to the results of standardized achievement tests, so the need for "ability level" groups like the blue/red/yellowbirds within the classroom became less pressing. And by the time you entered middle school or seventh grade, probably there wasn't much group work at all. In its place was "seat work," which meant some sort of writing. If you were like most students, you wrote alone. Nobody ever saw your writing except your teacher and, very rarely, other students, if they happened to look at the bulletin board where the teacher occasionally posted the "A" papers. If you were writing answers to questions or coming up with ideas in class, you were often reminded to "cover your work" so that your friend in the desk across from you wouldn't be tempted to copy. So you used a sheet of paper to cover your writing, or you hid your marks behind a wall you made with your hand, cupping it to keep what you wrote private. Covering your work became so natural that you might have even cupped your hand anytime you wrote *anything* in school—the beginning of a short story, a letter to the editor of your school paper or to your girlfriend— the kind of writing where "copying" would never occur. But you continued to cup your hand because by this time you had gotten the message: Writing is solitary, individual, something others can take away from you if you don't keep it from them, and something others don't see except when it's "clean."

These elementary school lessons about groups and about writing are deeply imbedded, so much so that you may react with suspicion or even hostility now when your writing class—a freshman composition course or some other—encourages group work. Your past experience with group work in reading hasn't led you to feel that it will do much more than put you in some category you'd rather not be in, and past experience with writing suggests that sharing your work with someone else is foolish or illegal. Your college, after all, probably has an honor code that says something about giving and receiving help. Why should a composition teacher force the connection between writing and the small group, asking you to come up with ideas together, make plans together, read and revise together, and, strangest of all, write together?

I try to answer that question here. One of the reasons that group work fails in the classroom is that neither our past experiences in the reading group nor those with the writing lesson have given us much of a rationale for working in groups. When a person doesn't know why she's doing something, doing it seems relatively useless. Working in small groups, even though it's an idea touted by theorists and teachers in composition, is limited in actual practice for just this reason: Students and sometimes their teachers don't know why they're doing what they're doing when they meet in the small group. Just as important, students and their teachers aren't aware of why they're often so disposed against working in groups. I describe what underlies these attitudes so that you can begin to understand why group work fails sometimes and why it's so potentially useful for your development as a writer.

Why Group Work Fails

I asked a group of students who will be student teaching in high school English classrooms this semester to use their own past experiences and their developing ideas about teaching to speculate about what makes groups fail in the classroom. Their list may mesh with your own feelings about the small group in the classroom:

Too Many Chefs; No Chefs; Untrustworthy Chefs

Students mentioned the possibility of the "one member who dominates," who "thinks he knows it all," who "can't let the group decide." Or the possibility of having several members who all wanted to lead. What some described as a domineering personality in the group, others saw as responsible. "Somebody always ends up doing most of the work. And that's usually me," says Beth, one of my first-year students at the beginning of the semester. "When I was in high school there were always a few who didn't want to do the work and goofed off, and they left the rest of us poor slobs to do it." The fear that the work won't be shared but shuffled off to one wimpy or guilty person is echoed in comments about who's prepared, who volunteers, who shows up. A student teacher reports on her experience with being given too much responsibility for her group's operation: "My classmates saw me as one of the smart kids and so in groups I was always expected to emerge as a leader and to get things done. There were many times when I felt I was carrying the load."

An even bigger fear about responsibility and personality centers on trust. "I don't know the other people in my group. Why would I want to talk to them about how I feel about anything?" asks a student teacher. And one freshman writer writing in her journal before her group met for the first time writes about her fears that the group won't be responsible to her: "What if they think my ideas are terrible? What if they think I'm stupid?"

Chaos Rules

At first, the fear of spinning out of control in th
marily to be a teacher complaint rather than
true that the fear that there will be too much
quickly get "off task" does prevent teachers '
all, or they use it only sparingly and with rig.
But students fear loss of control as well. When su
tioned to the quiet classroom where only one person has u.
talk (the teacher) and the rest have the right to remain silent (u.
students)—and this is the typical classroom—students aren't comfortable with a lot of noise and movement either. "It gets too disorga-
nized," one student lamented. "I'm an organized person. And I don't
like hearing what the other groups are saying."

If You Want Something Done Well—

One student teacher remembers her 101 class doing revision of essays
in small groups:

> We had writing groups to comment on each other's papers. This
> was fine except that no one would make any comments about my
> papers. I guess because my grammar is sound they couldn't find
> anything to say because they didn't know what else to look for.

A typical group dialogue went something like this:

> *First person*: I don't see anything wrong with your paper.
> *Second person*: Me neither.
> *Third person*: Yeah, it's a good paper. You'll get an A.
> *Me*: Well, what did you like about it?
> *First person*: Everything. The whole paper is fine.
> *Second person*: I liked your topic. How did you think of such a
> good topic?
> *Third person*: Yeah. You'll get an A.

> Not only did this fail to give me any useful feedback, but it also put
> me in an awkward position when the time came for me to comment
> on others' papers. They were so full of admiration and praise for
> mine, how could I say anything negative about theirs? So a vicious
> cycle where no one benefited was created.

Related to this feeling of the group not helping because no one knows
what to do within the group is the feeling that the work they do is not
very important. "It's a waste of time. I think teachers have us get in

ps when they don't have anything left to say and don't want to the class go. We just read the paper in my last class. Or maybe alked for five minutes and then read the paper." Another writer says, "I kept changing what my group said or changing what I said to match them. It would have taken a lot less time and been better just to do it myself."

Why—and How—A Group Works

These students tell the story of why group work fails in the classroom. The stories reveal deep and often unconscious beliefs about how the writing class is supposed to proceed, about how writers are supposed to work. The beliefs come from those old experiences with reading groups and with writing. But they also come from what we've all imagined about how people learn in school. School, we've determined, is competitive, not cooperative, and therefore it's the individual not the group effort that counts. And counting is what school is all about. Who has the most points, the most stars, the most A's? Who's the bluebird? The fact is we assume that effort can only be measured by a grade and that a grade can't fairly be given to a group. So attempts to work as a group seem futile and unnecessary given what we've assumed school is all about—keeping not sharing, winning not collaborating, cupping the hand, not opening the palm.

If it were true that people learn to think and write primarily alone—in solitary confinement so to speak—it might also be true that group work is wasted effort, or unhelpful or too chaotic or too hard. But the truth is that people don't learn—in fact, can't learn much at all—in isolation. They learn *by engaging in the world.* They come to terms with what's around them, understand it, through sound and movement, through talk. A child who never hears talk, as tragic cases show, never talks or talks only very little. Talking presumes at least one listener or commenter. Group work, then, because it encourages engagement—talk and reflection and response—mirrors the way people learn things inside and outside the classroom, the ways in which they make sense out of the world.

So conversation, communication with others, is vital to our understanding of others and ourselves. And people can't communicate unless they listen—work toward a shared notion about how to proceed. Do you know the movie *Airplane*? It's actually one long joke about how communication gets muddled when that shared notion doesn't exist.

"These people need to be taken to a hospital," the doctor says.

Walking up, stewardess Julie looks at them. "What is it?" she asks.

The doctor is impatient. "It's a big white building with sick peo-
ple in it. But that's not important right now." Or:
"Surely you can't mean it," Julie says.
"I mean it," the doctor says. "And stop calling me Shirley."

Julie and the doctor don't communicate because they haven't
decided on a shared basis for their talk. They mistake words and ideas
and don't care enough (because then it wouldn't be funny) to get it
right before they go on. In the classroom group, when shared work
and talk do take place, real communication can occur. People learn to
listen to one another and use one another's talk to test and explore
their own talk more fully. This notion of learning and understanding
as essentially shared rather than possessed by one individual can be
tested using a little game I came up with called Trivial Literacy (after
E. D. Hirsch's best-selling book *Cultural Literacy: What Every American Needs To Know*, 1987):

1. Choose part of Hirsch's list (or any list of words). A part of
   one list might read something like *hambone, harridan,
   Holden Caulfield, Huguenot.*

2. Mark every word you don't know or can't guess about.

3. In your group, see how many marks you can eliminate by
   getting information from others.

4. In class, see how many marks remain when the group pools
   all information.

5. Are there any words left? Guess about them. Ask somebody
   outside class.

You know what will happen before you do the test. You find out
more and more by talking. You hear the contexts people have for
knowing things like *Harlem Globetrotters*, and you bring up the context you have for knowing *Huguenot*. In other words, you'll illustrate
how your knowledge gets stronger, better developed, more insightful,
and more complete the more you combine your knowledge with others'. This combining always works better if it's informal, conversational, unpressured, in some way equal. That's why Trivial Literacy
usually teaches so much. Because it's a game—it's fun, and the stakes
aren't high. Group work needs to be nurtured because it works, often
playfully, to encourage the development of individual thought.

All writers need to hear their own voices, but I think they can
only hear them clearly when they find them in the chorus of lots of
other voices. Otherwise, for many writers the writing is hollow, without a sense of commitment or *investment* that characterizes the
voices of confident, effective writers. Kenneth Bruffee (1984), who's a

composition teacher and writer, makes this connection between the social and the individual explicit. "Thought is an artifact created by social interaction," he says. "We can think because we can talk, and we think in ways we have learned to talk" (p.640). We're stronger and better developed individual thinkers and writers because we interact with people in groups.

Partially because so much of writing is done in silence and solitude, college writers often fear the investment required in writing. They don't trust their voices; the only thing they do trust is the certain knowledge that they will be graded on what that voice is able to produce. They want control, and so they ask "How long does this have to be?" or "Can we use first person?" And they want to minimize risk, so they count words and number of footnotes, use simple sentences and forms they've read, and write with passive verbs that take them out of the writing. "It can be seen that Jane Austen was expressing feminist concerns," they might say, as a way of avoiding a declaration that *they've* been the ones to see it. They avoid the personal commitment that writing requires because it seems too dangerous to risk. It's as though you walked into a dark auditorium to speak to a group, knowing they were out there waiting but not knowing how many there were, how big the room was, or if you had a microphone. You'd probably clear your throat a few times, and test the sound, but if you could see nothing but your speech, and you knew you were being judged each time you opened your mouth, you might likely be stunned into silence.

Your small group functions as a visible audience, a literal sounding board for your voice, and, as Bruffee (1984) and others suggest, a source of your growing knowledge of the world. As such, the group alleviates the sense of powerlessness in writing (and thinking) that so many student writers feel and thus reduces the fear of commitment and investment by helping you to hear your voice clearly.

The Group at Work:
First Year Writers Writing Together

The group lessens writers' deep and real fear of taking responsibility for what's on the page in lots of ways—by supporting and strengthening individual writer's attempts, providing other perspectives on ideas, and sharing responsibility. All of these benefits for the writer occur when groups do all kinds of activities together—read, comment, discuss, plan, interpret—but they're most visible and dramatic when groups write together. That's why I'm using this example of the work of the group from my freshman writing course.

Students had been in their 101 class and in groups for five or six weeks when I gave the assignment. They were already comfortable talking about writing and ideas. But this task asked them to go a step farther, to write together a short (two- to three-page) collective response to Dorothy Parker's funny and bitter short story "You Were Perfectly Fine." The story is primarily a dialogue between a male and female character discussing the events at a party the night before. The man's guilt about getting drunk leads him to pretend he remembers a "promise" he's made to the woman, who pretends too in order to hold him to it. After reading the story and doing some quick in-class writing, groups met to begin to decide how they felt about the hungover, guilty man, the seemingly sympathetic woman, and the reasons for the dishonesty in the dialogue. As groups talked, they jotted down notes, often asking one another to repeat or clarify, often interrupting one another with revisions. Some groups talked mostly about the distinctions between social life in the twenties, when the story was written, and the present. Others concentrated on whether it was the man or the woman who was more to blame for the hypocrisy. In the next week and a half, groups argued about men and women and Dorothy Parker, and they worked out ways to allow for varying perspectives and to combine them. Everybody had to negotiate what to say and how to say it, who would write final copy, where they would revise. All the talk and writing helped them find new ways to make points and gave them finally the new voices they needed to write together.

Here's the first paragraph of one of the papers:

> Dorothy Parker's negative view of relationships between men and women is obvious in "You Were Perfectly Fine." We analyzed the story as readers and listeners. Reading it, we felt that the woman was basically honest and the man without credibility. Then listening to it our ideas changed. We got more of a sense of the female being manipulative, romantic and lovesick, but dishonest and deceitful. Peter, the man, seems sensitive and witty, although he ends up being weak and panic-stricken. They seem like real people. Between reading and listening, we've learned that both these characters are dishonest and the relationship probably doesn't stand a chance.

This group ends their piece with a modern tale of deceit that connects romance in Parker's time and in their own, using one of the group member's own experience with deceit in relationships: "It's hard for men and women to be honest with each other whether they live in the Roaring Twenties or right now. Nobody wants to hurt somebody or get hurt themselves."

Notice that the voice in this excerpt is strong. It's controlled; that is, students talk both about the story and the relationships within it, but they feel free enough to be personal too, using the personal pronoun "we" and including a real-life example. There's a clear sense of commitment, interest, and investment in the task.

Collaboration in the group removed or alleviated some of the most debilitating fears about writing for the freshman writers in my class, and this ability of the group to nurture confidence proves how useful the group can be in strengthening the writing process in individual writers. I bet that these fears about writing hit close to your own.

Fear of Starting

Many writers find a blank page of paper so intimidating that they delay beginning as long as possible, searching for the perfect sentence opening, the right title, the best word. But because in the group there were four or five sets of ideas about a particular sentence or a way to open or a character, no writer stared at her paper waiting for inspiration. Inspiration, in fact, came from the talk that went on in the group. "Wait a minute," a group writer would say. "Is this what you said?" And she'd read it back. Another member would say, "It sounds better like this." "And why don't we add something about his past?" another would add. Writing happened so fast that nobody had time to dread not being able to find the idea or the word they wanted to begin.

Fear of Stopping

One first-year writer told me once that her writing was like a faucet with no water pressure—"it won't turn on hard—it just dribbles till it stops." Lots of writers fear that once they get the one good thought said, or the two points down, they'll be left with nothing but dead air time, and that they'll have to fill it with what one of my students calls "marshmallow fluff." But none of the groups had difficulty maintaining writing after they began. The group kept ideas flowing, and changing, and if one person was losing momentum, another would be gathering it. Ken Kesey, the author of *One Flew Over the Cuckoo's Nest* (1962) and a teacher, comments on this effect as he describes a collaborative project—an entire novel—that his creative writing class worked on in one group: "Some days you just don't have any new sparkling stuff. But when you got thirteen people, somebody always has something neat and it's as though somebody on your team is on and you're off" (Knox-Quinn, 1990, p. 315).

Fear of Flying

When you have a personal stake in your writing, a belief in your voice and in what you're saying, and a trust in your reader to hear you out, your writing soars. "Everyone can, under certain conditions, speak with clarity and power," composition teacher Peter Elbow says. "These conditions usually involve a topic of personal importance and an urgent occasion." The group helped make the topic personally important since each writer had to justify decisions and ideas to the others, and the occasion was urgent since talk, writing, and real communication were necessary to make decisions in a limited time.

The Group and Changing the World

So what does this long example from my first year class prove? First, the group validates rather than hurts or lessens the individual voice. The group reinforces the effort involved in writing, talking, by the energy and specificity with which they both support and challenge the writer's thinking. Ken Kesey watched larger perspectives get developed on character and plot in the novel his class wrote: "When we would sit down around the table . . . and start writing our little section, boy you could hear the brain cells popping. They knew they had to write and had to fit in with the other stuff. You couldn't be too much yourself" (Knox-Quinn, 1990, p. 310). But knowing that gives writers a clearer sense of self when they write individually. Not being "too much yourself" is way of finding what your writing self really is.

"People think it's about competing with each other," Kesey says, speaking of writers and writing. "But the real things that you compete with are gravity and inertia—stagnation" (Knox-Quinn, 1990, p. 315). Writing is not some sort of contest between you and everybody else in the class, with the one who has the best grade—the fewest red marks—winning at the end of it, and that's why the cupped hand is a poor metaphor for what happens when you produce writing in a classroom. The struggle, the contest, is internal, between your desire to talk on paper and your fear or distrust of it. The group helps us compete with the real opponent of creative, critical thought—inertia, the fear of making a move.

As Kesey's work with his creative writers and my work with my first-year writers suggest, the group gives writers the strategies for winning that contest. I remember a few years ago, a freshman writer was writing an essay whose topic turned out to be something about the advantages of watching TV. She was bored with it, but chose it quickly as she was casting about for anything to do. The essay began, "There are many disadvantages to sitting in front of a TV. But there are some positive things about TV." Well, you get the idea. It was uncommitted, with no sense of the personal investment I've been describing, and a feeling in the writing of inertia. The writer wasn't just writing about couch potatoes; she was writing couch potato prose. When she read aloud her opening to her group the next day, she became aware that the group was growing glassy-eyed. She finally gave up. "It's bad, huh?" They laughed. Then she started talking. All of a sudden the couch potato had stood up. She was exploring an idea she was creating for and with her group.

Look back at the idealistic subheading that began this last section. Changing the world seems a pretty grandiose goal for group work, doesn't it? "Freshman Arrive But Not To Change the World" read the headline in an article this fall in the *Greensboro News and Record* that described how first-year students in colleges across the country didn't believe they would make real changes in the world outside themselves. I think the article was wrong. I think people want to change the worlds they live in, but they feel increasingly powerless to do it. And here's the last and best reason for the group. Because they force writers and thinkers to consciousness, groups foster action and change.

Deciding on what's significant about what you're reading, what you're writing, what you're listening to, what you're writing in a group, is the beginning of an understanding that you make knowledge in a classroom. You don't just find it in a book, and you don't just apply it from a lecture. You *create* it. That's a potentially powerful piece of information. Once you realize that you make knowledge, you see that you can act to change the knowledge that's there. As students of writing, your work in the group can help you become aware that the knowledge of the subject matter you work with, of voice, of forms and styles can be determined by you and those around you. The more your group meets to talk about reading, writing, and ideas, the more your group collaborates, the more *authoring* you do. What seat work and the bluebirds taught you to see as private and unique the group can help you recognize as also shared and social. And that realization really can help you make a difference in the world around you and within you.

Works Cited

Bruffee, Kenneth (1984). "Collaborative Learning and the Conversation of Mankind." *College English, 46,* 635–652.

Hirsh, E. D. (1987). *Cultural Literacy: What Every American Needs to Know.* Boston: Houghton Mifflin, 1987.

Kesey, Ken (1962). *One Flew Over the Cuckoo's Nest.* New York: New American Library.

Knox-Quinn, Carolyn (1990). "Collaboration in the Writing Classroom: An Interview with Ken Kesey." *College Composition and Communication, 41,* 309–317.

Parker, Dorothy (1942). "You Were Perfectly Fine." *Collected Stories of Dorothy Paker.* New York: Modern Library.

Sharing Ideas

- As a writing student, I've experienced positive and negative writing groups; Hephzibah's essay helps me understand why this is so. And, she explains that group work actually doesn't take place all that often. Is that true to your life in school?

- Imagine that you're in a writing group and it's spinning out of control: One member is talking too much, or one member is never prepared, or two members are ignoring you and stranding you with that fourth person who never talks. Still, you believe in groups because last week even your struggling group gave you a great idea for revising your paper. How might you cope with each of these scenarios (and any other nonworking scenarios you can dream up)?

- For you, what is at stake in your classroom groups?

- Hephzibah claims that groups help writers by giving them voice. Is that true for you and to what degree?

- Can groups be useful even if not every member agrees? In fact, how effective are groups when every member does agree?

- Say that it's Christmas break. You're going home and telling your parents or a good friend about your writing class and writing groups because they've never experienced this method for learning to write.

- Share some tips for sorting out the different advice you receive from peers when sharing ideas or writing in a group.

- If you were able to form a writing group composed of your favorite authors, who would the members be, and how might they get along?

- Before this class, did you align yourself with the cupped hand or the open palm model? Tell some stories.

15

Castles in the Air

Donavan Kienenberger

Born in Alaska, Donavan Kienenberger was a journalism-
broadcasting major at the University of Alaska Fairbanks when he wrote this essay.

It was 11 after 8 as his fingers clicked down on the computer keys.
Jon worked frantically on his essays. Hours earlier he had tried and
tried to work on it, but he had only sat there, blank before an empty
screen. Now, forced by passing time, he worked steadily. Each sentence slowly formed under his hands. Letter by letter, word by
word—until it seemed nearly done.

He looked at it, paused, and frowned. His ending was missing.
Nothing seemed to fit. Inspiration had left him. He removed a small
notepad from his desk drawer. He would have to do it the hard way.

*His mom was on the telephone. They talked about how Tom
Brokaw had become president. Before the conversation was finished,
the telephone melted in his hand. The connection seemed to be lost.
Oh well, a nice cup of tea would suffice. The spicy aroma smelled so
nice that he built a lovely castle, grain by grain, out of the tea. There
was a knock at the door. He went to answer it. His mom seemed mad.
She was frowning at him. Tom Brokaw was with her. She went over
to the chair where the castle floated. With the telephone in her hand
she battered the castle into dust. Tom and his mom left. He shut the
door, then sipped some tea.*

It wasn't much and it didn't seem to make sense, but the freewriting did get his inspiration flowing. He put his pen down and placed the notebook on the desk. He faced the keys once more and focused his thoughts. With his fingers typing on the keys, he slowly brought his first draft to an end.

Had it been a dream? The light of the sun sparkled from his dorm window on to his bed. He was tired, but he smiled as he remembered that it hadn't been a dream, more like a nightmare. His previous night's work was sitting on his desk, all finished and neatly typed.

Even though his head felt weighed down with sleep, the thought of his early morning class kicked him out of bed and into his clothes. He decided to skip the great golden arches of the cafeteria that morning. Instead, he looked over his essay again, but found no errors.

The cool air of the morning brought him into the class wide awake. It began as it usually did: a quick roll call, class highlights written in chalk on the board, many people scattered about the room with dazed looks reflecting the previous night's events on their faces. The pace of the class slowly picked up. Assigned chapter were discussed in detail. Questions were asked. Questions were answered. Then the moment arrived that most students didn't care about, some dreaded, some enjoyed. It was time to share essays.

Jon slowly went to his assigned group, unsure of what was to come. He sat at a desk near the corner. The others came and formed a circle around him. They all sat, some quietly, some not, waiting for the teacher's instructions. When all the groups merged, the teacher gave her instructions. Each person was to read his or her paper to the others, then listen to the constructive statements offered. They would start with the person closest to the teacher and go in a counterclockwise direction. That put Jon second in line. He was relieved. At least he wasn't first.

The group sat looking at the fellow who was to go first. He looked back at them with a look of fear. He seemed to be gathering his thoughts to try and express himself. Finally someone gave him a "We're waiting" nudge. He looked quickly towards the teacher and back again. He spoke. Jon was shocked. The person hadn't finished his paper; he had nothing to read!

Eyes turned to Jon. Jon shivered, then smiled faintly. He reached into his folder and removed his work. With a nervous voice, Jon focused on his essay. The words came off the paper slowly at first, then began to build. Sentence by sentence, block by block, his previous night's struggle formed before them. It was built with each word until it was finally complete.

With the essay floating before them, each person in the group looked at it, each seeing something different with their own eyes.

Some began to pick at it, slowly bringing it down. A few watched, saying nothing. Others began building on it, reshaping it. Ideas were exchanged. Many things happened, but in the end it was up to Jon how his essay would stand.

After class was over, Jon walked quietly home, sat down at his computer, and sipped some tea. The spicy aroma circled around his head.

Sharing Ideas

- Donovan has dramatized his experience of preparing a paper to share with a class writing group. Add to, amplify, or change his story by telling your own stories.

- When I read Donovan's narrative, I remembered how nervous I become before people talk about my work. I also remembered that I always try to be prepared so I won't let down my classmates. To discover what gets in the way of class sharing, retell this narrative from the unprepared fellow's point of view.

- How do you feel after a group response session? For instance, Jon seemed ready to sit down and write some more.

16

Journeys in Journaling

Chris M. Anson and Richard Beach

Chris M. Anson directs the composition program at the University of Minnesota, where he teaches all sorts of courses in language, literacy, and writing. He has written several textbooks on writing, as well as scholarly books and articles exploring how people write and can learn to write. He has a special interest in informal writing used across the college curriculum as a way to help students learn. In his spare time he writes, remodels old houses, runs, and enjoys the outdoors with his wife Geanie and his two little boys, Ian and Graham.

Richard Beach, a former high school English teacher, is Professor of English Education at the University of Minnesota, where he teaches courses on literature, composition, and media methods. He is coauthor of *Teaching Literature in the Secondary School* and co-editor of *Developing Discourse Practices in Adolescence and Adulthood*. He doodles in his own journal for at least an hour a day. He has also found that student journals, particularly dialogue journals, improve the quality of talk in his own classes. He enjoys running (even in below-zero Minnesota winters), going to movies, and reading spy thrillers.

Prologue, the Authors Explain Their Journey

When we first thought about writing a chapter on journal writing for this textbook, it was as if we were starting on a journey by choosing the most direct, boring route we could find. We talked about what we

165

could tell you about journal writing, what sort of *information* we could impart about this useful and complicated genre. To us, the landscape is familiar; we've traveled the journal road many times, both by keeping journals ourselves and by conducting research on how people, especially students, learn and write by journaling. We were planning to take you down a kind of textbook superhighway, telling you in a blur of ideas what you should think about journals and how you should use them.

But then we started wondering about the sort of journey we were mapping out for you. We would most certainly cover lots of ground and expose you to the "main ideas" about journal writing, even if at breakneck speed. Would you be interested? Possibly. Would you speculate much about journals? Maybe. Could we get across how varied and complex and interesting journal writing is? Doubtful. We could tell you all that, but you might not want to take our word for it.

Still undecided, we went home to do what we usually do when we're not sure how to begin a piece of writing: we journaled. And we kept journaling for many pages and many weeks, first writing to and for ourselves, in the form of "solo" journals and then, later, slipping into a kind of dialogue as we sent each other what we'd written.

Shortly before a draft of our (still unwritten) chapter was due, something curious happened. As we talked about all our journal writing, we began to realize that our own journey *into* this chapter was likely to be more interesting, with more (in)sights to see at a slower and more enjoyable pace, than the chapter we imagined producing for this book. Then it dawned on us that the best way we could tell you about journal writing would be to share with you what we did.

Our journey, then, begins early on in our journal writing, as we wrote loose, exploratory entries focusing on what we wanted to tell you. To help you to see us at work, we've inserted our initials in brackets to indicate who's writing [CMA] or [RB].

The Journey

November 10 [CMA]

Rick [RB] came up with a great idea: We simply journal our way into the essay for Wendy Bishop's book, and it could "show" us ideas that we'd otherwise have to conjure up academically. And even as I do this entry I feel that my usual journaling process is becoming different somehow, and I think it comes from knowing that maybe Rick will see this, not so much that it should be polished and formal but that someone is going to look into my thinking and my own learning as a way to understand this crazy genre. Because it *feels* more text-like. That may be a difference we want to explore in the piece because in most academic settings journals are, in fact, read by someone (a teacher? Other students?), which doesn't necessarily change their informality but makes the sentences more complete, fewer personal abbreviations and short cuts, maybe. Something to do with the syntax. This project should be fun.

November 11 [RB]

Academic journals vs. personal journals. In discussing the journal, we're really talking about "academic journals" used in college courses to write about and reflect on the class readings, discussions, observations, related experiences, presentations, lectures, etc. This probably differs from a more private "personal diary" form of journal or a journal often used in therapy or as an observation log in creative writing. We need to make this clear. Also, I think journals have gotten bad press from seeming too "wishy washy" in some educational circles. Journals may be informal, but they *lead* to and *require* hard thinking. That's their point.

I think we should include at least the following information:

- What's an academic journal? How does it differ from the stereotypical diary?
- How do you keep one? This seems basic (who cares what sort of actual notebook you use?). But people do feel that the physical side of journals make a difference.
- Different sort of journals. Monologues vs. dialogues.
- How do we show journals at work? I like the idea of including examples from students' work in different courses. Maybe we could include some of our own?

November 12 [CMA]

Rick wondered whether we should include anything about our own personal uses of journals. I'm not sure what he means—focus overtly on how we use journals? Who wants to read all our professional musings? But it occurs to me that he might have meant how we ourselves started using journals, our personal histories. Makes journal writing seem close to writing autobiography. So here goes.

I guess I was about 11 or 12 years old when I started journaling. It was back when the (now common) American gerbil had just made its way into a few pet shops around the country as some sort of exotic new rodent (I don't think anyone knew at that point how prolific the little beasts were going to be!). I had a tank full of tropical fish and some of those little chameleons (I think they were just a common form of lizard from Mexico but they did turn from brown to green occasionally) and a guinea pig or two. And one day, clutching my 26 cents for a replacement carbon filter for my aquarium aerator, I went into our local pet shop. I remember how the door jingled when I opened it, and I went past the cages and tanks and barrels of bird food and cracked corn and there, right next to the charcoal filters, was a 25-gallon tank containing two gerbils.

I stood there for what seemed like a good half an hour, transfixed by these two strange little creatures, dashing around in their cedar chips, burrowing and nuzzling in their frenzied way. There was something jerky about their movements that I'd never seen in any other pet-store animal, and that fascinated me. I stood there, mezmerized by the way the gerbils would sit up with their little front paws dangling in front of them and then move a few inches to the left or right in one single, split-second twitch, stop, then twitch again. Stop, twitch. Stop, twitch. I wondered what that would be like, moving in that way. I was fascinated, and I just had to have one.

Then came the shock. As I stood there, the pet store owner had been preparing a little sign, his magic marker squeaking across a piece of white cardboard. Finally he brought it over and taped it on to the wall next to the gerbil tank. "Gerbils (South American rodent): $7.50 apiece."

Seven fifty! Two month's allowance, not including a cage!

Somehow, and I think it was probably my all-time greatest feat of parental persuasion, I managed, within the week, to get not just one gerbil but both. And a tank. And food. And a bag of cedar chips. *And* a little glass water bottle with a metal drinking spout. My father, who did amateur carpentry in the cellar in his spare time, then decided to build five gerbil cages for me, so that when my pair started to breed (which Dad, in all his wisdom, predicted they would do with a vengeance), I could start up a kind of cottage industry. Twenty dollars for two gerbils and a fully set up cage. Who could resist? After all, these were new, exotic animals. (I think that image, of our entire cellar turned into a profit-making breeding station for gerbils, was what finally got to Dad and got me my gerbils.)

One minor problem. After waiting for several months, with our five empty cages neatly lined up on a cellar shelf, we began wondering whether our pair of gerbils were capable of breeding. My father had never really looked too closely at them (he was still, I think, immersed in his dream of becoming the state's largest producer of exotic rodents). Finally, one Saturday, he took the gerbils out of the cage to conduct a close inspection. The verdict was instant and final: they were both males.

The following week, I managed to get another pair of gerbils (both female) by agreeing to wash the windows for a year and take out the garbage when asked and even clean up the sawdust in the cellar whenever Dad retreated there to build something. By that time, they were only $5 each (and falling). Before long, my five cages each sported two or more young gerbils. I twisted my best friend's arm to take one cage off my hands for ten dollars, but in spite of this first sale it didn't take long for the remaining four cages to grow in population, each housing a little kibbutz of five, eight, twelve gerbils. Dad frantically built cages. The price continued to drop. And soon, within the year, I was begging our friends, neighbors, distant acquaintances to take them, cage and all, for free.

Now, I had other pets. And when I needed advice about them, I'd turn to one of my little 50-cent pamphlets on "Caring for Tropical Fish" or "The Domestic Guinea Pig." But nothing, anywhere, on gerbils. I tried the library. Nothing. I combed the pet shops in three nearby towns. Nothing. Not a single word about domestic gerbils. This was it—my very first forray into Authorship. "Gerbils as Pets" by Christopher Anson.

So in the dim light of the dusty basement, amid the squealing of the gerbils' exercise wheels and the weep-weeping of my two guinea pigs and the bubbling of my aquarium aerators, I started my first, almost Darwinian journal, a little lined notepage of clinical observations about my rapidly proliferating pets.

My gerbil journal lasted for over six months, page after page of the most scholarly notes a 12-year old could conjure up about his pets' behavior. Once a gerbil got out of the cage and was lost in the cluttered basement for three weeks. When I finally did find him behind a box of wood, he'd killed a small field mouse (whose little dried up body lay nearby) and taken up residence in the mouse's winter home, a nest of tiny pieces of newspaper, thread, insulation material, part of an old sock from the laundry area, straw, and bits of cedar chips that had fallen from the gerbil cages. Now wild, the gerbil bit me so hard when I tried to pick him up that my finger bled for half an hour. Worse still, when I reintroduced the prodigal gerbil to his commune, the entire cage instantly became a battlefield, father turning on son, brother on sister, cousin on cousin, in a frenzy of indiscriminate attacks. When the dust and cedar chips settled, my renegade gerbil was dead, two others had lost substantial pieces of ear, and a fourth was missing the end of his tail.

After this incident (and a ritual burial of my first gerbil casualty), I remember sitting for a couple of hours in the dank cellar, writing and writing and writing about what it all meant. I figured an entire chapter in my pamphlet would have to be devoted to this problem of the escaped gerbil. And there was more: what could make such peaceful, adorable creatures so aggressive? Why did the gerbil turn on me—his caretaker and source of life—and then on his own kin? And how could they so ruthlessly kill him in his madness? As I wrote, my entries began slipping from rodent to animal kingdom, domestication, zoos, cages. And then to the idea of hostility and war, and humanity. And then to who I was and what I wanted to be.

And that's it, that's all to tell, I guess. I started journal writing that year, the year of the gerbils. I never did finish my pamphlet, but I found out that wasn't really the point.

I've never stopped journaling since.

November 17 [RB]

I want to look at characteristics of journal writing (informal, etc.), to contrast them with formal academic writing. What I noticed about Chris' gerbil story is how it's a blend of "polished" and informal writing. When he sent it over he said he was surprised at how well it turned out for something just done very quickly. So in a way he *aimed* to write informally and then ended up doing something that could pass as a formal narrative. The usual difference between journal writing and academic papers looks like this:

Formal Writing	*Journal Writing*
Organized	Unorganized
Formal language	Informal language
Definitive	Exploratory
Polished	Unpolished
Used to communicate	Used to learn, think, reflect

Most of the journal writing used to help students *learn* is informal, etc. But it may be possible to see the act of journal writing as a great way to write your way into a formal piece.

November 18 [CMA]

The most powerful thing about journal writing, for me, can be visualized as a sort of wheel, a snake with its tail in its mouth. At some point, the wheel is labeled "writing." Somewhere on the other side, it's labeled "thinking" or "learning." Writing, in other words, *leads* to thinking and learning. Thinking and learning lead, in turn, to more writing. And on and on, like a mantra. I think this concept works especially well with journal writing because it suggests the exploratory nature of journals and emphasizes their chief value: contemplation.

November 20 [RB]

One use of the journal is to extend or explore your thinking in order to construct your own knowledge. Rather than simply restate or rehearse ideas shared in a course, you're using the journal to reformulate and reflect on ideas *in your own words*. In that way, you're assimilating these ideas into what you already know and believe. For example, you might begin in a philosophy class by restating or rehearsing what the text, students or instructor has said about the idea of "free will." To extend or explore your own thinking about free will, you may then consider the following ways of extending and exploring (etc., finish this thought):

1. A loping freewrite: Peter Elbow suggests that one way to extend your thinking is to pick out a word, phrase or key term, and do a 5- or 10-minute freewrite about that word, phrase, or key term.

2. Reflecting on your own thinking. You may also use your entries to reflect—to stand back and interpret or evaluate the larger meaning of your thinking.

3. Using the journal as prewriting. You may also use your journal entries as prewriting to develop ideas for your papers. As you begin to define and clarify a possible paper topic, you could highlight or circle material and entitle that material in the margin according to its relevance to your overall topic, etc. *Chris—What do you think of this sort of listing/bulleting?*

November 30 [CMA]

Rick: You notice that since we started exchanging journal entries we've slipped into a dialogue journal, and it's worth, I think, really making that distinction in the chapter for *The Subject is Writing*. Because some classes may involve students in just plain journal writing, for and to themselves, while others might get students writing in dialogues like this. And frankly I'd rather just dialogue about our journal writing from now on, because I think we have to start getting more specific about what direction we want to take.

December 9 [RB]

Chris: We need to explore more of those functions I started working on the other day. Another one I want to add is something like mapping—in keeping a journal, you may want to use some mapping to explore your thoughts (or something like that). For example, in an economics class, you may be discussing the differences between socialism and capitalism. Using a circle and spoke map, put the key ideas—socialism and capitalism—in central circles. Then draw spokes out from the central circles and make smaller circles that represent the different characteristics of the central ideas. (And so on—each smaller circle can then suggest other circles so you begin to fill the page with concepts. Then draw lines and label them with "d" or "s" to represent differences and similarities.) We could actually show a map or maybe one of our own. You didn't do anything like that for the gerbil thing, did you?

December 15 [CMA]

Rick—I like the idea of adding something conceptual/visual to journal writing, because it always seems so "wordy," if you know what I mean—all language, in full and sometimes very elaborated sentences (like these, I guess). It would be wise to show how appropriate it is to carry on even the most highly conceptual doodling, mapping, diagrams, and so on in a journal. I also like the way you stuck in a reference to economics, to show the academic diversity of journals.

You asked if I used mapping with the gerbil piece, and no, I didn't. For some reason I find it less useful for narrative, but the main difference was that I didn't think I was actually writing anything formal. This is, for me, one of the most powerful aspects of journal writing: I *tricked myself* into writing something that with a lot of work might actually become a fairly decent, lighthearted piece, but when I was writing it I was just writing as fast as I could to tell you about when I started journaling, and somehow, maybe because I felt so relaxed and uninhibited, my words started coming out more descriptively. It's wierd, but it never struck me as such a powerful way to start writing as it did then, and maybe it's precisely because I wasn't actually setting out to "start writing."

What do you want to do with the notion of dialogue journals? Since we started writing articles together (was it six years ago!?) I've noticed how much our stuff has really turned into dialogue journaling even when we're trying to do pretty formal chunks (notice, for example, how both of us, when we tire of writing a formal chunk, almost always do a kind of dialoguing at the moment we fizzle out, like "Rick, what else should we include here?" or (and you do this a lot) "Chris—fill in." It shows how dialoguing can become collaboration, and I like the idea of explaining that to students.

December 29 [RB]

Chris—here are some pieces on dialogue journals. Tell me what you think or just redo them.

Carrying on a written conversation. Keeping a dialogue journal differs from a solo journal in that you are sharing your thoughts with another person in a written conversation. You and your partner(s) can collaboratively explore your responses to readings, ideas, similar experiences, or difficulties. While you may do the same thing in an oral conversation, one advantage of using a written conversation is that you have time to reflect on each other's entries. There may be a gap of several days before you react. You can therefore mull over what your partner says in order to formulate a response.

Chris: How theoretical do you think we should get in this? I want to refer to Michael Halliday's finding that oral language portrays things more as unfolding processes, in a complex and dynamic way, while written language tends to describe products, turning those into a structure, so its complexity is static and dense. He notes that "writing creates a world of things; talking creates a world of happening." So that the dialogue journal, by combining the features of both oral and written language, encourages both an ongoing interactive exploration of ideas with the more structured exploration of written language. But that's a little too heavy, don't you think? Do you have any ideas for how to explain that?

January 5 [CMA]

Rick: I just looked back through the stuff we've been doing. I wondered whether instead of doing the same old boring *formal* kind of paper we could try to explore journals in a concrete and interesting way by actually *doing* what we're talking about. Do you think this could work? Because I'm worried that if we try too hard, we're going to end up doing a sort of "scholarly piece" disguising as a how-to chapter and maybe end up pandering too much or something.

I have one fear about this, and it's the conflict between the sort of journal writing we've been doing and the fact that if it's published in this form, then it sanctions sloppiness, random organization, etc. Let's face it, nothing is ever published unless it's formal and tidy and stylistically slick. We don't want to give the impression that a writer can be conceptually and linguistically messy and then just stop there. Do you think we'll be sending that message?

January 10 [RB]

Chris: The dialogue journal idea is tied up with the notion of building relationships, a kind of good conversation that leads to learning and thinking. So why not share the process we're going through?

January 15 [CMA]

Rick: Help! I don't know. I've read back through all this and I'm tempted to polish it up, especially my gerbil narrative (I was sort of amazed looking back at it to remember that it took me the lesser part of an hour to write, just blasting through.) But if we do that, we defeat the whole purpose of the chapter, which is to show journals in action, to go on a kind of journey in journaling. In other words, if the whole thing starts to look contrived and polished and slick, then it's not journal writing any more. And that's hard, because it takes a certain will power to resist "fixing it up."

We're putting ourselves on the line by going public with something so informal. But what I like about the idea is that we *had* to learn our way into and through this piece to begin with. We might have ended up with a polished article, but it wouldn't have shown *how* we learned our way into and through it.

And another thing I like about it in this form: We don't have all the answers about this sort of writing. It's too varied (I think we did five or six really different kinds of writing in the process of writing about it). I'd rather that people talk about journal writing and experiment with it than think that we have all the answers about just how and why it works. Again, that's a risk, don't you think? We're researchers, we have all sorts of data and expertise on journal writing. But I'd rather just be honest.

January 20 [RB]

Chris: I liked your phrase about a journey. Why don't we call it "Journeys in Journaling" and leave it at that?

Coda, the Authors Reflect on Their Travels

This is the first and probably the only time we will ever write about journaling by publishing our own journal writing. The advantage, for us, comes from the potential for our chapter to display some of the benefits of journaling: more and better thinking about a topic; less anxiety and procrastination because of the sense of having "started" a writing task; better planning for formal writing; and a more collaborative writing situation, especially when keeping a dialogue journal.

But, like the dramatic commercial in which someone flies over 10 piles of tires in a stock car or bungee-jumps 500 feet above a rocky river, we suggest that you don't try this at home. Turn in formal, polished writing. But by all means begin it by journaling. You'll find, as we do, that keeping a journal, alone or with someone else as a dialogue partner, really does work. Take our words for it.

Sharing Ideas

- Whenever I read other writer's journals, I tend to grab some of my old travel journals and start reading them again. Describe your own journeys in journaling. Have you kept journals? When, why, for how long, in or out of school, and so on.

- Chris and Rick have shown as much as told about journaling. Play teacher and draw some points from their presentation to share with a class of writing students—your own class.

- As they begin their essay, Chris and Rick point to a general problem in writing instruction. If writing is a process, then describing that process will not necessarily teach the process. Think about the essays in this book. Were there particular ones that helped you better understand and more ably produce your writing? Try to tease out the attributes of a useful "how to write" essay. Then write your own essay; to do this, you may also want to look ahead to the essays in the next section that explictly offer advice and explanations.

- Look at Rick's entry from November 11; did this essay manage to include the information he outlines as being essential? Can you provide additional information in these areas, based on your own journaling experiences.

- Chris and Rick's journal entries echo letter writing since they offer a dialog between writers. Some of my most engaging writing interactions these days are taking place on electronic mail where I "journal" with other writing teachers around the country. If you are using this form of journaling, share your experiences.

- At this point, what new ideas do you have about writers' conversations? Some of the essays in this book describe writers talking in class or in journals. Writers also hold many other conversations through electronic journals, letters, or phone and dinner conversations; writers hold conversations with themselves, aloud or internally, or on paper when they use invention exercises to hold a dialogue with a memory, and so on. How do you make sense of all this talking about writing?

- Finally, you might want to read ahead to Jim Corder's essay; Jim struggles with the degree to which he feels himself to be a writer alone and a writer in social conversations.

- Make yourself a promise about journaling and stick to it for a set period of time.

———————————

Part IV

To the Writer — Explanations and Advice

In the next four essays, experienced teachers provide general advice about writing. While earlier authors introduced you to the *new* college writing classroom, these essayists talk about some unchanging aspects of learning writing in school.

For instance, Pat Belanoff doesn't provide simple solutions for the grading concerns that arise in writing classrooms, but she does examine the beliefs we hold about objective and subjective methods of evaluation. And she offers suggestions for making grading and evaluation standards an important part of ongoing class discussions. In her essay on learning preferences, Muriel Harris encourages you to be alert and even somewhat skeptical when you review writing advice in this and other textbooks. She describes several measures of differences in human personality preferences and asks you to consider your writing processes in light of your personality and your learning style.

You've probably wondered about writing teachers. Do they just ask for more and more revision? Do they revise their own work and to the same degree? As Marcia Dickson tells how she composed her essay for this book, you learn that she uses most of the techniques she teaches, but she uses them in her own way. Marcia's narrative echoes the advice you receive in Muriel's essay; an individual writer develops a flexible set of writing strategies out of the options and techniques that are available to her.

17

What Is a Grade?

Pat Belanoff

Pat Belanoff directs the Writing Program at the State University of New York at Stony Brook, which is on the north shore of Long Island, a little more than an hour from New York City. She has co-authored two textbooks, one a freshman composition book with Peter Elbow called *A Community of Writers* and a somewhat off-beat grammar book with Betsy Rorschach and Mia Oberlink called *The Right Handbook*. She has also co-edited a collection of essays *(Portfolios: Process and Product)* with Marcia Dickson, one of the other authors in this book. Pat also writes about the women of Old English poetry and spends more time than she should doing crossword puzzles.

Grades and school seem synonymous. Grades are the evidence educators, parents, politicians, and other citizens cite to demonstrate that students have (or have not) learned what they should learn. Such reliance on grades presumes that the student who gets an A has learned more than the student who gets a B, who in turn has learned more than the student who gets a C and so on down the line to an F: the student who gets one of those has obviously not learned much. Many in our society and in the schools accept without question these connections between grades and the quality of student learning.

But those who accept these connections argue for their validity within some fields far more strongly than within other fields. For example, most people are more willing to credit a 90 on a math or physics test than on a composition or on a paper responding to some piece of literature. Students, reflecting this societal attitude, often complain to me about the nature of English studies—both literature and composition. It is the objectivity–subjectivity contrast that they usually bring up, lamenting that they wish grades on compositions could be objective like their math and physics grades. In those classes, they tell me, you know for sure what's right and what's wrong. In a writing class though, these same students say, everything is subjective: how well one does depends on what the teacher likes and dislikes—there's nothing substantial to guide one to better grades. Students come into my office to complain that a paper they got a poor mark on would have gotten an A or B from a previous teacher. And I suspect that among themselves they confess to the opposite: that some paper they just got an A or B on would never have gotten such a good grade from a previous teacher. They know from personal experience how greatly grading standards differ from teacher to teacher. Reacting to this, some students tell me that it isn't possible to get grades that mean anything in English classes and that they've come to hate English as a result.

Teachers of other subjects sometimes express similar judgments. I remember well, as a beginning faculty member, attending an interdepartmental meeting at which a member of the history faculty said that he envied English teachers because they didn't have to be bothered with "covering" a set range of materials every semester. When he was pressed to explain himself, he continued by saying that there was no "real" subject matter in English classes, only opinions and subjective ideas, no "facts." "How do you decide what grade to give?" he asked me. "It's all so subjective!"

How do I respond to these charges of subjectivity? First, I agree. I know, even better than they, that teachers do not give the same grades to the same pieces—particularly when these teachers work in unlike schools. But, rather than apologize for this lack of conformity, I actually celebrate it. I'll get back to why later in this essay.

After conceding the truth of these charges of subjectivity, I encourage those who make them to consider whether other subjects are as "objective" as they appear. Not all biology teachers cover the same material; not all of them focus on the same subjects when they make up their tests, and not all of them weigh answers in the same way. Biology teachers differ not only about what to teach but also about what's most important in the classroom. Some teachers think that how we discover information is more important than the information itself. They will teach and test quite differently from teachers who see their main goal as transferring information into the heads of their students. Furthermore, the deeper one goes into any subject, the less objective issues become. Astrophysicists look at the same data, but some posit a "big bang" theory for creation and others do not. Paleontologists study the same geology and the same bones and disagree about why dinosaurs disappeared from the earth. Newcomers in these fields gradually join these debates and earn the right to interpret data in their own ways.

Literature classes sometimes mimic the sequence I've just set forth for physical sciences: less and less agreement or objectivity as one moves deeper into the subject. Perhaps the teacher will give a test on the facts of a piece of literature: who wrote it, when, which character does what, where the figures of speech are, and so forth. Even literature teachers who approach their subject this way, however, move fairly quickly to interpretation, to an assessment of what the piece "means," which is equivalent to what the geologist does as he "reads" old bones and old geological formations. English teachers do seem to move to the level of interpretation more quickly than mathematicians do; but both fields deal with facts *and* interpretations. Both fields, that is, are objective *and* subjective.

I'm mainly a writing teacher, not a literature teacher, and must acknowledge that the objectivity–subjectivity issue is even more pronounced in a writing class than in a literature class. In the latter, there's at least some secure basis in that students are responding to published, established texts. But, in a writing class, there's a felt sense that the texts being produced are totally personal in a way nothing else in school is. We know, of course, that they're not totally personal: what we write is always partially determined by our backgrounds, our culture, our prior educational experiences, our past reading and writing activities. But all that is filtered through our sense of ourselves. Mikhail Bakhtin, a well-regarded Russian language scholar, once wrote that any word we use is only half ours, but that we can make words our own by saturating them with our own intentions and purposes. The more we're able to do that, the more individualized what we say and write becomes and the less likely it is to be like anything else a teacher has ever read. No A paper is exactly like another A paper in the same way as 2 + 2 is always 4. Thus, the grades of English teachers can never be based on exact correspondences between papers.

I celebrate and encourage this diversity. A major goal of the humanities is to guide students—not just while they're acquiring facts, but also while they're learning to interpret them. As a writing teacher, my task is to help students gain control *through words* over their developing interpretations. All of us struggle with language when we need to express ideas new to us. My particular students struggle as their already established ideas and thoughts interact with the new ideas and thoughts a new world (college) presents to them.

As they react, they will agree with some of their classmates in one way, with others in some different way and perhaps stand alone on still another issue. No one's ideas, opinions, and reactions are exactly like anyone else's. As a teacher I'm in the business of getting students to think, not of getting them to think like everyone else or even like me. Teachers who can get students to spit back information on tests will never know what these students are really thinking—or if they're thinking at all about what they're supposedly learning.

For the same reasons we do not react exactly like anyone else, none of us reads exactly like anyone else either. Thus possibilities multiply for diverse judgments—not only am I reading something I've never read before, I'm also reading in a way unique to me. It seems like common sense to see meaning as existing in the words on the page, but black marks on paper mean nothing until someone reads them. Meaning can only develop as a human mind interacts and inevitably interprets those black marks—and human minds come in all varieties. Quite simply, I never react to a student text exactly like any other teacher any more than I react exactly like anyone else when I read *Hamlet* or *The Color Purple*. And when the issue shifts to what these texts mean, differences multiply even more.

Many students do not like to hear this; it turns a world of seeming certainty into formless mush. It may be easier to have a teacher who tells you exactly how to write a paper. But once you realize that no teacher (because she is human) reads like any other teacher, you also realize that those directions for an A paper are valid only for that class. You don't learn much to carry to the next class if the teacher does not explain her standards for that A.

So far, I've written of the subjectivity resulting from the necessarily subjective acts of writing and reading. But subjectivity has other causes, one of which is the school setting. Because I've taught at a number of institutions of various kinds I've been forced to realize that grades are always relative to the institution where they're given. An A at one school isn't the same as an A at another school. What that means is that I'm judging each paper I read against other papers I've read at the particular school I'm teaching at. It also means that if that same paper were given to me at a different time at a different school, it would receive a different grade. And even within a department or program, grades are relative to the class in which they're assigned. A paper that earns a B in a developmental class will not be likely to get a B in freshman composition. And a B paper in freshman composition will not be likely to get a B in an advanced or upper-level writing class.

What's the alternative to this seeming unfairness or inconsistency? The alternative is to believe that somewhere out in the clouds is a model A paper, B paper, and so forth and that every paper I read (even though it is unique) can be graded relative to that model. Or, even more preposterous, that I was somehow born knowing what an A paper is. There are teachers who act as though they believe this is true, as though there is some absolute measure against which all student papers can be measured and that they know with absolute certainty what that measure is. Unfortunately for them no one seems to agree on any real, not-in-the-clouds paper which should serve as that model A paper. No sooner does a teacher offer one, than some other teacher finds fault with it and offers a different one. Usually teachers can only agree on the traits of good writing *in the abstract*. As soon as they start looking at individual papers, agreement disintegrates.

But even if we could get writing teachers together from all over the country and agree on a paper to which we would all give an A, we would not agree on how closely other papers approached our model, nor would we necessarily agree on what made that model A paper a model A paper. Some of us would cite its content first, some of us its organization, some of us its language, some of us the relevance of its arguments, some of us its originality, creativity, and imaginative power.

What I'm saying is that I inevitably judge the paper in front of me in terms of all other papers I've read. I make no apologies for that. That's the only way any of us ever judge anything: persons are beautiful in relation to others, movies are acclaimed or not in relation to other movies, scenery is lovely in relation to other scenes the observer has seen. I cannot know beauty, perfection, or loveliness apart from specific examples. It is hardly to be expected that decisions on the quality of writing could be made any differently. Thus the model of an A I have in my head is a product of all the papers I have read as well as of my own individual way of reading.

To be honest, I hate grading. I love teaching; I love talking to students about their writing, sharing my responses with them, discussing their subjects, listening and reacting to their ideas. But I hate grading papers. Most students work hard on their papers; many of them dig deep into themselves to express ideas and opinions important to them. It isn't easy to put "C" or "D" on such endeavors. It may be easy (I'm not really sure about this) for students and teachers in other classes to distance themselves a bit from the grades. A physics teacher gives problems to be worked out, formulas to be decoded and solved, and so forth. If a student does poorly, the teacher concludes that he didn't study or he's just not destined to be a physics student. The student can console himself by acknowledging that he should have studied more or that physics is just not his subject.

Somehow it's different when one writes a paper. It's hard to keep oneself out of it. The assumption—contrary to that about physics—is that everyone *can* "do" English. Everyone is assumed to have opinions and responses to events, to pieces of writing, to ideas presented by others; everyone is *not* expected to understand or master physics. Having an opinion on personal, social, and political issues or a reaction to a poem or an editorial is within the capabilities of all of us. We can't escape by saying that this isn't our subject. Thus we feel judged by grades on papers in ways we don't feel judged by a grade on a physics test. What we write (that is, if we genuinely commit ourselves to the writing) feels as though it comes from somewhere inside us; the answer to a physics problem feels like it comes from inside our heads only.

Perhaps the solution would be to abandon grading altogether in writing classes. I confess that this is a solution that appeals to me greatly. Instead of putting grades on a paper, I could simply respond to it: let the writer know my reactions to what it says and how it says it. If a student did all the assignments, met my attendance requirements, participated in class, and mostly got papers in on time, she would get a "Satisfactory" for the semester. There are colleges, universities, and even some high schools that have grading systems like this. Perhaps some of you reading this article may even attend such a school; if you do, you undoubtedly have an opinion about the value of it.

Unfortunately (for me, at any rate), most colleges and universities require grades. Mine does. Therefore, I've been forced to do a lot of thinking about what grades are and how to make them as fair as possible. Almost every time I sit down to grade papers, I ask myself: "What *are* grades; what do they measure?"

Despite my questions and doubts (or perhaps because of them), I argue for the validity of two kinds of grading in writing classes: grading by groups of teachers and grading by individual teachers who have worked through standards with their students. I am not going to argue that such grades are *not* subjective, but I will argue that they can be meaningful within the environment in which they're given.

If grades are only meaningful within limited environments, it's logical to argue for the joint awarding of grades by those within the environment. Gymnastics competitions come to mind as a possible model. For each performance of each gymnast, six or seven people give independent scores, and these are averaged or added up in some way. (It's interesting to consider that in gymnastics scoring the highest and the lowest scores are eliminated before the averaging is done.) In such situations, I don't have to convince anyone of my opinions; I just vote. Perhaps students' papers ought to be judged like gymnastics contests: six or seven teachers would give each paper a grade, and the actual grade would be an average or total of those given, after discounting both the best and the worst grade. The problem with such a scheme, as far as I'm concerned, is that I would be spending all my time grading papers! Since I hate grading, my enthusiasm for teaching might be considerably dampened. Although it isn't feasible to have every student's paper graded by six or seven other teachers, it *is* feasible for teachers to share grading once or twice during a semester. If two or three teachers jointly grade a set of each other's papers during the semester, both they and their students will develop a sense of community judgment.

Even teachers within an isolated classroom can make grades useful for themselves and their students. A teacher can, of course, simply put grades on papers and leave it up to students to figure out what she rewards and punishes. Some students are quite good at this. Quite a few are not. I believe that if students are going to get better, I have to explain the standards I use to arrive at grades. I consider this part of my responsibility.

I sometimes ask college freshmen to bring to class a graded paper they wrote in high school, especially if the paper has some comments on it in addition to the grade. Then the class and I together analyze the paper and draw some conclusions about what the teacher who graded it valued. I may also give my students some papers from other years and ask them to arrange them in order from the one they consider the most effective to the one they consider least effective. We then talk about our personal standards, where we agree and disagree and why. Often I do need to introduce some standards into the grading process that may not grow out of our discussions simply because freshmen are new to the academic community. At the same time, I aim to help them understand how the standards I introduce may be different from the standards of other writing teachers. I cannot do this honestly unless I make it my business to be more familiar with the standards of those with whom I work most closely: my colleagues in the department who are teaching the same courses I am and my colleagues who are assigning writing in other subjects areas.

On the basis of all these discussions, my students and I strive to reach some conclusions on standards without privileging any particular set of standards: mine, theirs, their former teachers. I then give them some papers to judge on the basis of the standards we've developed together. And, finally, I give them several assignments that will be graded on the basis of these standards. In the process, I am teaching what may be the most important lesson of all: the ability to write for a particular audience. If I can help students understand how to get an A or B in my class, I will be helping them learn to figure out how to analyze and impress other audiences too, both in and out of school. When I give assignments that will be judged by different standards, the class and I again discuss these fully.

No matter whether I grade individually or as a member of a group of teachers, putting one grade on one paper can be misleading because others (including the student who writes the paper) may deduce more from the grade than is warranted. Since neither I nor the student author can know whether she can write with equal skill on a different task, a grade can be meaningful only as a judgment of a particular paper, not as a judgment of a writer's overall skills. For this reason, I prefer to give a grade to two or more papers at a time. In fact, I prefer to grade a portfolio of a student's work at mid- and end-semester and give one grade for all the work with commentary explaining the strengths and weaknesses of the whole portfolio. Students can then get some sense of how I assess their overall skill in terms of what I, their classmates, my program, and my particular school value.

I recognize that not all teachers have either the time or the desire to discuss standards with students. If you have such a teacher, you can find ways to get at these standards. You can analyze graded papers and draw conclusions about what the teacher likes and dislikes and then make an appointment with the teacher to test these conclusions. (You'll learn more if you do some analysis too rather than just taking a paper in and asking for an explanation of the grade or for advice on getting a better grade.) Or you can ask a teacher if she is willing to read a draft of a paper several days before it's due. The worst she can do is say no. But most teachers are gratified to talk to a student who's willing to put in the time to improve his writing. My final suggestion in such situations is that you form study groups (research has shown that such groups result in better grades for participants) in which you share papers with one another before they're submitted for grading.

When I have this discussion with students in my classes, there's always more than one student who interprets me as saying that only conformity will lead to a good grade. My answer to that is not usually what they want to hear, for I tell them that language use always involves conformity. Speaking words others can understand means conforming to built-in rules of language. I can't give words my own meaning and adjust grammatical rules to my own liking. Creativity and originality can only develop *within* established meanings and rules. But that doesn't mean a language user cannot use the meanings and the rules in new, exciting ways—writers have been doing this for centuries. Taking into consideration a teacher's or class standards is the same as being tuned in to your audience. Once tuned in, you can decide whether to play to it or whether to try to influence these standards themselves—but, at least, you have a choice. And if you do strive to persuade your teacher and classmates of the validity of somewhat different standards and are able to meet them and thus demonstrate that validity, you may succeed in altering classroom standards. I've had students who could do that.

Frankly, I would be frightened about the future of our culture if we ever arrived at a point where I was sure that the grades I gave were the same as those all other teachers would give. This would suggest some rather unpleasant things about the future of discussion in the world. Not all of us think Shakespeare was the greatest writer the world has ever produced; not all of us think Jacqueline Suzanne is the worst writer the world has ever produced. Most of us fall somewhere in between on both these points. And most of us like it that way; but that means we have to accept and learn to value varying evaluations of student texts also.

Most decisions we make in our personal and professional lives are more like the problematic ones we wrestle with in English and writing classes; they're not usually as clear-cut as the answers on math tests. I'd like to think that coming to terms with the subjectivity of grades is good training for living with the subjectivity inherent in the world around us. But perhaps that's stretching my point too far. What is important within the world of the individual classroom is that grades can be useful and meaningful to students who understand the basis for them and who recognize that one grade on one paper can never be a judgment on all their writing.

Sharing Ideas

- Tell some stories of you, your writing, and grades.

- Have you encountered the subjectivity–objectivity problem before? What do you think about Pat's analogy to paper grading and gymnastics competitions?

- Are you "graded" in other (nonacademic) areas of your life? List the ways this happens. For instance, we may feel we receive grades in the workplace, on a date, when we go hunting and fishing, within our relationships, and so on.

- Are you willing to abolish grades and just get on with learning? What, for you, is at stake in earning grades in school?

- Have you ever learned in a nongraded and noncompetitive situation? Describe how that felt.

- How do you know when writing is "good"?

- Have you ever had to grade someone else? What did you do and what did it feel like?

- Using Pat's discussion, design your ideal writing class—how would grades work, matter, be assigned?
- If writing is a way of thinking, if writing is a recursive ongoing activity, leading to more and more revision and discovery through revision, what does it mean to stop the process and grade a paper?

18

Don't Believe Everything You're Taught
Matching Writing Processes and Personal Preferences

Muriel Harris

Muriel Harris is a professor of English and Director of the Writing Lab at Purdue University. She tutors in the Purdue Writing Lab and has written a variety of journal articles, book chapters, and books on working one-to-one with writers in writing lab tutorials or teacher–student conferences. Her children and husband claim to have survived living with someone who not only enjoys teaching writing but also wrote a grammar handbook, *The Prentice–Hall Reference Guide to Grammar and Usage* and her daughter even calls long distance now to the family Grammar Hotline. Muriel would very much like to hear from readers of her essay who are willing to share comments about it, their own writing processes, or bad textbook/classroom advice they've been suffering from. Write to her c/o English Department, Purdue University, West Lafayette, IN 47907.

Textbooks and teachers offer a great deal of well-meaning advice about how to write well. And while some of that advice may be helpful, not all of it may work for you. Recent scholarship on writing is beginning to help us understand that not every strategy about how to write effectively works uniformly well for everyone. In fact, you may be writing in ways that are not as productive as they should be—which is not to say that you should sell your textbook tomorrow morning or ask for a refund for your composition classes. The problem is that writing involves a variety of mental processes and habitual preferences for ways of proceeding that differ from one person to another, and we do better by matching our innate preferences with compatible writing processes, just as a right-handed person writes more easily with a pen in her right hand than in her left. But difficulties arise because we have all been through writing instruction of one kind or another, and as a result, we may be writing as we were taught to write, rather than as we might write if we were to try out a variety of options before choosing the ones that work best for us. When writers use inappropriate strategies and then find themselves struggling, they wrongly relegate themselves to the bottom of the heap in writing skills. "I'm just not a good writer" or "I just can't write," they say, when in fact they may actually be saying that the writing processes, assumptions, and strategies they are using don't fit them very well.

As a writing center tutor, I have had the opportunity to hear some of those "I can't write" comments, to see how some writers are hobbling themselves unnecessarily, and to observe first-hand how different writers really are. As a tutor sitting elbow to elbow with writers, I hear and observe them using a great variety of strategies—techniques that work well for them or techniques that are creating unnecessary barriers to writing more effectively. My attempts to understand why we respond so differently have led me to read about some of the windows into personal differences that relate to writing styles—for example, various types of learning styles, cognitive processing dimensions, and personality types—and to look at how some of those differences can be observed among writers. These dimensions help us to see that people naturally differ, and they do so in ways that—like being blue-eyed or brown-eyed—are neither right nor wrong (or better or worse), just different. However, unlike being blue-eyed or brown-eyed, we don't all neatly fall into one or the other of the categories. More often, the reality is that most of us tend to prefer one dimension more than another to some degree or to attack something first in a preferred way and then to come back and use a somewhat different mode.

When we use modes of behaving or acting that work against the grain and that are, therefore, not as productive as they should be, we can cause ourselves problems. The connection with writing in all of this is that not every textbook or teacher remembers to warn us against writing strategies that may not be appropriate for some of us who are asked to try out those strategies. To show you what I mean, I need to be more specific here, to describe these mental differences and to review some of the often repeated suggestions and tactics for writing that intersect with these differences.

Dimensions of Difference

One of the more interesting and widely used scales of differences in human personality preferences is the Myers–Briggs Type Inventory (MBTI). It is a scale that rates people according to how they answer questions such as the following:

1. Q. In a large group, do you more often
   a. introduce others, or
   b. get introduced.

2. Q. Does following a schedule
   a. appeal to you, or
   b. cramp you.

3. Q. Do you think it is more important to be able
   a. to see the possibilities in a situation, or
   b. to adjust to the facts as they are.

Two very readable and nontechnical introductions to the MBTI are David Keirsey and Marilyn Bates' *Please Understand Me* (1978) and Isabel Myers' *Gifts Differing* (1980). Career counseling offices often have copies of the MBTI for students to try out because the results can be useful in guiding people to careers that are most appropriate for them. A book-length study of how the MBTI interacts with writing skills is George Jensen and John DiTiberio's *Personality and the Teaching of Composition* (1989).

The answers to the MBTI questions, when scored, indicate the degree to which people sort themselves along a spectrum of four dimensions: Extrovert versus Introvert, Intuitive versus Sensing, Feeling versus Thinking, and Perceiving versus Judging. A quick overview of these types is as follows.

Extrovert versus Introvert. This distinction is based on the way we focus energy. People high on the Extrovert scale are energized by conversation and being with others, and they tend to value outer experience (talking and acting). They often leap into tasks with little planning because they rely a lot on trial and error to complete the task. Extroverts think more clearly and develop more ideas while in action or conversation. Introverts, however, predominantly focus their energy inward through contemplation. They are more cautious about the outer world and prefer to anticipate and reflect before becoming involved with it in order to avoid errors. Introverts think best and develop more ideas when they are alone, uninterrupted by people and events.

Sensing versus Intuition.   This distinction is based on alternative ways of perceiving or taking in information. Sensing types prefer direct and conscious use of their senses (seeing, hearing, etc.), and they like things to be concrete, practical, and matter of fact. They are detail-oriented as well. For example, a sensor might start a story with a solid grounding in reality—what happened, when, to whom, and so on. Sensors learn better when concrete examples are given, and they usually do better with detailed, specific instructions, and by proceeding step by step. As writers, they tend to get ready to write by collecting large amounts of data so that first drafts are primarily recordings of facts. When they revise, they need help with moving to the level of generalizations and implications. Intuitive types, on the other hand, move more easily in the realm of impressions, hunches, and imagination; they prefer the abstract and are idea-oriented and imaginative. When Intuitives begin a story, they will start with its meaning and will prefer to find unique approaches to it. Their early drafts may contain only ideas and generalities unsupported by concrete examples, which have to be added later during revision.

Thinking versus Feeling.   This distinction is based on how we make decisions and evaluations. Thinking types prefer to make decisions based on objective criteria. They prefer to do what is right even if feelings are hurt. They excel at categorizing, are analytical and logical, and prefer to follow outlines or organizational patterns. Feeling types, on the other hand, prefer to select topics in which they can express more personal values and—when it is appropriate—their feelings. They also prefer to make decisions on the basis of subjective factors such as values, are more concerned with how they are connecting to their audience, and are more comfortable following the flow of their thoughts rather than an outline.

Judging versus Perceiving.   This dimension is based on how we approach tasks in the outer world. Judging types like to complete projects, are decisive, may seem a bit rigid, and tend to limit their writing topics quickly and set manageable goals as they write. They need to finish tasks and are less likely to go back and keep reworking something. Perceiving types, on the other hand, are more comfortable with leaving the world unstructured, and tasks can remain unfinished. Perceivers are usually more flexible than judgers, are more spontaneous, and like lots of alternatives to choose from.

I particularly enjoy the discussions after introducing the MBTI dimensions to groups of writers because of the buzz of conversation as writers recognize themselves and their friends among these types. Some writers enjoy leaping to generalizations about causes of personality clashes they observe in their lives (e.g., the perceiver who begins to suspect that her fights with her roommate in the residence hall are a result of the roommate being a super judger) and about different writing habits (the extrovert who suddenly doesn't feel quite so peculiar about sitting in the student union coffee shop while he writes or listening to his stereo in his room, even though he's read that writers should always find a quiet place to write).

In addition to the MBTI, another way to look at our differences is to consider learning styles. A learning style is a predisposition on a person's part to adopt a particular learning strategy. There is a large body of research on learning styles, and if you are interested in learning more about this, the psychology section of your campus library will have a number of books on the subject. Two you might start with are *Learning Strategies and Learning Styles: Perspectives on Individual Differences* (1988) and Volume 1 of *Individual Differences in Cognition* (1983). Two of the most widely accepted differences in learning styles (among many that have been identified) are the following.

Global/Analytical Processing (or Holist/Serialist). People who use global strategies tend to be deductive rather than inductive and are better at seeing the whole. Because they first try to build up the big picture before determining where any details fit in, they are more liable to jump to conclusions on the basis of too little evidence than are analytical types. Those who use analytical processes are more prone to going step by step, moving inductively, and are better at seeing the parts of the whole and the specific details. They progress linearly from one topic to the next and, because they are concerned with operational details and procedures, are in danger of seeing the trees but not the forest.

Visual/Verbal Processing. Work on right brain/left brain orientations indicates that left-brain processing is more word-oriented, analytical, and sequential as distinct from right-brain processing, which is more visual and spatially oriented. Psychologists believe that the brain's two hemispheres function in specialized, distinct ways. The left hemisphere, which controls the right side of the body, is predominantly involved with logical thinking, especially in verbal and mathematical functions. The right hemisphere, which controls the left side of the body, is predominantly involved with visual/intuitive, nonlinear information and is responsible for orientation in space and artistic endeavor.

Yet another way to look at differences, this time more closely tied to writing habits, is to consider the different planning and writing habits of writers in terms of how they create drafts of papers. In an article entitled "Analyzing Revision," Lester Faigley and Stephen Witte (1981) looked at expert writers and found a wide spectrum of differences: some of these writers made almost no revisions on their papers, others started with almost stream-of-consciousness writing and then converted it into organized writing in second drafts, one writer made one long insert as a revision, and another revised mostly by pruning. In my study of writers who differ according to revision habits (Harris, 1989), I looked especially at people who tend to fall at either end of the spectrum, those who only write one draft and those who only write many drafts. Not everyone falls into this category, of course, but it was surprisingly easy to find people for this study who told me either that they never rewrite what they've written or that they seem to write many drafts of almost everything they write. For instance, one of the multidrafters told me she even revises letters home to her family.

One-drafters, as I found out, are quite different from the multi-drafters in the processes they use. All the one-drafters I studied explain that they can only start writing after they have a main point and an organization in their minds. One writer told me that outlines were useless for him—although teachers often asked for them—because he really relied on planning everything in his head first. Several other one-drafters said that they cannot freewrite (writing without planning or stopping during the act of writing). When the one-drafters are done with a paper, it's done. They don't want to look back through it, and one person said that she normally has been through a paper so many times in her head that the act of rereading it even one more time on paper (to check for typos or minor grammar problems) is sheer torture for her.

True multidrafters are quite different. One of these writers said that he can't stand the idea of writing what he already knows as that would be boring. He prefers to plunge in and write to see where it takes him. He doesn't actually do many separate drafts as he prefers to work and rework his opening section until he knows where he is going. The other multidrafters I studied said they can't really visualize their arguments until they see their writing. When there are choices to be made, they spend a lot of time trying out options or writing them out to see which they prefer. The multidrafters I met prefer to keep reworking a paper and talked about feeling as if no paper is ever really done—it just has to get handed in at some point because of deadlines.

This difference in how and when people revise is evident in the essays in Tom Waldrep's two-volume collection of articles written by people who write about and teach writing, *Writers on Writing* (1985, 1988). One professor, who writes a great deal, says he does extensive writing in his mind. He writes and revises and writes and revises in his head so that often he "can write pages without pause and with very little, if any, revision or even minor changes" (p. 187). Another of these teacher/writers says that she cannot predict at the outset a great deal of what she is going to say. She only knows by writing how her essay will develop.

Yet one more variation among writers that has been studied is the difference between what Donald Graves (1975) calls "reactives" and "reflectives" among young children. In his research report, "An Examination of the Writing Processes of Seven-Year-Old Children," Graves noticed that some children had a decided need to verbalize before they wrote. The reactive children used overt language to accompany their prewriting and their composing while the reflective children showed little or no tendency to rehearse out loud before they wrote or to talk aloud as they wrote.

Using Textbook Advice

With all those differences among writers in mind, we can now turn to advice offered in composition textbooks to see how various suggestions will be very helpful to some writers but not to others. I won't quote word-for-word from particular textbooks; instead, I'll paraphrase from a few freshman composition texts that are bestsellers—that is, widely used around the nation in college freshman writing courses. Since I can't cover all the topics of a textbook in this brief article, I limit the discussion here to a few of the most important ones—advice on planning your writing, developing it, and revising it. Most of this advice should sound very familiar, as if it came from some textbook you read at one time or another—because it did.

Planning

There are a number of different planning suggestions offered in various texts, but these are some of the most widely accepted strategies.

Group discussion is an aid to planning your writing. While many textbooks suggest that you talk over your ideas with a friend or in planning sessions in classes, the Myers–Briggs Type Inventory dimensions remind us that while extroverts are likely to benefit from such discussions and planning sessions, introverts are more likely to be more productive when they work alone because they profit from sitting quietly working out their thoughts in their heads. Extroverts, who think more clearly and develop more ideas while in action or in conversation, will find many forms of discussion useful, so useful in fact that introverts in the group are in danger of thinking of themselves as brain dead when they watch others more inclined toward the extrovert end of the scale bursting with possible directions for papers. "I usually feel like the world's worst dud, sitting there not contributing a thing" one student told me, although I suspect what she should have said was that instead of in-class writing groups, she needed to be alone somewhere to spin out her ideas. The work of Donald Graves (1975) also reminds us that some writers need to talk aloud before or during writing. In short, discussions and writing groups may be of some or great benefit to you, or they may be wasting time that you could use more productively if left alone.

Write to discover your ideas. You will find your subject as you write. Your thoughts will emerge and interconnect in ways unavailable until the physical act of writing begins. Writers may have promising ideas, but until they have written them down and tried to develop them, they cannot know if their ideas make sense and are worthwhile. Many texts now stress this idea of using writing to develop your ideas, and there are various exercises to try, such as freewriting and journal keeping. Some texts even call early drafts "discovery drafts" and suggest that you can go back to these planning drafts and use whatever looks appropriate. Since the MBTI tells us that extroverts find their ideas while writing, they can be comfortable with trial and error approaches, and multidrafters certainly confirm for us the usefulness of writing yourself into your subject. But the one-drafters I have met are definitely not comfortable with this approach. They talk about being uneasy or uncomfortable about plunging in without knowing where they are going. They are also disconnecting themselves from their preferred method of planning in their heads. Now, most of us may be somewhere in between the one-drafters and multidrafters (and are equally likely to score somewhere in the middle of some or all of the MBTI dimensions), so we can try both methods to see what works best and when. Different tasks may seem to get done more easily in different ways, that is, more time for mental planning for some writing tasks and more freewriting or discovery drafts for others. The only real problem here is the one that results when a true multidrafter tells herself she will get it all organized in her head first (and fails) or when the true one-drafter tries to freewrite and can't produce more than a few sad sentences that go nowhere. They might both wind up confessing to their teacher or writing center tutor that they can't write.

You should start by having your thesis sentence clearly in mind. Then, write an outline that you can follow as you write. This will keep you from drifting off your topic. This is an older set of strategies that some books and teachers still promote, and the whole approach of figuring out mentally where your paper is headed is certainly comfortable for one-drafters and for those who score highly as thinking types in the MBTI. Sensing types profit from sorting all the data that they tend to collect, especially for long research papers or reports, and those who learn analytically (who may also score highly as sensors) are equally comfortable with step-by-step approaches, but there is also some evidence that it is the global learner, not the analytical one, who can make better use of outlines because outlines call for seeing hierarchies, an ability that comes more easily to global (or possibly right-brain) thinkers. The emphasis on outlines at the beginning of writing is, therefore, helpful for some people but not for others who would do better to wait until a later draft to try an outline. Now this may seem obvious, but that isn't the case for the student who comes to our writing lab and whispers forlornly, as if admitting that she is a social and academic reject or a mental midget, that she can't follow her outline. For the same reasons, you ought to look carefully at the types of comments in textbooks such as the following:

For your own benefit, write your main idea (or topic sentence) in a statement so that you will be able to keep it clearly in mind before you as you plan and write. Writers who score high on the introvert scale on the MBTI can follow such advice to some degree because they generally want most of their ideas clarified before writing. They find it easier to write when much of the essay is written mentally before they start. If they are global learners, more adept at seeing the whole first, they can easily rearrange parts of the paper in their minds beforehand. People who score high as extroverts may not be as successful as mental planners, although they may feel guilty or force themselves to do it.

Try a variety of planning strategies such as mapping, tree-ing, or clustering in which you liberate yourself from lines on a page and are free to connect ideas in a variety of creative ways. These forms of planning have various names and ways of proceeding, but they generally involve writing down phrases or topics or words on blank paper and then circling them. Writers are then encouraged to draw connecting lines between circles to reveal relationships. Thus, the beginning of such a visual plan on the subject of advertisements might look like Figure 18.1.

This highly visual approach can be very useful for visual learners who think comfortably in nonlinear ways, but for analytical or verbal learners a step-by-step sequencing can be far more productive. Again, it is a matter that sometimes these visual planning strategies are not appropriate for various tasks, or it may be the case that particularly

Figure 18–1

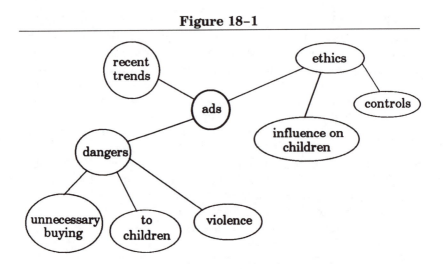

nonvisual learners never quite succeed as well with lots of diagrams and lines connecting circles.

Revising

Revising is another major aspect of writing, one that we have to approach differently according to our own particular skills and preferences. Thus textbooks have a lot to say and to emphasize about the complex act of revising. By now, having read all the above descriptions of different personality and learning styles, you should be looking at textbook advice with a slightly skeptical eye and asking yourself how much of it applies to you. I don't mean to downplay revising because it is important. I do, though, mean to emphasize that you have to revise in ways that best suit you. Which of the following summaries of comments from textbooks are truly useful for you? How different are your choices among ways of revising from choices your friends might make?

- As you write and rewrite, you will move closer to what you want to say. Good writing is rewriting. Good writers add, delete, rearrange, and reword.

- In most writing situations you will not be certain that all parts of a thesis statement accurately reflect what you say in the essay until you have written one or more drafts. Expect to revise your thesis statement as you write successive drafts of your essay.

- A rough draft is a necessary step to a finished paper. Writers who go from an outline to what they consider the final copy usually produce a much less effective paper than they could have otherwise. Don't worry about how you are expressing your ideas in your draft—simply get them down. After that, you can make improvements.

- Professional writers are thorough revisers. They are rarely satisfied with the first draft of their work.

- Think of the initial draft as something you have to get off your chest, not something to labor over.

- It is wisest to resist rewriting until you get to the end of your initial draft; otherwise, you may not get to the end.

For many writers all of the suggestions above are quite useful, but some writers do a large amount of redrafting in their heads. They expend effort mentally and don't need or profit from lots of scratched out pages or the cut-and-paste approach. All of this, however, is quite different from the all-too-human reluctance to do any more work on a paper at 2 a.m. when there is a chem quiz the next morning to study for. Rejecting the notion of revising because of lack of time and/or motivation is not the subject here. Instead, think about people who might score highly as judgers in the MBTI and their need for closure. If they have planned and planned and revised and planned and then revised and revised some more before they actually get the words on paper, then they may need to do some minor rereading, but the notion of going back into a finished paper to consider major rework-ing is about as appealing as doing last week's laundry all over again.

Once you tune in to the possibility that some of the advice you hear about writing varies with different individuals, you may want to start collecting examples of strategies and suggestions that sound like absolute rules but, in fact, are merely possibilities. Think about those suggestions that we should use our senses as a starting point for descriptive writing. People who score higher in the sensing category may indeed begin there and move later to generalizations or implications, while those who are inclined toward being intuitive types will more likely begin with ideas and generalities and need to add the sensory details afterward. Suggestions about sharing early drafts of your papers may or may not work for you as you might find that there is a more productive time for you to get other people's feedback—perhaps at a later stage of writing. If you are a verbalizer who benefits from talking before writing (like those kids Graves watched), talking into a tape recorder may be a good planning or early drafting strategy. Or the act of talking first may merely be a distraction that keeps you from thinking. Find a quiet place if that starts your thoughts churning, or sit in a coffee shop or talk to a writing center tutor. Start by gathering your evidence first, or begin with the whole picture of your topic and then go back and fill in the evidence. Use outlines before, during, or after you write—whichever helps you organize better. When you are asked to write with an expressive aim (that is, to focus on expressing personal insights and feelings), you may feel comfortable doing so if you are inclined toward the feeling end of the scale in the Myer–Briggs Type Inventory, or you may feel decidedly less adept at expressive writing if you score high on the thinking end of that spectrum. The situation changes when you are asked to argue logically for or against some issue, as thinking types are more comfortable using facts and logic (but have to work harder to find emotional appeals), while feeling types are more inclined toward using emotional appeals (and need to remember to incorporate factual appeals also).

What can we make of all this? Don't toss out those textbooks on writing as there may be some useful suggestions for you. But don't expect that you and I (and your roommate or the person sitting next to you in class or your cousin) are likely to agree about which is the most helpful. Textbooks and teachers are sincerely trying to help students become better writers. But you are the person in control of deciding what works best for you. Some people don't want to accept that responsibility because it takes some effort and experimentation to find out how they write most effectively. They'd rather have someone tell them exactly what to do—it's a "no brain" activity since they then merely have to do what they are told. Other people shy away from the close consideration involved in making choices because they are so unsure of their skills. They'd rather trust "the experts." But you are the expert on the subject of yourself. In fact, recognize that you are expert enough to figure out exactly what parts of this essay are of any use to you.

Works Cited

Dillon, Ronna, & Schmeck, Ronald (Eds.). (1983). *Individual Differences in Cognition* (Vol 1). New York: Academic Press.

Faigley, Lester, & Witte, Stephen (1981). "Analyzing Revision," *College Composition and Communication, 32,* 400–414.

Graves, Donald (1975). "An Examination of the Writing Process of Seven-Year-Old Children," *Research in the Teaching of English, 9,* 227–241.

Harris, Muriel (1989). "Composing Behaviors of One- and Multi-draft Writers," *College English, 51,* 174–191.

Jensen, George, & DiTiberio, John (1989). *Personality and the Teaching of Composition.* Norwood, NJ: Ablex.

Keirsey, David, & Bates, Marilyn (1978). *Please Understand Me*. Del Mar, CA: Promethean Books.

Myers, Isabel (1980). *Gifts Differing*. Palo Alto, CA: Consulting Psychologists Press.

Schemck, Ronald (Ed.). (1988). *Learning Strategies and Learning Styles: Perspectives on Individual Differences*. New York: Plenum Press.

Waldrep, Tom (1985, 1988). *Writers on Writing* (Vols I and II). New York: Random House.

Sharing Ideas

- As you read Muriel's essay, I'm sure that you did the same thing I did; I tried to decide where I fit in any of these personality categories and learning models. For instance, I believe I'm an introverted intuitive who judges. I'm less clear on whether I'm a feeler or a thinker since I do a lot of both. Still, I tend to think globally and jump to conclusions and I'm very visually oriented. Write an informal profile of yourself based on this essay and share it with people who know you. Do they contradict you or agree?

- Using this essay, consider a group of people you know pretty well—family members or a set of friends; can you estimate with any degree of accuracy what type of learners they are?

- Muriel talks about one-drafters and multidrafters. What is your drafting process and what has it felt like to try to change it? For instance, many writing teachers require several drafts from students. How do you decide if you're a *true* single drafter or just a reluctant multidrafter?

- Have you ever encountered the contradictory textbook advice that this essay shares? What have you done when that happens? How have you negotiated those contradictions?

- Many authors in these essays offer writing advice and rules. When do rules start to inhibit rather than help a writer? Tell some stories from your own experience.

- This essay focuses on you, the writer, and your writing and learning and personality preferences. Think back to Jeanette Harris' essay on writing and reading processes. What happens if we bring the reader into the preference equation?

19

Practicing What I Preach
A Writing Instructor's
True Confession

Marcia Dickson

Marcia Dickson works at Ohio State University–Marion,
where she divides her time between writing and teaching. As a
teacher/researcher/writer, she co-edited *Portfolios: Process
and Product* with Pat Belanoff, and she's practicing what she
preaches while she completes *It's Not Like That Here:
Teaching Academic Discourse to Basic Writers*, to be published
by Heinemann Boynton/Cook. As a writer/storyteller interested in people's lives and histories, she plans a book on her
grandparents' west Texas hometown, Spur. How she's going
to schedule all this writing and teaching remains a mystery,
but one she can solve with the help of her friends and a few
peanut butter sandwiches.

I confess: I don't practice what I preach. I don't follow a textbook system for the composing process. Am I a disgrace to my profession or a
consummate hypocrite? No. I practice process writing, but not necessarily in a manner my students would recognize. Some of you are
wondering "Who cares? How is some teacher's true confession going
to help me to write better?" I'll attempt to answer these questions
upfront because I think they are important ones for students and
teachers alike.

We learn as much from listening to stories as we do from memorizing rules and following rigid formulas for creating perfect essays. In fact, some of us learn better when information is placed in familiar contexts, and I think most of you will find my writing process similar to yours. Real writers have to struggle to fit writing into their lives outside of school. They don't just sit down at a computer or a typewriter, pull out the rules they learned in freshman composition, and start banging out perfect prose.

Even people like me, teachers who love to write, have a hard time finding ideas, organizing them, and getting to a finished product. I procrastinate and get frantic, just like my students, but I do manage to finish most of the writing projects I start. And I feel great when the final product sounds like me and not some robot English teacher. That's why I'm confessing, not lecturing; I'm telling the truth about how I write at home rather than pretending that it's all effortless. In my struggle to finish this paper, perhaps you can see your own struggles with writing, and in my solutions to writing problems, I hope you will find solutions to yours.

In class, teachers tend to emphasize putting words on paper. Working out a rhetorical strategy, creating lively images, organizing material, supporting a thesis, all become written activities. This writing process seems to be, for the most part, a solitary activity—which takes place between pen, writer, and paper—interrupted only by a couple of in-class peer reviews and a conference with the teacher. You would think that finding a quiet place to write, and being rich enough to afford reams of paper, constitute the only writing problems a student encounters. Neither the teachers nor the books discuss what you really do at home or in the dorm while you write.

At home, I begin writing a paper by wandering about the house, whimpering, before I settle at the computer. Generally I'm saying something like:

"Why did say I'd write this paper? What made me think I could tell people how to write? I don't know anything about how to write—I just do it. Okay, I'm committed to this, I can't pull out now; I write; therefore, I know how to write. Sure. Now how do I do it? I think I'd better fix a sandwich. . . . "

I leave my computer and sally forth into the kitchen, seeking peanut butter sandwiches. The amount of time it takes to create an open-faced sandwich is exactly the amount of time it takes to stop worrying about my ability to write an essay. By the time I get the peanut butter on the bread, I can usually bear to sit down at the computer and stare at the screen. But I can't write the essay yet.

A writing teacher will tell you, as my writing teacher friends often tell me, that they can't think without using a pencil (or a word processor) and paper. They love to quote the novelist E. M. Forster: "How do I know what I think until I see what I say?" But they seem to imply that no thought occurs until they pick up their pens and decide, "Now I will write about the Evils of Capital Punishment."

The truth is this: When I have to compose an essay, I sometimes spend more time *not writing* than *writing*. I know this goes against what teachers usually tell you, so perhaps I should define what I mean by *not writing*. Not writing isn't a state of doing nothing; in fact, I'm very actively engaged in composing my paper—working with the topic, refining words, working out concepts—but I'm not putting words on paper in any form whatsoever.

Some of us need only short periods before we're willing, or able, to sit down, pencil in hand, and start writing. I have to think before I write and think mightily. And I don't think while sitting at a desk, pen poised to write. I usually try to study the assignment for about 15 minutes, but almost immediately I discover that I really need to straighten out the assignment file. Then I determine that the desk itself needs tidying; the office needs organizing; the floor needs sweeping. By the time I've finished this step in the not writing process, I've done the laundry.

Don't be fooled by what seems to be procrastination. The entire time I'm bringing order to my household chaos, I'm bringing order to the topic. Mostly because I am questioning myself all the time. As I tidy the desk, I tidy my thoughts, indulge in a sort of question-and-answer game where I play all parts of the conversation. Talking to yourself can be a good method of figuring out what to write about:

"Why are you tidying your desk? You have to write a paper on the writing process."

"Right. I'm thinking. Should I begin with a story of how I write or with a story of how my friends write? Do I have a thesis here? I think I want to say that the real writing process is incredibly messy and yet really based on the nice neat theories that we learn in school."

"So what? How do the stories connect?"

"I knew you'd ask that. OH MY! Look at this floor! It's covered with scrap computer paper! The ecology suffers because of this. I'll clean it up so no one will suspect how wasteful I am."

"Stop procrastinating."

"Okay. What if I opened with a description of how I write and forgot the examples of my friends until later on?"

And so it goes for hours and sometimes for days. An outsider looking at this process would say, as your friends and relatives have probably said, "You're not working. Get to that desk." But I am working; I'm not just to the desk stage yet.

Next, I engage in another not writing activity: I read more about my topic. This allows me to pull my thoughts together and to put off writing a little longer. Many people use this not writing activity regularly, but it can be overdone. For example, my friend Lynda habitually gathers copious notes on her topic before she writes. She sits in the library for hours, reading books, taking notes, finding out what everyone on earth thinks about the subject. Her notes to herself are a writing teacher's dream: quotations, comments, interpretations, page numbers for future reference. More often than not, she goes under from the sheer mass of material—too many theses develop, too many ideas present themselves.

I'd like to claim that I always start with a narrow focus and read with this tentative thesis in mind, working diligently to discover whether or not I'm correct. But that's not what really happens. When I'm reading, I'm either looking for confirmation of what I think about a subject or when I'm desperately looking for an idea to think about. Reading helps, not because it gives me the definitive truths, although I always secretly hope that I will chance upon the "right" answer in the process, but because it helps me to figure out what I think.

As I read, I find clues that help me to write my paper. I measure my ideas against the ideas of people who are considered experts. Their ideas force me to rethink my own. I conduct a dialogue between the author and me that sometimes causes me to change my mind and sometimes merely reconfirms my original ideas. But a book or article seldom leaves my thinking unchanged, and it always helps me put new words on the page.

Reading can be a frustrating experience because often I discover that two, three, even four writers, all of whom hold different opinions, can be *right*. I never cease to be amazed at this phenomenon. Many freshmen, confronted with this reading/critical thinking factor, bog down and want to quit writing at this point, certain that whatever conflict they've encountered can't be resolved in their papers. However, experience has proved to me that nothing is straightforward, that in university studies nothing is easy, nothing can go unexamined, and one person's *educated* guess is often as good as another's. I italicize the word educated because that's where reading before writing becomes important.

If I have an opinion on the topic I'm writing about, even a topic I understand a little about, it's merely my opinion. For instance, my Great-Uncle Joe had Alzheimer's disease, but that fact doesn't make my opinion on the care of Alzheimer's patients an expert opinion nor does it make my paper a good guide to the disease. However, my experience with Alzheimer's Disease *combined* with information from experts in the field gives me an *educated* opinion, one that has credibility and can be helpful to readers. Whom do I call an expert? Several experts come to mind: Great-Aunt Helen, who nursed Uncle Joe; Uncle Joe's doctor; and the authors of the latest reports in *Scientific*

American and *American Nurse*. Credibility comes only from reading and—if you didn't notice when I mentioned it briefly—talking to people who might have experiences to share. That's the next step in *nonwriting*; I leave the library and go to McDonald's for French fries and conversation.

Talking can't provide answers to writing problems any more than reading can. But good friends, willing to listen, even if they aren't immensely interested in the topic, can help me express my thoughts and provide a means of determining how others will react to those thoughts. I always choose good friends for these conversations because I'm about to risk appearing stupid. Early in the development of the essay, I really just need to talk.

"I'm having a devil of a time with this paper on writing," I confess as we're sitting around munching Chicken McNuggets. "All the books I read insist that writing is somehow manageable, not magic. Look at any freshman text. *'Freewrite.' 'Loop.' 'Cube.' 'Outline.'* As if that was all there was to it!"

"But don't you do that?" Amy asks.

"Naw. . . " Tim drawls. "She's a teacher. You can't expect her to practice what she preaches."

"Now wait a minute," I retort. "I never ask my students to do anything I don't do myself."

"Really?" Amy questions. "Then why did you speak about all those freelooping things so disparagingly?"

"They're not bad ways of writing, but using them at home is not like using them in class."

"How do you use them at home?" Lynda pushes gently. "Maybe that's what you need to write about. Could it be valuable for students to see what a real teacher does when she sits down to write an essay?"

That's how I came up with the idea for this essay. All I needed was a few good friends who were willing to talk about my writing problems as well as my family and job problems. Only one of them teaches writing, yet none of them considers my paper unimportant. They see my writing problems as I do, as interesting intellectual problems, and they help me solve them not only because they feel a commitment to me but also because they find all manner of things interesting. Probably I would have eventually worked out a topic by myself. But it would have been much harder and infinitely less fun. And you need to have fun before going to the desk stage.

What drives me to the desk?

Desperation, usually.

When I've read all I can read, talked all that it's useful to talk, and the final deadline starts to corner me, I write. Why do I wait so long? Because, like my students, I put off writing until I can't avoid it any longer.

And I love to write. I fancy myself a writer. However, like the people in my class, I consider writing only one part of my very busy, somewhat chaotic life. If I didn't have to write for a living, my writing would probably be just casual and sporadic, something to share with my friends or send to my mother on Christmas. But my job, and at least for now, *your* job as a student, requires that we write and write well. That's why, out of necessity, I combine the *not-writing* stage with my daily activities (cleaning, lunch with friends) and my desk and revision stages with the deadlines that run the rest of my life. My writing practice resembles carefully planned emergency situations.

For example, I never end up without time to proofread. I may put off writing at first, but I generally know how much time I need once I get to the desk, and I allow for it. Finding out how much time you need requires trial, error, and practice. The first few times you try to time yourself, you'll probably end up rushing through. Let that be a lesson: add more time to your schedule the next time a paper is due. Eventually you'll get so good at setting aside time that writing will only seem partially intimidating.

So, to get back to the subject. What happens at the desk stage? A lot of prewriting that looks like a waste of time. I make grocery lists, appointment lists, and lists of friends whom I need to write. I write notes to myself. This isn't wasting time; this is limbering up. I do warm-up exercises for writing, just like pianists pound out finger exercises before they play the concert piece, or opera singers trill their way up and down a scale before they sing an aria. Making lists gets the brain in gear, forces it to talk to the hands that operate the keyboard. After the lists, 10 minutes of freewriting rids me of most of my anxieties and helps me put aside all the other things that I have to do before the day is over.

Then, warmed-up and ready to go, I throw myself at the keyboard and start writing in one of two ways: If I'm really primed, I write until the ideas disappear or until I realize that I don't have a point. If I'm still unsure of what I want to say, I just start writing down everything I know about the subject.

Either of these approaches usually results in about an hour of writing, but sometimes the words won't come. When this happens, I use a technique I read about in an article by Virginia Valian (1977). In "Learning to Work," Valian describes how she learned to write at home while creating a book. Desperate because she could only concentrate for 15 minutes at a time—which is really not unnatural when you're starting a project, she bought a simple kitchen timer for her desk. She'd set the timer for 15 minutes and work as hard as she could until the little bell rang. Then she would get up and get a snack, run a short errand, read part of the newspaper. After her break, she could sit down and concentrate again—at least for another 15 minutes.

This may sound like an unusual way to write, but it worked for her, and it may have implications for all of us. When you're trying to begin a project, the timer method creates the sort of structure a classroom provides. Time is limited; any exercise that becomes unmanageable can be terminated legitimately—you stop because you run out of time rather than because you're too stupid to make it from the beginning of the essay to the end. Fairly soon you can ignore the magic pings of the timer and write for longer periods. Writing this way usually gets me through the first draft.

Then I take a nap.

A long nap.

I'm not kidding. Writing makes me tired. The exhaustion may result from the anxiety of revealing what I think on paper or merely from putting words together. It doesn't matter; I go to sleep every time. When I wake up, I'm usually calm enough to go on, and I can read what I wrote from a distance, as if someone else wrote it.

It's impossible to underestimate the importance of that first draft, that first beautiful version fresh from the printer or neatly copied by hand. Until you get to this first *finished* draft (the italics indicate the level of self-deception), you can't see if your idea works. And usually, this draft is far more disappointing than you anticipated. Real words appear on the paper; they make sense. But they don't say what you meant, exactly, and the mistakes in grammar and mechanics appear as if by magic.

If only slightly unhappy with the draft, I'll cover the pages with arrows, bubbles, and reference marks: insert paragraph three into the middle of paragraph twenty-seven; use "the students" instead of "they"; take out this reference to reading; add that idea about talking.

If incredibly depressed by what I've written, I change the essay until it takes on new physical dimensions; I cut the draft in pieces, reassemble the pieces I don't trash, and add filler to reconnect everything. The new work looks like it was shredded by accident and then pasted back together.

Whatever the condition of this second draft, I make a friend read it. This time I want my consultant to save me from making a fool of myself. Away from school, away from feedback sheets, and away from the structures of formal rhetoric, I ask a writing partner to make sense of a piece of writing.

A confused and sloppy piece of writing.

A possibly dumb piece of writing.

The first type of conversation was casual; anybody could participate. The second kind of writing conversation must be with writer friends, who can serve as writer/editors, or writing partners. They read as critics, not just as friends. On this paper, my friend Anne, who also is my colleague, worked with me through the entire desk stage and multiple revision stages. We had similar tasks to complete. I had this paper; she had to write an article for a journal. The stakes were big; getting an article in a major journal is like getting an A+ on a major research paper; getting an essay in a collection like this one gets the same type of reward. We need published articles for our careers like you need A+ essays for your GPA.

Such writing is hard and scary because so much rides on writing well. To support each other, to keep writing, and to avoid true procrastination, Anne and I worked out a reasonable writing schedule and arranged to meet for writing sessions once every two weeks for a two month period. Anne, whose keen sense of organization I trust, pointed out that in the original version of this article no relationship existed between the example on one page and the statements that followed it. It hung there, all by itself, without a point to support. I had left a big blank space between the *not writing* and the *writing* process.

"You were busy cleaning your desk and talking to friends—*not writing*—and then suddenly you're at the desk—*writing*," Anne comments, "But I don't understand what finally got you to put words on paper."

When I explain what I meant, she confirmed that I was right—but she suggested that I write my idea down instead of just assuming that all my readers understand the point. I revised.

Sometimes I ask more than one person to read my draft. Each of the people serves a distinct purpose. Lynda will talk about how *wonderful* the essay is—then she'll "make a few suggestions." These suggestions make me realize that "wonderful" may not be an appropriate adjective for this essay. For instance, the question "Who's the audience for this piece?" hardly indicates that I've written the perfect essay for student writers.

Richard, the Mr. Spock of our group, concerns himself with logic and becomes the defender of the English language. He's quick to point out that my thesis statement has little relationship to the essay as a whole. Then he moves in for the kill—the evidence doesn't support the claim. He starts to talk of warrants and red herrings, of logical fallacies and qualified positions, speaking in formal rhetoric terms. I thank him and move away quickly so that I can figure out what he means. Richard's comments take a bit of interpretation.

About this essay he might rightly ask: "Marcia, what does all this have to do with practicing what you preach?" And I guess I'd have to echo what I said at the first: disguised by all the housework, the conversation, and the whimpering and complaining are the writing techniques that I teach my students. The kind of nonwriting I do is a sort of *mental* and *oral* freewriting. And once I start writing, the short journals, freewrites, lists, and other writing activities clear my mind before I write my rough draft. Sometimes I even *outline*—right after I finish my rough draft—to make sense of what I've said. By the time I get a first draft that I can *cut and paste*, I've gone through several types of writing activities and engaged constantly in *peer and group editing*. And I'm not finished by a long shot. In writing this piece I created nine drafts and used practically every type of writing process activity that I teach.

The textbooks and the composition teachers present the writing process at its finest and most abstract. No composition text ever told me to fix a peanut butter sandwich so that I could calm down enough to think. I invented that myself, just as all writers have to invent their own variations of the writing and not writing process. Reality changes outside trappings of composing, not the essence. When writers leave the composition class and become real writers who write under real conditions, in real homes, they have to find ways to make classroom writing techniques work under less than perfect conditions. I've given you my strategies; I wish you luck in developing your own.

Works Cited

Valian, Virginia (1977). "Learning to Work" in Sara Ruddick and Pamela Daniels (Eds.), *Working It Out: 23 Women Writers, Scholars, Scientists and Scholars Talk About Their Lives and Work*. New York: Pantheon.

Sharing Ideas

- Marcia explains that sharing stories about writing may be as important as sharing advice, or perhaps stories offer a more accessible way of sharing a writer's wisdom. Think back through the stories told in this book and then compose a writing story for an audience of your choice.

- Marcia tells you about the many individuals with whom she discusses her work in progress. Describe your set of listeners and what each does for your writing process. If you don't have enough listeners, think of ways you might find more.

- What do you do to avoid writing? When is this delay profitable and why? I know I get a lot of housecleaning done, like Marcia, when I work on projects like this one. I'm not into peanut butter sandwiches, but I do tend to fiddle a lot with coffee makers.

- For you, what is the connection between messiness and neatness and writing?

- How important are books—other authors' voices—to your writing, and what would more reading do for your writing?

- Many authors talk about loving to write but hating or avoiding the process of writing. Explain your own feelings on this issue.

- Marcia's story is one of great effort and concentration; when she stops writing she's tired and sometimes quite critical of the draft. Use your own experiences and the observations of other essayists in this book to explain why humans continue to go through such a complicated and sometimes draining (and sometimes exhilarating) process.

- Marcia says, "No composition text ever told me to fix a peanut butter sandwich so that I could calm down enough to think." Try to provide some other advice that rarely makes it into textbooks for the next class of writers who will work with your current writing teacher.

20

How to Get the Writing Done

Donald M. Murray

Donald M. Murray is a writer who publishes novels, poetry, a
newspaper column, and textbooks on writing and teaching
writing. He is Professor Emeritus of English at the University
of New Hampshire. As a journalist, Murray won a number of
awards including the Pulitzer Prize for editorial writing on
The Boston Herald in 1954. Currently, he writes a weekly column, *Over Sixty*, for *The Boston Globe*. His most recent
books include, new editions of *Write to Learn* and *Read to
Write*, as well as *The Craft of Revision, Expecting the Unexpected*, and *Shoptalk: Learning to Write with Writers* were
published by Boynton/Cook.

Famous writers and writers who hope they will become famous, published writers and unpublished writers, master writers and miserable
writers, good students and poor students have one problem in common: How can we get the writing done?

I am going to take you into the back room of the writing shop that
readers never see and show you how one professional produces his
daily quota of words.

There is no one way to get the writing done. Many of my strategies are contradictory, what works on one project will not work on the
next. I have to keep trying new ways—or retrying old ways—to produce effective writing. The strategies keep changing as I steal a technique from a fellow writer or from another craft, remember one I
have forgotten, or discard another that works for someone else but

never seems to work for me. Here are the strategies hung above my workbench this morning:

1. Write Now.   Write before you know what you have to say or how to say it. Ignorance is a great starting place. Write as fast as you can—and then increase the speed! Don't worry about penmanship or typing, punctuation or correctness, making sense or being silly. Velocity is as important in writing as in bicycle riding—speed gets you ahead of the censor and causes the accidents of meaning and language essential to good writing.

Later you can read what you have written and the draft, rough as it is, will often reveal what you have to say and how you can say it.

2. Rewrite.   Take a rough draft and get into the writing by rewriting. The old draft will stimulate a new one. I used to revise by hand, cutting (I love to cut—this chapter is growing shorter at the moment), adding, moving around. Now I work on a computer, and I write right over what I have written, layering new meanings on top of old ones the way you build up an oil painting.

Rewriting is not failure but an essential part of the process of writing, each draft leads us to our meaning and allows us to tune our voices to that meaning.

3. Delay.   But sometimes writing early doesn't work. In that case stand back. E. B. White says, "Delay is natural to a writer. He is like a surfer—he bides his time, waits for the perfect wave on which to ride in. Delay is instinctive with him. He waits for the surge (of emotion? of strength? of courage?) that will carry him along." And Virginia Woolf wrote: "As for my next book, I am going to hold myself from writing it till I have it impending in me: grown heavy in my mind like a ripe pear; pendant, gravid, asking to be cut or it will fall."

I find it helpful sometimes to take a walk, drive somewhere and do errands, watch the Celtics on TV, take a nap or assign my subconscious to consider a writing problem as I go to sleep at night. The writing goes on, and when I return to the writing desk I discover I know what to say and how to say it.

4. Rehearse.   We rehearse plays and concerts, rehearse what we will say when applying for a job or a loan from a parent, and rehearse our approach to a member of the opposite sex, and writers rehearse writing. Talk to yourself, try beginnings and key paragraphs in your head before you get to the page, hear what you may say before you see it. I am at my desk a couple of hours a morning but I write in my head during the 22 or so hours I am away from the writing desk. To help me in this process I keep small cards in my shirt pocket so I can catch a phrase or thought if one flies through my head. I also keep a day-book, a writing log or journal, in which I can talk to myself in writing, playing with what I may write when I return to my writing desk.

5. Consult.   Develop a writing community with which you can talk about what you may write, what you are writing—and rewriting. I have developed my own community by sharing my writing first. Then some of them share theirs. We consult on what we may write, what we are writing, what works, and what needs work. I not only receive help from the writers in my community; I hear the answers to my writing problems in what I say to them.

I have one rule for admission to my writing community: I only invite people to join who make me want to write when I finish talking to them.

6. Plan.   Some writing is unplanned. You free write and a text seems to arise spontaneously from the page. Wonderful. Accept the gift, but don't count on it happening regularly like the six o'clock news. Most writing is planned. But rarely do writers plan in rigid detail, outlining with complete sentences—"The Harvard Outline"—or an intricate A, a, B, b; Ii, Iii; 1.1, 1.1.1 sequence. The planning techniques I find most helpful are

Line.   I know I have a piece of writing when I have a line, a fragment of language, sometimes a word, most likely a phrase, rarely a sentence, which contains the essential conflict or tension within the subject. I knew I could write this piece when I heard the phrase "master writers and students have the same problem: how . . . " The article would be released by the tension within those words.

Title.   I find the title helps me get started if it contains the energy to push the writer—and the reader—forward. Write a title such as "How to Get the Writing Done" and the draft follows directly.

Lead.   As a journalist, I have to get the lead right, the first few sentences or paragraphs, before I go on. I play with those lines in my head, in my daybook, on my computer screen, drafting half a dozen or three dozen leads quickly until the essential tension within the piece is established, the voice is clear, and the reader is drawn in, as I hope I did in developing the line into the lead, or first paragraph, of this article.

Cross Heads.   In writing most nonfiction, I write the headings and subheadings first, as I did in this article. They may change as I go along but as I draft the heads I can see the sequence and pattern the article will take.

7. *Attitude.* Every writer goes to the writing desk with a set of assumptions that may make the writing difficult or easy. For years I wanted to impress teachers, editors, and associates I didn't even like. I also wanted to write perfect copy the first time out. But I learned to follow William Stafford's advice:

> I believe that the so-called "writing block" is a product of some kind of disproportion between your standards and your performance. . . . [O]ne should lower his standards until there is no felt threshold to go over in writing. It's easy to write. You just shouldn't have standards that inhibit you from writing.

> I can imagine a person beginning to feel he's not able to write up to that standard he imagines the world has set for him. But to me that's surrealistic. The only standard I can rationally have is the standard I'm meeting right now. . . . You should be more willing to forgive yourself. It doesn't make any difference if you are good or bad today. The assessment of the product is something that happens after you've done it.

Now I go to the desk determined to write as well as I can write each morning but no better. If I lower my standards, I receive a draft. Then I can rewrite.

8. *Habit.* Right there, in the center over my workbench are four words in big black letters: *NULLA DIES SINE LINEA.* The Latin command—"never a day without a line" is attributed to both Horace and Pliny. Never mind who said it, it is the motto of most writers, ancient and modern, men and women. Jogging and writing require habit. And it is more productive to write every day for a short time than one day for a long time.

Brief writing periods can be amazingly effective. One prolific— and excellent—writer, Anthony Burgess, pointed out that by writing only 1 page a day, you can have a 365-page book drafted in a year. I find that I can get an amazing amount of writing done in bursts of half-an-hour a day, 20 minutes, 15; 3 pages a day, 1 page, half a page; 500 words, 300, 200, 100.

9. *Deadlines.* There's little that clarifies the mind and increases the concentration better than a deadline, a point upon which you pass and you are dead. As the deadline approaches, the adrenaline flows and copy comes; it is too late for excessive thought: don't think, write.

But *their* deadline should not necessarily be your deadline. My deadline for my Tuesday column is Monday—a week ahead. And I stick to it.

Work backward in time and establish your own deadlines, saying, "On the 12th the research will be done, on the 14th I'll have the lead and a list of the main points to be covered, on the 19th I'll have a first draft, on the 22nd the final draft."

10. When interrupted as you wr. . . .   Stop in the middle of a sentence so that you can finish the sentence and be involved in the writing immediately after the interruption or the next day when you return to your writing desk. If you have an idea of the sequence of things to be written scribble them down at the same time.

11.Change your working style.   What works on one project may not on another. I advocate fast writing, but sometimes I have to slow down and work with pen on paper. I am an early morning writer, but once in a while a project will seem to require days of ruminations as I do errands, and I end up writing in late afternoon. I usually outline nonfiction texts and plunge into fiction, but sometimes I have to plunge into nonfiction and stop to plan fiction.

Know your working patterns, but when a project isn't going well—or even going—experiment with other styles to see if they fit this new project. New projects may require new work patterns.

12. Count Words, Pages, or Hours.   While writing, never ask yourself or answer the question: "How good was my writing today?" You have no idea. You can't tell in the middle of a project. Forgive yourself. Follow the counsel of Jonwillum van der Wettering that has kept me productive:

> To write you have to set up a routine, to promise yourself that you will write. Just state in a loud voice that you will write so many pages a day, or write for so many hours a day. Keep the number of pages or hours within reason, and don't be upset if a day slips by. Start again; pick up the routine. Don't look for results. Just write, easily, quietly.

13. Work within the draft.   When the writing doesn't come easily, do not look outside the draft to textbooks, including mine; to the principles and traditions of writing; to the expectations of teacher, editor, or reader; but first look within the text. Read the paragraph you have just drafted. It will tell you what to deal with next; it will call for more description, an opinion, some evidence, whatever is needed to develop what you have to say, paragraph by paragraph.

14. Answer the reader's questions.   Effective writing is a conversation with a reader. Anticipate the reader's questions—and answer them.

15. Make what works better.   I used to write the way most schools teach writing, by pointing out the errors in a draft and then trying to correct them. I always felt guilty, unsure, hesitant, and, more and more, a stranger to the draft. It was less and less mine.

Then I photocopied each page of my first draft on a large sheet of paper and made notes on what I was doing when the revising went well. I was increasing and strengthening those qualities and elements in the writing that went well. If the draft was well organized, I worked on making it even better; if the voice was clear, then I made it clearer; and if the documentation seemed the strength of my argument, I made it even stronger.

My writing went easier when I learned this lesson, the drafts were more my own, and most of the problems of the early draft disappeared. If they didn't, then I corrected them—in the context of an effective working draft that had established its own method and its own standards.

16. Make Use of Failure. I continue to learn to write from what works well and from the instructive failures that are a necessary part of any writing act. I do not like to fail, but I no longer see my writing failures as judgments against me personally as if I were flunking the human race. They are the normal, instructive failures of an experimental art in which you commit yourself to discover what works and what needs work.

17. Write in Chunks. John Steinbeck once wrote:

> When I face the desolate impossibility of writing 500 pages a sick sense of failure falls on me and I know I can never do it. Then gradually I write one page and then another. One day's work is all I can permit myself to contemplate.

All of us feel despair and hopelessness when we contemplate a long writing project. I was comforted by Steinbeck's quotation and by the answer of a woman who spent many days and nights climbing a huge rock face in California. When asked how she stuck it out, she answered: "You eat an elephant one bite at a time." Break long writing tasks into daily bites.

18. Write with force; unleash the draft. Let it rip. As Annie Dillard states:

> One of the few things I know about writing is this: spend it all, shoot it, play it, lose it, all, right away, every time. Do not hoard what seems good for a later place in the book, or for another book; give it, give it all, give it now. The impulse to save something good for a better place later is the signal to spend it now. Something more will arise for later, something better. These things fill from behind, from beneath, like well water.

You can cut later, but you cannot cut from an undeveloped, under written text. Write from abundance to get the draft done, let the energy rise out of the writing; cut, shape, polish later.

19. Write.   Write when you think you don't have anything to say. Write when you are tired. Write between classes. Write during TV commercials. Write when what you see on the page makes you want to vomit. Write when the writing isn't going well—and when it is. Write fast. Write slowly. Use a pencil, use a pen; type on typewriter and on a computer. Dictate to a tape recorder. Write when you are sick. Write. Write. Write. Write, and something will begin to happen, a word, a line, a sentence, and when you least expect it, the writing will come.

Writing is the way to get the writing done.

Sharing Ideas

- Don provides you with several provocative quotes by poets and novelists. Use one as a starting point for a freewrite of your own, considering or expanding on that author's advice.

- Decide which 5 of the 19 categories of advice you find here are the most important to you as a writer. Are those 5 the same as the ones chosen by other class writers? Consider how your learning and personality preferences may influence your choices.

- Think about ways to break out of school imposed deadlines. Decide when it might be useful to set your own writing deadlines. For instance, in any class there are always some writers who get work done ahead of schedule. It's certainly not cool, but it is productive. What would you have to do to be one step ahead of your normal production schedule and what, if anything, would you gain?

- What do you think about the suggestion that writers should write every day? Chris Anson and Richard Beach's discussion of journaling shows you one way to get the words down. What would happen if you set your own word count, as Don suggests, and what would that word count be—100, 200, 300, 500 words?

- Spend a week changing your working style and report on the results.

- Don's section 14 on readers is quite brief. Spend some time deciding who your readers are, and how they do (and should) affect your writing.

- It's certainly hard to accept, but we all fail as writers sometimes. Tell stories of times when you learned from writing that didn't quite work.
- What writing conditions are necessary if you want to follow the advice to unleash a draft and let it rip?
- Think more deeply about Don's advice that writing anything at any time is *always* better than not writing.

Part V

Writers, School, and Writing

A common thread runs through the last five essays: writers in school are always negotiating their identities and this negotiation is never simple or easy, although negotiation seems to be essential to personal *and* to academic development.

Beth Daniell and Art Young use the story of one of Art's classes to study resistance. They examine the way a student in that class responded to Art's classroom authority, and this examination leads them to reflect, once again, on the new writing classroom advocated to different degrees by all of the authors in this book. These classrooms of necessity create new roles for learners; writers are asked to actively question and analyze their learning. Since this model is different from the banking model of education that many of us are used to—teachers depositing information into the minds of passive student learners—it is no surprise that students might be taken aback by classroom demands and resist their teachers.

Kevin Davis looks at academic acculturation from a slightly different angle as he relates his own journey—that of an outsider who finally chooses to become an insider in English studies—and the journeys taken by two students he studied in a research project. Kevin shows how movement into new communities can put learners at risk, sometimes alienating them from their community or family, but movement can also transform learners, turning them into new people, people they want to be. In a similar manner, James Zebroski shows you his own struggles with developing an academic identity,

221

and he lets you see that your teachers did not always come to their professions with less struggle than you yourself may be feeling. You'll notice how journaling has helped Jim make sense of his own academic odyssey.

My essay relies heavily on journal entries, also. In this case, I let you see how my classes and I have struggled to understand writing categories. Together we have asked questions about writing, creative writing, and literary writing. Together, we have come to see that writing categories—like writing rules—are sometimes useful but at other times inhibiting or confusing to writers. Like Beth, Art, Kevin, and Jim, I find that writing communities are essential to my unraveling and understanding of these issues.

Jim Corder ends this book for us with a narrative about the contradictions any writer feels when he works within the academy. Jim considers the degree to which he is composed by his writing and reading communities and the degree to which he composes himself. In doing this, he struggles with questions all writers struggle with: Who am I, what am I writing, why am I writing, and who am I writing for? These are good questions, ones you have begun to explore yourself, I hope, in the company of the writers in this book, and will continue to explore the rest of your writing lives.

21

Resisting Writing/Resisting Writing Teachers

Beth Daniell and Art Young

A former high school teacher, Beth Daniell now writes about literacy and teaches composition, literature, and women's studies courses at Clemson University. Her idea of fun and relaxation is to read murder mysteries and spy novels and to write in her journal. As a native of Georgia who has lived in Texas, West Virginia, and Illinois, she is happy to be back in the South. In upstate South Carolina, she explains, the dirt is red, the pine trees are tall, when it snows there's a holiday, and you can play tennis outdoors in February.

Art Young holds an unique appointment at Clemson University in South Carolina, where he is Campbell Professor of English and Engineering. In addition to teaching English courses, he works with engineering students and faculty in the Effective Technical Communication Program. He is the father of three teenage daughters who generously help him with his writing. When he is not involved with school work (and sometimes when he is), he enjoys traveling, sports, hiking, and fishing.

Last year Steve sat in the back row of Art Young's English 102 class. Steve was about 20 years old, a couple of years older than most students in this class, and when he volunteered in discussions, it was usually with a cryptic or sarcastic remark that elicited a few chuckles from his classmates and teacher. At Clemson University, where we teach, English 102 is the second in the required first-year sequence in composition; its purpose is to develop students' abilities in argumentative writing, library research, and the academic essay. In such essays, students write about academic rather than personal subjects, develop an original thesis or perspective on a course subject, and integrate appropriate sources from their research to provide a knowledgeable context for their own contribution to the issue at hand. The first academic essay assigned in Art's class that semester was to be on the topic of civil disobedience. The class had read and discussed several articles on the subject in their textbook. In this persuasive essay students were to use these sources as background for developing an informed opinion about civil disobedience. A traditional assignment, to be sure.

The students read and critiqued each other's rough drafts in small groups; after they revised these drafts, they submitted them for Art's feedback before the final copy was due. When he returned their drafts with his comments, he asked the students to take a few moments of class time to reread their essays and consider his comments. He then asked them to write a brief response on how useful his comments were to them. Art had hoped such responses would give him constructive feedback, open communication between him and the students early in the course, and enable him to see each of his 22 students as individual writers. Steve wrote:

> I don't know what I am supposed to be writing to you. I read your critique and I think I disagree with 95% of them. It seems to me you want us to be robots and make the same argument. I can care less whether I'm right or wrong for two reasons. One I don't care about this topic. There is no relevence to real life. I came to college to learn about finance not English, History, and Biology. Yet I've spend my money taking an entire year of these bullshit courses. That money comes out of my pocket and I shouldn't have to pay an entire year's tuition for useless info that I learned in high school. Secondly, I got plenty of other classes and don't have 3 or 4 hours a night wasting time on this. Give me a damn D or F I don't care, and neither will my employer who's already offered me a job. This is my essay, and not going to do anymore than I have to. If you don't like it then give me a bad grade. If you don't like this response, well tough luck!!

Steve's response to Art is behavior that we would call resistance. Resistance can be defined as those games or strategies, ranging from fun to deadly seriousness, played by those with little or no power against those with power; the point of resistance is to diffuse authority, to thwart the plans of the bosses. Resistance can be as simple as a joke about an authority figure, or it can be, as in Nazi-occupied France, an act of violence like blowing up a munitions train. Resistance also can be an act of civil disobedience, as in Alabama in 1956 when Rosa Parks decided to face arrest and sit in the front of the bus. History tells us that students have always resisted the authority of teachers. And in one sense they should. How can students learn to think for themselves if they don't resist the authority of teachers and other powerful figures in their lives like parents and government officials? Sometimes students need to resist to protect themselves from dishonest or oppressive teachers or administrators. An example occurs at the end of *Dead Poets' Society*, when the boys stand on their desks as a salute to the teacher, played by Robin Williams, who had been fired because he tried to instill in his students a sense of individualism. The teacher in *Dead Poets' Society* wanted the boys he taught to resist the unthinking conformity he saw both in the school and in American society, but in this scene they do even more: They resist the headmaster's lies. If we study acts of resistance, we may come to understand a particular situation better than we did before. That is, resistance can offer a critique. An act of resistance may not be malicious disobedience but rather a criticism of injustice or a protest of events that are unfolding in a way the resistor does not endorse.

Students often resist writing and writing teachers, and such resistance can be either healthy or unhealthy. As part of the classroom dynamic, resistance can play a role in promoting learning and critical thinking or it can be a way to refuse to learn or to become critically engaged. For example, with hours of drill on *lie/lay* and *sit/set*, tests on the eight comma rules, fill-in-the-blank questions about the ways to develop a paragraph, five points off for every misspelled word, students are probably right to resist such mindless "drill and kill" exercises often associated with being taught to write. Of course, usage, punctuation, paragraph development, and spelling are important in writing well, but we think that students realize that heavy emphasis on these issues by teachers often deflects attention from what students are thinking and saying. Unfortunately, schooling sometimes teaches students that the teacher is the enemy and that school work is irrelevant and alien to their concerns.

But not all resistance in school provides a critical examination of abusive situations. Some resistance is habit: resist the teacher, any teacher; resist the work, any work. As writing teachers, we are frustrated when students resist for the sake of resisting. After all, we are teachers who try, admittedly not always successfully, to make our classes and our assignments fulfill institutional goals and also be relevant to our students' lives. But sometimes, despite our good intentions, students—like Steve—resist our teaching. In this essay, we speculate about why Steve and other students resist writing and writing teachers. Further, we suggest that sometimes students who resist our approach to teaching writing don't realize that they are resisting a kind of teaching that is also critical of the traditional "drill and kill" approach to teaching writing.

But perhaps an instructive way to continue our discussion of student resistance is to focus on teacher perception, to explore Art's reaction to Steve and his writing.

When Art read Steve's response, his first reaction was defensive. What had he done to create such hostility? What could he have done to avoid it? Although none of the other students wrote a similar response, was it because they were too timid to do so? Did Steve speak for many students who dared not speak for themselves? Next, Art realized that Steve was making this a personal matter, as if Art were forcing him to do something that was against his best interests. Steve may have targeted Art's writing course as symbolic of a more pervasive problem created by an educational system with its "useless" general education courses. For neither Art nor the English Department required that Steve take this course; Steve's major department required it. Art might explain that to Steve, refer him to the Head of the Finance Department for answers on why they required useless courses, and thus deflect responsibility from his own teaching.

Art's third reaction was anger. He was working hard to provide Steve and his classmates with a meaningful educational experience, and this was the thanks he got. He had taken the time and trouble to provide constructive feedback on Steve's essay, while many of his colleagues skipped this step and saved themselves several hours of effort and the hassles of dealing with unappreciative students like Steve. Who did Steve think he was anyway—to speak to a teacher that way? This student seemed to delight in challenging the teacher's authority; he had passed around his response so that several classmates could read it before he turned it in. He flouted the power Art held over his grades. Maybe that was the best response—take him up on his offer to receive an F. Steve already implied the course was a waste of his time—which meant any time Art spent reading and thinking about Steve's writing was a waste of both their time. Hadn't Steve said that neither he nor his employer would care if he received an F in the course? So Art could give him an F on this essay and promise him further F's unless his attitude changed. Or Steve could drop the course. If he didn't like this response, "well tough luck!!"

As his anger continued to grow, Art's next reaction was to use Steve's own writing to refute his argument, a very clever and academic thing to do. Did he learn in high school to make pronoun reference errors (critique/them) or misspell "relevence"? Do his employers really want his writing to be full of errors? So civil disobedience has no relevance to real life? Who says? Can he prove this claim? Maybe faculty in the Finance Department believe students like Steve harbor misconceptions about real life, which is why they require courses in English, history, and biology, or why they require students to think and write about academic topics as well as immediately personal ones. Maybe Steve's next essay could be a definition of "real life" that Art and the rest of the class could examine critically?

Eventually, Art's anger abated, and he reassessed the situation. Art realized he had initiated Steve's response by asking him for an "honest" reaction to the commentary, and from one perspective, Steve had given Art just that. In his first sentence, Steve said he didn't know what he was supposed to be writing, and it is true that Art did not provide further directions, preferring to leave the assignment open-ended to provide the freedom necessary to encourage a wide range of responses. Indeed, Steve may not have been asked previously by a teacher to write this kind of response, and so he may not have known the protocol apparently familiar to the rest of his classmates. Art had asked for these responses hoping to create a dialogue about their mutual enterprise, and Steve had obliged.

And so Art reread Steve's writing from a sympathetic perspective, trying to understand Steve's viewpoint, his experience, and his apparent anger, and this was the perspective Art communicated to Steve. We can't be sure how appropriate Art's response was nor how Steve actually received it. We do know that the relationship between Art and Steve settled into a civil give-and-take in which Steve revised his essays and modified his attitude somewhat, and Art often took note in class discussions of the reasons for Steve's original protest.

Reflecting on this incident, we now see both Art and Steve as part of the "paradigm shift" that Maxine Hairston (1982), who teaches writing at the University of Texas at Austin, says is taking place in the teaching of composition. A paradigm is a model, a pattern, a set of forms to follow. Philosopher of science Thomas Kuhn has used the term paradigm shift to describe a major change in theoretical orientation; it was a paradigm shift, for example, when people began to believe that the world was round and not flat, because that new belief, that new set of "forms" for the mind, changed not only how people thought about the world and the universe but also how they did things like sail boats and build buildings. The theory of relativity has changed the model of matter and energy, initiating another paradigm shift. Professor Hairston borrows Kuhn's term to explain what has happened with composition teaching over the last three decades.

In the 1960s, many teachers of writing became dissatisfied with the way composition was being taught on their campuses. They argued that composition classes often seemed concerned more about following rules than about writing. Some of those teachers, especially those who taught in open enrollment colleges, saw that the traditional ways of teaching writing really didn't work with students described as "under-prepared." Nowadays, the name given to the old way of teaching writing that those teachers were rebelling against is "current-traditional." Here's basically how it worked: You thought of a topic; then you wrote an outline, often a Roman numeral outline; then you wrote the paper; next you proofread, paying a lot of attention to commas, spelling, and usage (that is, things like *lie* and *lay*); you handed the paper in; and a few days (or weeks) later you got it back with a grade and with all your errors in punctuation, spelling, and usage marked, usually in red. Sometimes there was a comment in the margin like "awk" or "frag" or even "good," but usually you didn't know what those abbreviations meant or what was good in the paragraph. Then you did the same thing over again, often eight times in one semester. Class was devoted to lectures on commas, sentence structure, and synonyms and to the analysis of essays by great writers.

In the current-traditional paradigm, what was important was the student's essay, the product. Under the new model, the process of writing became as important as the product. Sometimes called the "process method," it works like this: you spend a lot time in class on prewriting activities—journal entries, making lists, freewriting, journalist's questions (who? what? where? when? why?), small-group discussion; then you write; you revise; you bring your paper to class for workshops or peer-editing sessions; you write another draft; you might go for a conference with your teacher; the teacher reads a draft and comments on the strengths and weaknesses of your paper, paying particular attention to purpose, audience, and organizational strategies; you might write still another draft; you may or may not get a traditional grade; and you might even revise again.

One problem with the process method is that it keeps changing. In the 1960s, writing teachers wanted to help students find authentic voices and so spent a lot of time on prewriting activities. In the 1970s, composition teachers began studying the process of writing more systematically than they had before. As they observed successful adult writers, they began to emphasize setting goals, making plans, organizing, revising drafts, and editing; they recognized that good writers can and do move back and forth among these activities. In the 1980s, scholars began to look at writing not just as an individual act, but as a social act as well. These teachers argued that what we write is a social artifact and that how we write results from the social situation we are in. They began to pay attention to both the product—that is, the text, its genre, and its conventions—and to collaborative learning—that is, the ways writers and readers work together to create a text. To sum up, there are lots of different ways to teach the process of writing, probably as many different ways as there are teachers who say they teach it.

With this background in mind, we now see Steve's resistance to writing and to Art a little differently. First, if Steve's high school teachers were old paradigm teachers, then he may have been expecting a class where he could get by just following orders. Many students figure out rather quickly that a current-traditional teacher may lose enthusiasm for students' ideas under the time-consuming obligation to find all surface errors. Such teachers often become so bored marking errors that they forget that students do have important things to say, and they don't remember that helping writers state their messages appropriately is more important than telling them one more time that they misspelled *relevance*. If Steve has had enough old paradigm teachers, then he may know that what he has to say will be of little interest. In such a case, writing multiple drafts is not just a chore but in truth a waste of time.

Furthermore, students trained under the old paradigm often learn to manipulate the system to get by with a minimal amount of work and mental engagement. Since Steve believes that English doesn't matter to him personally or to his employer, perhaps this is what he wanted: a course that would make few demands on his time or energy. But here he is in Art Young's class, where Art asks him to write a draft, then another draft, then still another draft, all the while paying attention to what the other students and Art have to say. Art asks Steve to look at his own writing process, to change his text in response to comments and suggestions, and to make decisions about what to keep and what to leave out, about what to add and what to change to a different place. Art is asking Steve to do more work and more thinking than in the old way.

The heart of the clash between Steve and Art may be a student trained in the old paradigm resisting a new paradigm teacher. Steve may be thinking, Why spend all this time trying to write an effective essay on civil disobedience when no one cares what I think anyway? Since it is not an important or relevant topic for me, I'm not even sure I know what I think about civil disobedience. He may deduce that, to take the process of learning to write seriously, he will have to take ideas (his own and those of interest to others) seriously. Perhaps this class, full of unfamiliar tasks, interferes with Steve's plans for his semester or triggers his insecurities about English or about school.

Indeed, many students resist the new paradigm simply because it is unfamiliar. The old way carries with it a lot of certainty—"two fragments and you flunk," for example—and certainty makes all of us feel secure. "The devil you know is better than the devil you don't," according to folk wisdom. In other words, some students may resist simply because this new teacher does it differently from the way other teachers have done it. Perhaps the rules for getting a good grade don't seem as clear as they were before. Perhaps because Art's class doesn't fit familiar patterns, Steve becomes defensive. Perhaps Steve prefers a class in which he writes a paper, the teacher grades it, and then it is forgotten—filed or thrown away.

Let us suppose, on the other hand, that Steve has had a process teacher before. In such a case, he may not recognize the familiar in another process teacher's classroom. This is because those of us who claim to teach process don't all teach it the same way. One teacher may hold conferences with individuals or with small groups; another may use collaborative learning techniques for editing workshops; one process teacher may give grades on the third draft; and another may give no grades at all until the end of the semester when she grades students' portfolios.

Maybe Steve's teacher in English 101 was a new paradigm teacher. Maybe he or she also required drafts, group work, conferences, journals, freewriting. Maybe Steve did all that and still got a C. Even if he got a grade better than C, perhaps he did all this work but never felt that he learned anything new. Maybe it all felt like "busy work" to him. So perhaps when Steve gets to Art's class and realizes what is required, his reaction is, Oh no, not more revising. I learned that in 101. Maybe the other teacher's comments on drafts were not suggestions but orders. And so perhaps Steve sees feedback from his audience, whether peers' responses or Art's, not as help in clarifying his thinking for this specific audience (his teacher and his peers) but as an infringement on his freedom to say what he thinks in any way he wants.

One thing that undoubtedly makes composition confusing for students is that their teachers are themselves caught in the transition period of this paradigm shift. Many teachers prefer the process approach to the traditional approach, but there is no general consensus among these teachers on how most effectively to use the writing process in support of teaching students to think and write clearly. In other words, it isn't just students like Steve who are caught in the paradigm shift, but teachers as well. Some teachers proclaim process but give objective tests on how to write a paper, or they count off a letter grade for every comma splice, or they use peer-editing groups but fail to help students know how be effective editors. Some talk a lot about the process but consider only products in grading.

But the shift to process is not just a change in classroom practices. The paradigm shift in composition is part of a larger shift in looking at knowledge. In many fields, from literature to physics, knowledge is no longer regarded as something that exists separately from human beings. This shift has been described by Paulo Freire, a professor of education in Brazil in his book *Pedagogy of the Oppressed*, (1970). Freire believes that knowledge is not a *thing* that teachers possess that they can just pass on unchanged to students. Instead, according to Freire, knowledge is what we—teacher and students—make together as we talk to each other, as we ask questions and put into our own words our experiences with the world. Freire believes that together we can use language and literacy to "rename" our world, to change the world, to make it more equitable and more humane for everyone. For Freire, the purpose of education is to help students (and teachers) develop "critical consciousness"—that is, an attitude of questioning and analyzing the world as it has been given to us.

The old way of teaching writing, the current-traditional approach, resembles what Freire has called the banking concept of education. In the banking model, the teacher makes deposits of knowledge into the pupil's mind; the student only receives this knowledge but doesn't do anything with it. The student is required, in fact, to be a passive learner, not an active one. When the student has accumulated enough deposits, he or she can cash them in on a grade or a degree. In America, we expect to trade the degree in on a "good" job. The university is often seen as merely a hoop to jump through on the way to economic security, not as a place to learn to use both spoken and written language to engage in dialogue about how the world is and how it ought to be. Steve appears to accept the banking concept of education. He seems to have been convinced long ago that English as well as history and biology has little relevance to finance or business or to his life. For Steve, the purpose of higher education is to prepare students for jobs, not to get them to think about and discuss such concepts as civil disobedience.

If in fact this is how Steve views education, he has lots of company. Historically and statistically, in the United States the level of education correlates highly with income. Although there are exceptions, the general rule in our economic system is that without an education there is little if any economic security. So Steve's point of view has validity, and we are not so naive as to try to ignore that fact. But we—and faculty in the Finance Department—also believe that Steve should know that important decisions even in the business world are rarely made on only the "bottom line"; the equations also include human values. And human beings are the subjects of such courses as English, history, and biology. Coming to decisions in the "real" world that Steve wants to be a part of requires conversation, argument, dialogue, language—the traditional concerns of rhetoric, which is what we are trying to teach in our writing courses.

In addition, although we may not initially like Steve's resistance to the way we teach writing, we believe his resistance to authority is valuable, and we want to help him learn to resist effectively. We see a connection between some forms of resistance and the ability to think critically. Learning to resist effectively includes creating a context for critically reexamining generally accepted ideas and practices. Such resistance is based on courage, self-respect, and respect for others. These attributes cannot be measured in dollars and cents but instead often require difficult and even unpopular actions. Our country has a long tradition of civil disobedience, of resisting government policies that people consider immoral, unjust, or unfair. We honor individuals like Rosa Parks who have the courage to nonviolently disobey laws with which they disagree and thereby challenge governments to change laws in order to create a more just society. But this concept is not limited only to laws; sometimes it is necessary to resist at work. Sometimes individuals in business and technology have to say no to company policy. The tragic example of the NASA space craft Challenger comes to mind: Some of the engineers and scientists resisted and some of them succumbed to company pressure to change the temperature safety rating of the O-rings that were used on that fatal flight. While it is true that Americans expect education to serve economic ends, we also expect it to serve a higher purpose: Education should help students learn how to make moral decisions and how to argue for them.

As teachers of rhetoric, we hope that we can contribute to this purpose by helping our students learn to read carefully, write effectively, and think critically. Ideally, the new way of teaching writing, the process approach, requires that students and teachers work together. Through questions, feedback, answers, and suggestions, both texts and ideas are revised. This process creates knowledge. The new paradigm asks students not to be passive writers, saying only what they are told to say the way someone else wants them to say it but active writers, making decisions about what they want to say and the most effective way to say it to a particular audience, learning to construct through conversations with others their own interpretations of the world.

The new pedagogy, or way of teaching, makes all of us—students and teachers—uncomfortable because it critiques schooling as it has usually been carried out. The new paradigm resists the old model that has taught us that knowledge is a set of facts that we have no influence over. It resists teaching that implies that obeying a set of rules is more important than questioning, thinking, seeing inconsistencies, or speaking in one's own voice. Because many students who come to college have been successful with the old methods, with Freire's banking concept, they don't want to question familiar methods and standards or their own success. The new pedagogy asks students to take charge of their own writing and their own learning. In addition, the new paradigm asks teachers to reconsider their role, to look at students not as empty vessels into which knowledge is poured, but as persons who also help create knowledge and whose view of reality must be taken seriously. It is easier for teachers to slip into their old role as authorities than to share power with students. It is easier for students to resist participating actively in their own learning. Sometimes we all resist the responsibility for creating our world. It is easier to accept someone else's view of it.

In a writing class, the new pedagogy asks students not only to think and question but to take risks and to live with some uncertainty, all activities that create anxiety. Maybe it will help our students—Steve, for example—to know that the new paradigm requires us teachers to question tradition, to think critically about our roles in educating students, to take risks, and to tolerate uncertainty. We are all—students and teachers—caught up in this paradigm shift. The changing view of knowledge and of the world is scary, but at the same time exciting, for we can contribute to it. In this new paradigm, Steve's resistance in Art's class last year is no longer a disrespectful gesture but an opportunity to analyze the circumstances in which teachers and students now find themselves. We think our consideration of Steve's resistance has helped us better understand both our students' situation and our own profession. We hope it has proved enlightening for our readers who may resist both writing and writing teachers.

Works Cited

Freire, Paulo (1970). *Pedagogy of the Oppressed.* New York: Seabury.

Hairston, Maxine (1982). "The Winds of Change: Thomas Kuhn and the Revolution in Teaching Writing, *"College Composition and Communication, 33,* 78–86.

Sharing Ideas

- Pretend you were in Steve's writing group all semester as he wrote in Art's class. Then try to add to Beth and Art's analysis.

- Share a story of a time you resisted a teacher. If you've never resisted, explore why that is so.

- Have you ever seen a teacher go through some or all of the stages Art and Beth describe—anger at student behaviors, refuting a student with the student's own arguments, reassessing and changing the classroom in response to student comments, then giving the resisting student a more sympathetic reading?

- What are your thoughts on the Freirian model of education and the banking model of education? Consider whether they are at work in your own classes.

- Do you think there is a connection between resistance in the writing classroom and the tradition of civil disobedience?

- Share ways you have worked to change institutions or institutional practices.

- What are your feelings on the possibility of students sharing educational power and authority.

- Describe what you view as ideal roles for teachers and for students in writing classrooms.

- Have you ever been in a class where a student seems to be resisting the teacher for reasons you don't understand? In light of Beth and Art's essay, try to describe what that student's reasons might have been; also, detail the impact that student's resistance had on you and your classmates' learning.

22

Does Coming to College Mean Becoming Someone New?

Kevin Davis

Kevin Davis, father of two teenagers, is an avid baseball fan (St. Louis), bicycle rider, and pasta maker. He writes an occasional poem and enjoys woodworking projects. In his spare time, he teaches writing and directs the writing center at East Central University in Ada, Oklahoma, where he received an award for teaching excellence in 1991.

As an undergraduate English major, I felt like an outsider. I originally chose to major in English because of my love for reading and writing, but the reading and writing college expected of me was not the reading and writing I was prepared to do. Sure, I could read the assigned literature, and I could make my own good sense of it. Yet that was not enough for my English professors. They wanted me to make their sense of the literature, to understand the texts as they understood them. Not only that, they expected me to write about this alien sense-making in turgid, impersonal, passive-voiced prose. When I became an English major, I didn't just learn certain understandings of what I read; I also had to learn a particular way of reading and writing. Right from the start, it was clear that if I was to become a member of the English-majors community, I had to do more than read and think and write; I had to turn into someone new.

Perhaps that is why I was never a very successful English major and why, eventually, I left the academic world and joined the business

235

community. I was living on the boundary between academic and home communities, between maintaining my identity and accepting another. I found I didn't like the someone new I was being asked to become.

Eventually, I returned to the academic world and discovered I fit into the community of outsiders known as rhetoricians (people who study the way other people effectively communicate). I'm not sure if I fit into this community because I wanted to join it more than I had wanted to join the English studies community, because it was willing to accept me as I already was, or because I had matured enough to be willing to become someone new. I do know, however, that this second attempt at entrance into the academic community has been as successful as my earlier attempt was a flop.

As a rhetorician and because of my past experience, I have become interested in issues of community membership. Everyone is a member of several discourse communities (the term rhetoricians use to describe groups of people who share patterns and strategies of communication). We're all members of a home discourse community, based on our family's regional, social, and economic lifestyles. And many of us are members of other discourse communities because we are familiar with particular language communities through experiences such as jobs or hobbies. But entering the academic discourse communities present on college campuses can produce problems and anxieties for students who are attempting the transitions.

In the rest of this essay, I want to use my own experiences and research to answer several questions: What happens as students try to become members of new academic discourse communities? What special writing and thinking abilities are required? What personal investments must be made?

When I was 18, my writing was an extremely personal activity. I didn't just throw words on pages; I invested myself into the work. Everything I wrote was full of personal insights, personal style, and voice. A good writer, I was regularly praised and awarded for my high school writing efforts. I was totally unprepared for the shocking comments that my college professors would place on my writing.

Part of the problem came from a natural maturing process: The valued and original insights of a high school senior were suddenly the trite and common repetitions of a college student. And part of the problem came from style: The original, personal, whimsical voice of a young writer was not enough to assure my spot in the academic community.

I have now discovered that rhetoricians have an insightful way of looking at the split I experienced (North, 1986b). "Formalists," people who think that the most important aspect of a particular discourse community is the forms the community's writers use, would suggest that I didn't know the appropriate forms for academic writing. I didn't know what academic writing sounded like, and I didn't know how to present my ideas in the lingo that would bring the ideas recognition and acceptance. On the other hand, "epistemics," people who think that the most important aspect of a particular discourse community is the way the community thinks and solves problems, would suggest that I was not thinking like members of the academic world are supposed to think. I didn't process my thoughts in appropriate academic ways, according to the epistemics, and I wasn't positively involved with my studies.

Several composition scholars have completed research studies that try to understand more fully what happens with students trying to enter academic discourse communities. Recently, for example, Stephen North (1986) investigated the ways three students changed during one philosophy course. He relied solely on his readings of the papers the students wrote in order to describe three contexts in which the students changed: the *rhetorical* (the students' sense of their audience and their purpose for writing), the *intellectual or epistemic* (how the students struggled to understand the ideas they were studying), and the *disciplinary or formalistic* (how the students used language to show membership in the discourse community). By looking at papers similar to those that I wrote as an undergraduate, North was able to ascertain these three changes in writing for students entering new discourse communities.

Another research project, completed by Lucille McCarthy (1987), studied one student as he learned to negotiate his way through new discourse communities in several different freshman and sophomore courses. McCarthy made several conclusions from her work. First, she found that her subject used the same writing process to figure out how to complete a variety of writing tasks; this would imply that a student who can write in one situation, like I could, can extrapolate a process for writing into other situations. Second, she found that the purpose for the writing task and the student's involvement with the task were important to the writer's success; this implies that students write better if they are actively involved in the topic they are writing about, which is certainly true in my own experience. Finally, McCarthy concluded that writing tasks that are familiar in one situation were considered different when the student encountered them in a different situation; this implies that epistemic knowledge of a discourse community is important for a writer to succeed.

These adaptations writers make to new discourse communities are not limited, of course, to undergraduate college students. Everyone enters new communities throughout life. Carol Berkenkotter, Thomas Hucklin, and John Ackerman (1988) verified this when they examined the experiences of a teacher who returned to graduate school after several years of teaching. In their study, they ended up agreeing with both the formalists and the epistemics: They concluded that student writers have to assimilate both the forms and the thoughts of an academic discourse community to function within it. Their subject had to change the nature of his writing, from personal exploration to impersonal declaration, but he also had to change his community allegiance: he had to learn to think like a member of the community.

By looking at these studies and at my experience, then, I can begin to make some conclusions about how students have to adapt their writing and thinking to succeed in a college's unfamiliar academic discourse community. First, we have to recognize and accept the forms of the community; we have to make our writing look and sound like that of the field. Second, we have to learn to think in the ways that are valued by the field we are entering; we have to be personal or impersonal, focused on ideas or numbers, as the field demands. Third, we have to have a reliable, comfortable writing process that we can take with us from task to task, community to community; once established, the process will probably serve us in a variety of settings. Finally, we have to become personally and intellectually involved with the community, wanting to be a part of it; without personal involvement, the formalistic and epistemic changes are merely window dressing.

As I look back on my own experience, I can clearly identify that last change as the most problematic for me. As an undergraduate English major, I never completed the personal commitment important for my success in the field. Eventually, I learned to mimic the writing and thinking activities that the field valued, but I remained unwilling to submit to the authority of those form and thought patterns. To personally endorse the English studies discourse community I would have had to abandon much of what I believed about life. Later, when I returned to graduate school to study rhetoric, however, I easily endorsed the field, finding it much more palatable to my native ways of being.

As I began my own research into discourse community membership, I was particularly interested in the personal involvement issues. Did other people reject communities, as I had done, because they were hesitant to make the personal commitments necessary for success? Could individuals only join communities that endorsed their native ways of thinking? Or did other people accept the communities and, in the process, give up something of their native ways of being in the world?

To investigate the personal changes students make as they enter new discourse communities, I interviewed, several times over six months, two undergraduates who were taking their first courses toward a degree and eventual licenses in social work.

Stella (the names are changed) was in her early twenties and in college for the second time, having delayed her education for a marriage. As Stella engaged the social work community, she became more accepting of differences in others, developing a new sense of open-mindedness. As she put it, "I try to see people as they are and not make judgements. . . . Through my social work classes, I've learned that everybody should be treated that way." But sometimes this open, non-judgmental attitude caused problems for Stella who suddenly found that her husband was prejudiced in several ways: "My husband is racially prejudiced, and I'm real open and have no problem with that"; "My husband's family thinks welfare people are lazy. I really stand up for people they don't understand." Through her entrance into the new community, her attitudes toward others changed, and she adopted a socially accepting world view even when that new world view was in direct conflict with her family. In the process, she became more committed to the community of social workers.

The other participant in the study, Charlotte, had graduated from high school in 1957. After raising a family and working as both a cosmetologist and a practical nurse, Charlotte was finally returning to college to get the degree she had long cherished. Charlotte, too, was willing to make the personal commitment that membership in the social work community required. As she put it, "This course is really making a difference in my thoughts. I had not recognized that I was biased in my way of thinking." Further, Charlotte suggested that self awareness and open-mindedness were mandatory for a social worker: "If you don't understand yourself, you can't help anyone else. Not in the way that will help people take control of a situation." Her studies in social work, she said, changed her overall view of people and communities and culture. And, like Stella, Charlotte tried to become a change agent for those around her: "Just this weekend my husband made a comment, and I said 'Now just a minute; that's not the way it is at all.'"

In attempting to enter the social work discourse community, both Stella and Charlotte underwent a great deal of self-realization. Both acknowledged their native social world view, critiqued it, began to develop new social world views, and even tried to become change agents for their spouses' world views. Through this progression, both women began to develop what their instructor described as the "social work frame of reference," a socially accepting world view that is necessary for an individual to help members of diverse social groups try to improve their position in life. In the process, they became increasingly estranged from their home communities.

Research—my own and others'—exploring discourse communities verifies what my personal experiences taught me: Learning to write within an academic discourse community is not a simple procedure.

First, we have to learn to put down words and ideas in community acceptable ways. We have to internalize and apply the form limitations of the discourse community; our writing has to look like writing in the community is supposed to look. In my own experience, this formalistic community entrance was easy to master, quick to develop; I learned to sound like an English major early in my education.

But there is more. We also have to learn to explore ideas by employing the intellectual manners that are important to a particular field. We have to accept and use the epistemic processes of the discourse community. This can be more difficult than the forms, but new ways of thinking usually develop easily through repeated contact. In my own experience, the epistemic knowledge developed a bit more slowly than the formalistic, but it, too, grew rapidly; I was soon thinking and sounding like an English major.

Finally—and I think most importantly—personal commitment to a particular community is involved in entering that new discourse community. Students can develop the sound of a community and apply the thought processes of the community without adopting the world views of the community, without truly accepting membership in that community. In my own case, I was unwilling to become the person the literary studies community required me to be and to develop the world view the community expected. As a result, I pursued careers in two different communities, business and rhetoric. Literary studies expected me to become somebody new, somebody I was unwilling to become. I was willing to become a business manager and, later, a rhetorician.

In my research, however, I found that Stella and Charlotte were willing to make the total transition, to write in social worker ways, to solve problems using social worker methods, and finally to adopt a social worker world view, no matter how alien it was to their native communities. In the process of coming to college, Stella and Charlotte found themselves becoming someone new.

Works Cited

Berkenkotter, Carol; Hucklin, Thomas; & Ackerman, John (1988). "Conventions, Conversations, and the Writer: Case Study of a Student in a Rhetoric Ph.D. Program," *Research in the Teaching of English, 22*, 9–44.

McCarthy, Lucille (1987). "A Stranger in Strange Lands: A College Student Writing Across the Curriculum," *Research in the Teaching of English, 21,* 233–265.

North, Stephen (1986). "Writing in a Philosophy Class: Three Case Studies," *Research in the Teaching of English, 20,* 225–262.

———— (1985). *The Making of Knowledge in Composition: Portrait of an Emerging Field.* Upper Montclair, NJ: Boynton/Cook.

Sharing Ideas

- Draw a diagram of your discourse communities.

- I'm very sympathetic to all three stories Kevin shares—his own and those of Stella and Charlotte. You've probably known people (they may be you) who have changed their minds several times about majors and future professions. How do these stories illuminate such changes and choices?

- For you, what is at risk when you think about succeeding in your chosen field and major? Who agrees or disagrees with your goals and why? Consider your family, your significant other, your teacher, your friends? How do their opinions affect you?

- What is involved in personally investing in your education?

- How important has writing been to your success in school?

- Kevin claims adaptation to college requires that learners recognize the forms of writing used in their new communities, to think in ways that are valued in those communities, and to become personally and intellectually involved in their communities. How are these three elements playing out in your own college life? The lives of your close friends?

23

Writing Does Not Equal Schoolwriting

James Thomas Zebroski

James Zebroski has had the great opportunity of teaching all
kinds of students for almost 20 years. He received all three of his
degrees from Ohio State University in Columbus, Ohio (Go
Bucks!) and presently teaches writing and English graduate
courses at Syracuse University. He started out as a physics major but switched to English because he had been writing since
sixth grade and enjoyed it and found he could get credit and even
get paid to do it and teach it. He loves all kinds of books and
old second-hand bookstores, hiking, cooking, and old-fashioned
Neil Young-type rock and roll. He writes and publishes about
the psychology and the anthropology of writing and literacy and,
as a third generation Polish-American, is especially interested
in learning more about his Slavic ethnic heritage.

A Preview

I have always thought it was a bit hypocritical for me to ask my composition students to write so much for me but not share any of my
writing with them. So whenever I teach composition I make it a point
to let students see my writing in its various stages and for its varied
purposes. In this essay, I try to do something similar. I share reflections on my writing process to make a point about the "why" of writing. To do this means that I have had to experiment with the way this
essay has been put together and even with the way I use language, so

that my writing "does" what it "says," so that it, in effect, practices what it preaches. This essay then takes a form unlike most pieces of schoolwriting precisely because it is arguing against most pieces of schoolwriting.

I am trying to give the reader an experience, and to do this I have composed this piece on purpose so that a reader will have to get through the whole thing before any part will make sense. So if as you are reading along you feel a little uncomfortable or are not entirely sure of where the essay is going, that's great. You should know that that is exactly what you should feel since I am trying to argue that that is often the way real writing works. It isn't enough to say it. You also have to have the experience. Maybe the most helpful way you could approach this text is to imagine that you are the character described in the story, a student new to the university, finding it very difficult to keep up, and also very lonely at times. . . .

Going Back to School

In September of 1979 as I was getting ready to go back to graduate school at Ohio State, I reflected on my first year. It had been a lot different from what I had expected. I had known when I left teaching to go back to school to get a Ph.D. that it would be tough, but I just wasn't ready for the demands that school would make on me. Never before in my life had I read so much. Never before had I been called upon to think so deeply about issues of language, mind, and society. It was hard just keeping up with the reading, let alone mastering the content and being able to talk with others intelligently. As usual, I was impressed—no, intimidated is a better term—by the other students and professors who not only appeared to know so much, certainly so much more than I, but were able to talk so beautifully about what they knew. They all sounded so articulate. While I was stuttering and sputtering, they seemed to talk fluently, quickly, and quietly in whole, coherent paragraphs. Whenever I tried to speak, even if it was about things I knew about, I always sounded so—what's the right word?—"clumpy." They were always so "smooth."

As my first year wore on, I wrote more and more, but enjoyed it less and less. It was really frustrating to put so much time and energy into this stupid writing activity. That year I wrote many 20-page papers in a variety of courses and disciplines, including English, philosophy, anthropology, linguistics, and geography. I pushed hard to write well. By school standards, I suppose I was successful. I got an A- on a 55-page monster paper I wrote at the end of spring term. But in another sense, that huge 55-page paper was a complete failure.

Writing, when all is going well, leads to more writing. Good writing generates surprising words and ideas that invite us to write more, to explore more in writing. Successful writing is writing that creates a desire in us for more.

But that monster paper . . . I hated that paper. I can still remember the topic with dread: It was on the fiscal crisis of the state and the inequalities created in the schools by the extraction, appropriation, and ebb and flow of surplus value in and out of local school districts. A typical piece of "schoolwriting." Very theoretical, lots of researched facts, very correct, and very dull. I gathered a huge amount of information, webbed it out on a single sheet of paper covering my entire dining room table, then outlined it and wrote it up. That paper was the end of my schoolwriting for more than a year. It hurt for me to write schoolwriting after I finished that paper. Because I couldn't write more than a few sentences at a time, I decided for more than a year to take only courses that had no required writing. This then was the end of my *schoolwriting* for a long time. Writer's block at its worst. And the irony was that my area of specialization was composition. Writer heal thyself! Here I was trying to get a Ph.D. in composition to teach freshmen to write and I couldn't even put words on paper myself.

So the moral to this story? Writing does not equal schoolwriting.

In September of 1979, while Hurricane David was wreaking havoc on Florida and I was becoming more and more depressed about school starting and about eventually having to do schoolwriting, I was writing journal entries. I didn't write regularly, every day. Sometimes I didn't even write once a week. I usually wrote very short entries. I never wrote about school or intellectual topics. Instead I wrote about ordinary things. I wrote about my life, everything from the girls I was dating to changes in the seasons and the weather. Hurricane David survives in this essay because he was tracked in the writing in my journals as he slammed into Columbus that early autumn and howled and blew and dumped a pile of rain there. As writing flickered and went out in my school life, it continued to burn bright in the rest of my life. True, I might have gone weeks, even months, without scratching a page, but later I would always come back, the prodigal son. My journals, started back in August of 1969, persisted through this dark September of 1979, and continue to this day.

Writing Out of My Life

I feel sorry for people—and you would be surprised by the number of composition teachers who fit this category—who think that writing equals schoolwriting, who believe that the only writing in their lives that really counts is "official" writing that we do for our teachers, and also later for our coworkers and bosses.

I'm not suggesting that schoolwriting (or writing for work) is unimportant or that it is somehow fake. I obviously would not have continued my education and teaching if I were that cynical about school and schoolwriting. Still, what I find most absent from the composition classes that I have taken is the notion that writing includes a lot more than this. Sure schoolwriting is important. Sure that is one of the reasons you are taking and I am teaching composition courses—to improve your schoolwriting. But I also want my students to leave my class with some experience of the unexpected pleasures and values of other sorts of writing. Writing is bigger and more interesting than schoolwriting.

Here is an entry from my journal from the time of Hurricane David. The writing is recorded here as it is. It's not pretty writing, but it is writing out of my life.

Tuesday, August 14, 1979

A strange but in a sense kind of nice dream. My family and I back in Poland from United States. Outbreak of World War III. The Germans AGAIN. Even Hitler has somehow resurfaced. A stormy night. Bombs and lights in the distance. The advance of the Germans. Again. If they did to Warsaw in particular and Poland in general what they did LAST time think what they are going to do THIS time. And me of draftable army age—if and when they find me there's little doubt I'll be shot. So with a storm beginning, though I don't know where I am going, though I am scared to death, I decide to start walking away. Maybe I can get away by taking the back roads—or even better yet the railroads?

I kiss my mother goodbye and tell her not to give up EVER because I am not going to and I'll be back. Shake my father's hand and talk briefly with him before leaving—he's a bit more realistic and has a firmer grasp of the situation and what's really going on and how desparate it is. Leave my parents and brother and sisters at the old farmhouse in Poland we had returned to and set out thinking can you imagine Hitler in the age of nuclear bombs? An electric truck right outside on the road. It's dark out. Perhaps fifth column Germans? Lights flashing. Cars going down the road—away from the advancing Germans? Why do they always pick on Poland? Why must we go through this again and again? How many times can we become the "perfect holocaust"? If I take the railroad tracks, it's less likely I'll be seen and caught though my chances still are not good. How far is it likely I'll get in this storm? In the rain? Not knowing the land? Without food, shelter?

The entry breaks off here. Now what in the world are we to make of this little piece? What can this try at writing possibly say to me (or anyone else, for that matter)? I wrote this immediately upon waking when I was still half asleep, a habit I still try to encourage. The best writing happens early in the day, before the mind gets frittered away by stupid detail, at least for me.

I was puzzled even as I wrote this entry. What could it mean, and why had I felt compelled to write it? A few minutes later in the shower, after I had written the journal, it dawned on me. It hit me like lightning. The illumination was so unexpected, so unintended, and so sharp that 12 years later as I write these words I can recall in minute detail that moment, recall what I saw, smelled, heard, felt, thought.

I had been very close for nine years to college friends who were still in town. But at that time I realized I was losing these close friends when I needed them most, when I was frustrated and intimidated by my first year in the Ph.D. program. My friends were by this time all doctors or lawyers, making money, raising families, less and less interested in ideas and talk. But I hadn't yet really made any friends in graduate school. I felt alone and friendless and frightened. In fact, worse. I felt my close and dear friends were betraying me, abandoning me. It hit me in the shower—their names were all German-American. I am Polish-American. This dream and entry seemed as much about my close friends (Germany) at "war" with me when I was in a "new" country, forging a new identity in graduate school (Poland) as about history. The dream writing was about a kind of world at war, but in my world and my soul. Schoolwriting had gone out in my life, but the writing that continued and kept me going came from my life.

Writing for the Right Reasons

I am a writer today because I believe that I would never have been able to make this kind of sense of my life and world if I hadn't kept at writing and kept at it for my own reasons and my own purposes. That's the payoff. That's why writers write. Since writing is often hard and always takes considerable time and energy, there has to be some trade-off. I have to get something from writing. What I get is the unexpected. Writing always reveals and conceals far more than I ever intend it to. Writing marks, tracks, orders, preserves, and transforms my world(s). I enjoy discovering things about myself and my world(s) that I had not known, and could not know, before I wrote. Without tries at writing, I know I could not ever have discovered precisely these things. It's the recurring *attempt*, that *try*, that is what writing is all about.

Too often writers forget that the word *essay*, which we bandy about to mean a finished, perfected, almost gem-like polished piece, originally meant a test, a try, an attempt, at writing. The essay seems to have originated with Montaigne a kind of adult French Bart Simpson, who seemed to hate the schools, schoolmasters, and schoolwriting of that time, but who wrote for his own purposes, in his own way. Montaigne wrote very untraditional little sets of explorations, of tentative wonderings, about himself and his world that he called essays. Writers would do well to recover Montaigne's sense of essaying. Writing is a dialogue with one's world, open, unfinished, not always pretty, but ongoing. Writing is in this sense a bit like our talk with friends. We don't know exactly what will happen next in talking with a friend. That's the fun of it. Sometimes its a horrendous flop. We wonder why we even bothered. We keep at it, keep trying. Through good times and bad. Writing is the same sort of dialogue, the same sort of try.

Joan Didion is probably my favorite writer. She says a writer is "a person whose most absorbed and passionate hours are spent arranging words on pieces of paper." Notice what she doesn't say. She doesn't say that writers are born or writers are the ones who put together the good stuff and get into literature books; she doesn't say writers are the ones who can sell their writing for money. She doesn't even mention that writers are the people in school who put together papers. Rather, she opens the community of writers to anyone who would become absorbed and passionate about writing words. I like that. That's very democratic. The door to writing is open to anyone who wants to come in. If you have ever felt passionate about something or someone and have sat down and poured it onto the paper, no matter the form, and felt a great release afterward, that is the beginning of this attempt to be and to become a writer. So writing instead of being limited to schoolwriting, a false voice, a way of passing for something the writer doesn't really want to become, becomes a dialogue with the world.

And so the frightened graduate student, who in September of 1979 could barely put one word down after another, is writing this essay, this try, this attempt, to you.

Sharing Ideas

- Imitate this essay and talk about a time when education wasn't working for you. Particularly, explore a writing block or a time when classroom performance demands made you avoid performing, and so on.
- Jim's Hurricane David journal entry reminds me in a way of Chris Anson's journal entry on buying gerbils. Both journal

experiences only hint at issues, both are exploratory, both are unshaped yet deeply important to their authors. Try collecting dream or informal freewritings for a week and then analyze the events of your life, using those writings as a mirror.

- Do you agree that writing reveals and conceals far more than the writer ever intends it to?

- This essay brings us back to central questions, ones we've encountered earlier: What is a writer? What are a writer's subjects? Why is it so hard to experiment and take chances in writing? Now Jim adds the question of authenticity. Is your school writing *just* writing for school, for teachers, or is it authentic, important to you, and full of your voice?

- My last question raises further questions, such as what is authentic writing, how do we identify a writer's voice, and do writer's have only one voice?

- Kate Ronald claims that teachers look for a certain style of writing. Explore how this essay makes the same argument, even if from a slightly different perspective.

24

When All Writing Is Creative and Student Writing Is Literature

Wendy Bishop

Wendy Bishop works with writers and writing teachers at Florida State University. She arrived in Tallahassee after some years living and teaching in Alaska, Arizona, Nigeria, and California. She writes about the connection between composition and creative writing; she writes poems, stories, and essays. And she enjoys seeing her young children—Morgan and Tait— grow into writing and reading. They take particular pleasure when her books include their names, which they always do.

Here are journal excerpts from two writing students:

June

If we are to accept the definition of a writer as one who writes, we must accept the fact that writers are not a special type of person. Those who write might be of any age, shape, background or interest. They may produce a technical manual or a provocative essay or a piece of artistic prose. The one thing they hold in common is the use of language.

If I write a letter to my friend, I am a writer. If I submit a term paper of the same caliber of technique to a committee judging a dissertation, they might dispute whether or not I am a writer! Perhaps writing, like beauty, is in the eye of the beholder.

On the other hand, I can consider myself a writer if no one beholds that I write. Emily Dickinson certainly was a writer during her lifetime, not just after the discovery of her wealth of poetry. The first grader who tells in scrawled words and pictures of the arrival of a baby sister should be encouraged to call herself and be called the writer of that piece.

Perhaps by widening the definition of writer and dissolving the aura of specialness as a prerequisite, we might better encourage possible writing artists to give it a try. Ah-ha! Now there is another category—the writing artist. All writers won't enter that category, due to lack of talent, or dedication, or luck or some mysterious something that can't be pinned down. But with a recognition of a larger pool of writers as those who write, we are more likely to find among us those who write well.

Chris

The suggestion about how "art" writing may be similar or different from regular writing particularly intrigues me. After spending this school semester learning about composing as a process, I am more apt to see similarities between "art" and regular writing. Similarities exist in the process itself. The stages are the same whether you are writing a sonnet or an essay, pre-writing, writing, and revision. It happens over and over no matter what the outlet. The stages may vary slightly but by and large they remain similar. By learning about the composing process a writer can become more fluent in the language of writing.

In journal entries like these, collected for several years, my writing students often voice strong ideas about what constitutes good and bad writing. Many feel, or have learned to feel, that a writer either has *it* or hasn't got *it*. Sometimes, students enter my composition classroom remarking on differences between essay writing and "literary writing." Sometimes, they don't see differences, easily calling their essays "stories" and their stories "essays." Equally, many student writers are confused about the distinctions between types of writing classes they may enroll in—creative writing or composition. Is a composition class a place where they won't be allowed to be "creative"? Or a place where they just can't write poetry and fiction? And, when they move from composition to creative writing, will they be asked to put away all their compositional skills and never again write essays?

Fran

Is creative writing stuff that is done for fun, and composition stuff that the teacher makes you do? That's what it meant in elementary school, and later. Composition was writing about a specific topic, picked out by the teacher and had to be a certain length and certain form. Creative writing was anything you felt like putting down on paper.

As someone who teaches both kinds of classes and does both kinds of writing, I know that in the past composition was often taught as a skills class. Students were asked to write in particular essay forms (narration, description, exposition, argumentation) and to bring in a finished essay each week for grading. Such classes are now labeled current-traditional. Being product-oriented, those classes resulted in formulaic writing and rarely offered students glimpses into the messy, generative, exciting process of writing. Creative writing classes, too, for many years were taught in predictable ways; master poets or fiction writers asked students to share and critique a story or poem each week (again, almost always this writing represented a "finished" product). Workshops were stimulating in that 20 or more writers examined a single work. They were also frightening since a traditional creative writing workshop could feel like a performance, making new writers eager to conform to what they assumed were the expectations of their teachers or the models of "excellent" literature found in their particular class anthology.

But I don't believe either of those teaching approaches serves the writer in you very well, and my teaching strategies for both classrooms have become increasingly similar and more process-oriented. I aim to let writers see how writing is put together and to explore the necessary risks of sharing multiple drafts. I think a well taught composition or creative writing class should allow you to explore writing beliefs, writing types (genres) and their attributes, and your own writing process. You will be successful to the degree that you become invested in your work. And you need to be willing to experiment and to study your own progress.

I realize not everyone feels this way, and I believe I know why. In some classrooms, teachers encourage writing students to believe that literature consists only of famous (old) examples of poetry, fiction, and drama.

Robbie

Student 'lit' is not old enough. Student writing can be literature, if it's published and recognized, and read by a lot of people. If it's just in the classroom, then it's a bill and not a law. Literature is Shakespeare, Chaucer, Coleridge, Shelly, Joyce.

But in other classrooms, teachers broaden the definition of literature to include more than texts in the traditional categories of poetry, fiction, and drama; they include nonfiction and the writings of many modern experimental writers. Students then learn to broaden their definitions, too.

David

Literature, to me, is just about anything that has been published. There are, of course, different levels of literature ranging from journals to novels, comics to compilations.

And in still other writing classrooms, teachers expand categories to include student writing as literature, encouraging writers to consider how their work functions in a universe of texts and text categories.

Karen

Student writing can be literature—it just may not necessarily be 'good' literature.

Sean

There's not a reason why a student can't do it [write literature]. In fact, judging from what I've read of the students here over the last couple of semesters, they are pumping out literature.

If, during the course of your college career, you encounter two or even three writing teachers who make you feel strongly but differently about these issues, you may reasonably be confused. This essay won't resolve your confusion, but it will begin to talk about these points by letting you hear some student writers, and teachers who are writers, voicing their opinions.

Risk Taking, Creativity, Engagement

Creativity involves risk taking. It's likely that in your writing past, you were not praised for taking risks. Rather, you were told that you had to follow the conventions for the type of writing focused on in that class, writing an academic essay, a short story, or a research report. You were rarely asked to look at your research report in "new" ways, nor were you asked to "publish" several drafts of your creative writing in workshop; instead, you were asked to produce a polished research paper and a finished story.

When writing classes don't highlight risk taking, it's hard to see the complicated ways authors go about their work. Sometimes it's difficult to realize that the "finished products" you read in anthologies often went through days, weeks, months, and years of change, alterations, false starts, and even sometimes temporary abandonment. For most of us, risk taking in writing spells disaster and failure rather than excitement and discovery. We haven't often been graded A on our outrageously playful parodies or our intelligent-but-still-problematic third drafts.

Since you generally write within classrooms and under the direction of teachers who value particular models of excellent writing, it's no wonder that you want always to present your best, most polished, most finished work to peers and your teachers. In doing this, it's natural to play it safe, but safe work is often conventional and derivative.

All this is understandable, too, since the penalty for risk taking in the traditional writing class is failure if your work is judged ineffective, unfinished, inexpert. And no one wants to fail in a writing class. Most of us remember too many past failures. We all have stories of teachers correcting our grammar and marking in red ink across every white and open space in our texts. As we grew up as school writers, there was so much to learn about spelling and sentences and paragraphs and citation systems that trying and failing in order to find a new, better, more original way of saying something would have sounded like a recipe for academic suicide. Yet without risk and experimentation, most writers remain disengaged with their work.

Fran

Then I wrote a paper that was required, and it turned out to be fun. What??!? Yes, and it was an English (ugh! don't say it!) *term* paper. I chose my own topic, so I wouldn't get bored with it. Something *totally* off the wall, so fascinating that it's appeal overwhelmed my intense hatred of term papers. It was on parapsychology.

Another writer found that writing expository prose and creative prose was not a matter of inspirational difference; rather, it was a matter of cognitive difference, thinking in somewhat different ways for different purposes.

Juan

I don't find a difference when writing expository prose and when doing "creative writing." To me, it's all essentially writing. To me, they're very similar, just the writing research comes from two different areas: internal source or external source.

For Juan, the creative writer conducts mainly "inner" research while the expository essayist conducts mainly "outer" research to support his text-in-progress.

Writing teacher Stephen Tchudi (1991) also feels that his experience writing in several genres—children's fiction to essays on teaching writing—have shown him fewer differences than similarities: "It's okay to put a little jelly on your bread-and-butter writing. My nonfiction prose style has been greatly aided by my ventures into imaginative writing" (p. 105).

I'm suggesting then that writers need classes that allow them to take risks and experiment with prose, and they need to see similarities between the types of composing they do, adding a little jelly to their bread-and-butter writing (and I might guess that sometimes their jelly writing would benefit if it grew from the solid base of bread-and-butter prose).

Genre, Subgenres, Popular Genres, and Literary Genres

None of these suggestions mean, however, that in writing classes you should stop valuing the work of professional writers or fail to study the forms their writings take. Traditionally, a great deal of student time in English classes has been spent acquiring genre knowlege, examining strategies for making poems seem like poems, stories like stories, and essays like essays. So part of the writing classroom, too, always involves the study of exemplary or expert writing in the forms you hope to learn. But you also always need the opportunity to write against and experiment with those forms. *You have to try it to do it,* whether bread and butter *or* jelly writing.

All of us can learn to value literary forms just as all of us value nonliterary forms or literary subgenres. My own not-so-hidden secret is that I love the writing of women detective novelists as well as the finest, most famous academic poetry I've ever read (and I've read a lot of both). Within her genre, for my money, Agatha Christie is still tops. Just as within his genre of lyric English verse, Gerard Manley Hopkins produced writing of incredible power.

Further, I've seen that my students have the same ability to perform well in many types of writing—many genres—if they choose and therefore value those forms. Over several years of writing and publishing student work in books about writing, I've come to like the works of Ken Waldman, Pam Miller, and Sean Carswell—who were writing essays, journal entries, in-class writing experiments, nonfiction, and parody—as well as any writing I've ever read. And these writers have strong feelings about their work because they are involved with it; they take risks, but also they take writing seriously.

Sean

I like to think all of my expository prose is creative. I like to think that the only difference is that it's focussed on something that bores the hell out of most people. Also, my expository prose generally doesn't have characters, a plot, or foul language. Not that the language in my "creative" writing is foul, just a bit more vulgar.

Everything I write is literature and I'm offended that you'd doubt me. Sure student writing is literature. F. Scott Fitzgerald wrote the first half of *This Side of Paradise* while he was at Princeton. I've seen pieces go through the workshops here that are better than any John Updike I've read. Langston Hughes poem "Poem for English B" or something like that was written in college, and that's a great poem. I think Kerouac started his first novel at Columbia. I guess all that literature is is taking on a theme worth reading about, writing well, i.e. good images, powerful language, different levels of meaning, none of the shit that's in Danielle Steel. There's no reason why a student can't do it.

You can see from Sean's remarks that widening what we define as creative and literary and viewing student writing as literature doesn't prevent us from categorizing and judging writing; humans understand their world through categories and judgements. I would simply argue that we shouldn't assume that there is only one way to categorize or that those categories should (or could) hold fast for all people, in all cultures, in all historical times.

Current theories of reading and writing suggest that there is no ideal, exemplary "best poem" or "great American novel" out there, waiting to be written. Rather, once texts are composed, we find them more or less like other texts that we have already sorted by general categories, *and* we do this sorting by community agreement: We do it within the worlds of literary critics, the worlds of English departments, the worlds of writing classrooms, the worlds of independent reading groups, and so on.

Karen

Literature to me can be just about anything. The word "literature" is kind of lofty and snobbish to me. The distinction I'd make is between "good" literature and "bad" literature. I don't have any rules for that—I think for example, that something like an article in the *Enquirer* is bad literature compared to maybe *Moby Dick*—then, again, if an *Enquirer* article was taken from its context and issued as a satire of comedy piece, it might be good (author's intent can be important in *some* instances. . . .).

Karen is grappling with a category system here that says *Moby Dick* is better than an article in the *National Enquirer* just as I for many years felt a bit silly that I enjoyed Agatha Christie (and the subgenre of detective novels) as well as the work of Gerard Manley Hopkins (academic poetry).

Of course, most writers aim for a genre at some point in their drafting process. These days, we know writers can incorporate a lot of what they hope to share, but not all that they wish to share; they are unable to *fix* a text so that each reader will read it in exactly the same way because readers bring themselves, their backgrounds, associations, experience with texts, and so on, to each reading occasion.

Since a text can never be completely fixed, it is open to interpretation. Readers can offer several possible readings of your text without doing the work a disservice, although certainly some readings appear more "sophisticated" or may turn out to be closer to your original intention than others. At the same time, often you fail in your intentions and are unable to incorporate some of the genre characteristics you had hoped to incorporate, leading to a less than successful text.

For instance, your argument may be based on shaky facts, your "serious" story may be sewn together from absurd and unbelievable events, your *free* verse may go "Ta-dum, Ta-dum, Ta-dum" with constrained regularity, or your informal journal may be knotted up with self-consciousness. It takes study and time and practice to turn out a "traditional" piece of work in an accepted form and style (essay or novel or newspaper article) just as it takes study and time and practice to loosen the bounds of accepted conventions to write an exciting, experimental, or exploratory piece.

Equally, readers depend on the conventions they have learned to understand your work, yet they also need to be willing to suspend their judgements in order to understand *each* new work they encounter. A reader has to identify the genre you are attempting as well as decide to what degree *you intended to deviate* from the standards of that genre.

Reading and writing are *both* interpretive acts, then, requiring intricate intellectual negotiations from all parties concerned. And literature, traditionally, has been a set of texts, all having features that a group of readers and writers have agreed upon. This set of texts changes as the community changes, for, over time, agreement about common features of those texts changes. It's always been that way, even though English teachers often prefer their set—called a canon— of texts fixed, and therefore easier to "cover."

But sermons and letters have gone "out" of the set and stories and poems *of certain agreed upon quality* have been put "in." Women and racial, ethnic, and class minorities have often been out but nowadays many are arguing for including them as in. Students have often been out, but they know better, seeing themselves as in. After all, *someone* has to write literature before it can be classified as such.

Charles

Student writing is definitely literature. Literature is not only found in textbooks, it has to start somewhere.

Gordon

Student writing is always literature; however, the quality of that literature is never determined by the writer, but by the readers of that work.

Bill

To me, if a piece of written work is read by even a few people and enjoyed by at least one—then it was worth writing. The amount of popularity a piece gets is not NECESSARILY how good a piece of writing is, but what is most readily accepted at that time. What I'm writing now is not literature, but it could be if I spent a lot of time editing, and rewriting it would probably sound a whole lot different. I think that student literature can be considered literature if the student perfects the piece through revision. Many students disbelieve this because a lot of work is involved and many papers turned in are not up to literary standards and students are discouraged.

I believe student writing is literature, too.

I understand that conventional standards for judging writing always affect us.

At the same time, we, in our classroom communities, always affect those standards when we discuss together what we know about and appreciate in the writing we review.

That's how writing and reading work.

I hope you can see how certain questions about texts—When should writers obey or break writing conventions? What is successful work and unsuccessful work? What makes a poem a poem, a story a story, and an essay an essay?—have always interested those who write and study writing. Such questions are perhaps answered best by the nonanswer of overlapping genre categories; that is, categories don't start and stop but shade into each other. You can learn to write a traditional poem, and you can take risks with that form, exploring prose poems and short short fiction along the way. You can learn to write the traditional first-year writing essay, and you can enliven that form by taking risks with your voice and your style as you adopt first person (I), add some unexpected narration, and/or use logic lightly. Sometimes you'll fail, but you'll always find that you learn from exploring conventions, sometimes—often—you learn as much by breaking those conventions.

Literature in the Writing Student

The questions and voices I've shared here suggest that you should approach composition classes and creative writing classes in pretty similar ways. Overall, both types of classrooms need to encourage *and reward* risk taking and experimentation as you learn to conform to and break genre conventions. Mimi Schwartz (1989) writes:

> To value self-investment, to avoid premature closure, to see revision as discovery, to go beyond the predictable, to risk experimentation, and, above all, to trust your own creative powers are necessary for all good writing, whether it is a freshman theme, a poem, a term paper. . . . Few of us reward risk taking that fails with a better grade than polished but pedestrian texts. We are more product-oriented, judging assignments as independent of one another rather than as part of a collective and ongoing body of work. No wonder that students interpret our message as "Be careful, not creative!" (p. 204)

If you are creative before you are careful, you will be more likely to gain an understanding of the writing process of professionals. This will happen when your workshops focus on drafting (being creative), revision, style experiments, editing (being careful), and use of portfolio evaluation (which allows you to share both experiments and final products). And being part of such a classroom doesn't mean that you won't still have to examine and explore some of these issues for yourself.

Anji

> Of course student writing can be literature. If critics consider some of the trash out today to be literature, you better believe that students can write literature too. The ability to write something that is considered literature is not only a God-given talent. Most people can do it if they just make the time and collect their thoughts.

Like Anji, most of us are given to grand pronouncements about the quality of this or that piece of writing, but we need to temper our value judgements with an understanding of genre conventions, how they developed, and how they have gained value in particular communities.

Summer

> *Literature* what is canonized by the unknown people who create anthologies and textbooks, is a formal definition. In an informal definition, literature is a completed piece which has been published or disseminated to an audience, and has been read by a number of persons (which would include everything, even graffiti and advertisements). To narrow the definition, it is not intended for business or propaganda purposes, is received in a "legal" form (NO graffiti, etc.) and is meant to be enjoyed by readers and meets cultural standards of literature (circular argument). Unpublished works can never be literature, no matter how worthy.

You start acquiring this knowledge as you learn about category systems and how texts work in the classroom community; you also

learn that it is possible for you to become part of that writing community. The questions you have, the beliefs you hold, the worries you
may feel, can all be explored and should be explored. Remember, risk-
taking and experimentation results in knowledge, not in anarchy. At
the same time, if your writing goal is, ultimately, to become a mystery
novelist, you won't be tempted completely to ignore the requirements
and limitations of that type of writing. A consummate mystery writer,
Agatha Christie (1977) once wrote:

> If you were a carpenter, it would be no good making a chair, the seat
> of which was five feet up from the floor. It wouldn't be what anyone
> wanted to sit on. It is no good saying that you think the chair looks
> handsome that way. If you want to write a book, study what sizes
> books are, and write within the limits of that size. If you want to
> write a certain type of short story for a certain type of magazine you
> have to make it the length and it has to be the type of story that is
> printed in the magazine. If you like to write for yourself only, that is
> a different manner—you can make it any length, and write it in any
> way you wish; but then you will probably have to be content with the
> pleasure alone of having written it (pp. 334—335).

When you view your writing as literature—through a broad definition and understanding of that word—you allow yourself to share a
supremely satisfying human activity. For most of us, writing is never
easy, but it is made worthwhile when we "publish" in the writing
classroom and when we are "read by even a few people and enjoyed by
at least one."

Works Cited

Christie, Agatha (1977). *An Autobiography.* London, Great Britain: Collins.

Schwartz, Mimi (1989). "Wearing the Shoe on the Other Foot" in Joseph
Moxley (Ed.), *Creative Writing in America.* Urbana, IL: National Council of Teachers of English.

Tchudi, Stephen (1991). "Confession of a Failed Bookmaker" in Mimi
Schwartz (Ed.), *Writer's Craft, Teachers's Art.* Portsmouth, NH:
Boynton/Cook.

Sharing Ideas

- Since it's hard to be objective and to maintain distance from my
  own writing, I'll ask you to play editor here. Make up five questions about this essay and/or relate it to other essays in the book.
  Then work with other writers to explore those questions.

- Choose any quote in my essay and write your own informal response to the issues the writer raises. Put yourself in dialogue with this essay and these writers; add to our conversation.

25

At Last Report, I Was Still Here

Jim W. Corder

Jim W. Corder has been exploring the ideas he shares in this essay in articles published in *College English, Freshman English News*, and *Rhetoric Review*. In addition, he is the author of *Lost in West Texas* and *Chronicle of a Small Town*. He has taught at Texas Christian University since 1958, serving as chair of the English Department, dean of the College of Arts and Sciences and associate vice chancellor. Several years ago, Jim started to write his own essay assignments with his freshman students, a practice that he continues each semester.

I'm pretty certain sometimes even insistent, about which pipe tobacco I want to smoke and which coffee and white wine I want to drink. I want—need—burley tobacco that's cut coarse for my pipe. I buy it in bulk at a pipe shop; it's pure tobacco, has none of the additives that some packaged tobaccos and all cigarettes have. About coffee, I'm not so particular, so long as it's made strong. The white wine has to be cheap and in a big jug. I prefer Carlo Rossi Rhine Wine, made on the Rhine River, which wanders from Germany through parts of northern California.

But about most other things, I'm mostly uncertain. I sometimes admire—but always at a careful distance—people who seem to have a sure sense of themselves, who are sure in their integrity and judgment. I'm mostly not. Sometimes, I'm not even sure of my own identity. Some people have found me gentle, dear, and easy going, but others apparently have found me arrogant and domineering. It's little wonder that sometimes I can't find myself at all.

But I keep looking. I hope that people haven't noticed, but I take frequent ritual surveys of myself. I read myself like Braille to find out if I am there. I check my pockets to be sure that my tobacco is in my left hip pocket, my handkerchief in my right hip pocket, my wallet in my left front pocket. My right front pocket takes longer to check; I have to be sure that my keys are there, and my pocket knife and two white rocks from Grandpa's farm and an arrow point that I found on the Brazos River and a 1921 silver dollar. Finally, I check my shirt pocket to be sure I have my pens and pencil, the little spiral notebook, and the loose bills I keep out for daily expenses. If you're as uncertain as I am, you don't want to be getting your wallet out all of the time. Mine has the last sure signs of my identity, and I want to keep it safe. I check my pockets pretty often. I reason that if everything is there, then maybe I am, too.

When arguments come up, as you might by now guess, I'm easily unsettled, easily disturbed into doubt. Sometimes, I feel strongly both ways as the argument progresses, and sometimes add a third and fourth. It doesn't take too much to ruin any calm I've previously achieved. An argument that appears to make sense, even if it contradicts what I thought I had earlier believed, is likely to bring everything into question. I begin to doubt what I had thought, or what I thought I had thought, and the first thing you know I have to check my pockets again to find out whether or not I'm here.

Such arguments sometimes occur just before I'm supposed to go to class. There I am, trying to be wise, or at least serene, or at least competent as I head for class, and someone reminds me that things may be otherwise than what I think. Or maybe I read something that tells me I've got it all wrong. What am I to do? Go on to class and get it all wrong there, too? Then go to class another time and say everything in an altogether different way? That sometimes happens.

All of us have been, whether knowingly or not, whether directly or not, part of a rhetorical tradition that has been with us for 2500 years. This tradition allowed and encouraged us to believe that we could achieve identity not just in what we do, but also in what we say and write, and that others could know us in what we say and write, and that they could tell themselves back to us with their words. That tradition—it goes back to Aristotle and before—still predicts and influences much of what teachers do in composition classes.

In that old tradition, we believed or wanted to believe that the author was in the text that he or she wrote, making a self-known. Aristotle said in his *Rhetoric* that *ethos* is potent, that ethical argument is more persuasive than logical argument or emotional appeal. *Ethos*, as he and others since have used it, means character, the character of the speaker or writer, as it is revealed in the text—not as it was known previously, but as it emerges in speech and writing. Ethical argument, then is argument that rests upon the revealed *ethos*, or character. Something like that is what I've been waiting to read in the work of composition students.

I want student writers to show themselves to me in what they write, to give themselves to me, as I try to show and to give myself back to them in what I write. I want them to remember their lives, their histories, the particularities of their existence, and to show them to me. I want to know what they think and how they think and why they think that way, and I want to know the particular experiences that count to them. I want them to cherish themselves at least enough to understand who and what they are. I want them to cherish what they write. I want them to believe that I cherish them as authors. I want us all to be there, present to each other. I wish we could all be here forever, each of us cherished. I had hoped that it would someday be possible.

But that's on Monday in my freshman composition class. On Tuesday, I have to go to my junior literature class, and the confusion and uncertainty begin again. Something altogether otherwise happens there.

When I go to my literature class on Tuesday, I'm obliged to listen to writers of our time who tell me that I've been wrong, who tell me that old rhetorical tradition never had things quite right. What they say is compelling; I begin to listen and to doubt what I thought I formerly thought. They tell me, and make sense of doing so, that I cannot know the author in his or her text. I can only know my interpretation of the author. In *Image, Music, Text,* Roland Barthes (1978) remarks that "the birth of the reader must be at the cost of the death of the author." And besides, they tell, me, the author is not who I think, not some solitary self singlehandedly creating a text. The author is a social construction, always a crowd. Stanley Fish (1980) says in *Is There a Text in This Class?* that "selves are constituted by the ways of thinking and seeing that inhere in social organizations." If *ethos* exists, it exists in the perceiving minds of the readers. It is not the creation of a solitary author; it is what readers find in the text or project upon the text. The solitary author is dead. Language writes us, rather than the other way around: We write what the language of our community will let us write. The notion of the self as a source of meaning, they tell me, is outdated and was always wrong, or at least more complicated than we thought. The language by which we view and construct the world comes from society, not from the individual, who is already gone and was never there. If there is character, it is character as interpreted by readers as they respond to the text.

Confusion begins, and uncertainty comes. I wonder what I'm to do when I go back to my composition class on Wednesday. I check my pockets again and wonder if I've lost my chance for identity. I begin to be afraid that I don't exist. I can't turn away from what I've learned from my literature class, and don't want to, for it's often exhilarating and provocative. I can't deny the power of the reader to determine the meaning of a text—*Gulliver's Travels* is mine; I don't allow it to be Swift's property. I can't deny what some call social constructionist and intertextual thought. It challenges the habits that we sometimes call thoughts and reminds us, for we need to be reminded, that reality is what we have decided to call reality, that facts and logic are what some community has decided they are, that a self exists only in and through the interpretation of a community.

Such thoughts leave me lonely. Will no one find me if I manage to say or to write something? Later, will all forget that I was here, or never notice? I had decided that the text of what I wrote was just about all there is to me, but the me that's there is not myself, only some self created out there by others, if they happen to notice.

I don't want to think such thoughts, but then find myself providing evidence that I should. A book I wrote, called *Chronicle of a Small Town* (Corder, 1989) was published not long ago. A newspaper reviewer said some nice things about it, said some nice things about my "character" and "voice." I was excited. I existed. I ran to show my wife and decided to call my cousins to notify them that I was real. I danced a little jig.

And then I stopped. I was talking back to the reviewer, who was not there, anyway. "Wait just a damn minute,"I said to him. "Don't think you've caught me so easily," I advise him. "There's more to me than what you've seen on the pages," I insist, " and my voice is sometimes much louder and more strident than what you think you've heard, and sometimes much sweeter."

I don't even exist in my own text, and it's not my text any more, but the reviewer's.

What am I to do? I check my pockets again.

I can't keep things sorted out. Things won't stay in tidy files or neat compartments for me. What they say about literary theory is true, that it slops over into everything else, and I begin to go fuzzy around the edges, on my way toward disappearance. A colleague tries to reassure me. "Now, now," he says, "it's going to be all right. When Barthes says that the author dies, he doesn't mean that the *person* dies." He pats me on the shoulder. "How do you keep them separate?" I ask, but he doesn't answer.

If the author of an essay in the literature anthology is dead to me, if I can never find him or her, must I learn that I will never find my composition students either? And will I vanish when I write something for them? Arguments inside the composition community seem oftener and oftener to say that we are lost to each other. Increasingly insistent demands, no longer taken as controversial, for collaborative forms of learning and writing seem to leave fewer opportunities for individual achievement, and besides, out there in the larger public community more are saying that individualism has been allowed to run rampant too long, far too long.

That last sounds ominous to me.

Will I vanish? Have I already?

I don't think so, but I'm a little uncertain.

I check my pockets again and find the rocks and the arrow point and slowly begin to remember what I might have remembered all along.

When you write, you're always alone and with someone. Everything anyone ever wrote intrudes upon, alters, blesses, and damns anything anyone writes. The language doesn't belong to me.

Still, I think I'm here, though I'm a little uncertain. I think I'm here and I think the language does belong to me. I think you may be here. I think composition students may be here. A little while back, I said that ". . . I'm obliged to listen to writers of our time who tell me that I've been wrong." I'm obliged because they compel me. They pull at me. They are real.

If they are real, there's a chance that I might be, too, some day.

And there's one other thing I remember.

I can hold them accountable for what they say. They can hold me accountable for what I say. If I slander someone in what I write, interpreting readers won't go with me to court and sit bedside me as codefendants. I'll be alone, and I'll be held accountable. If I lie in what I write, the social group that constructed me won't sit beside me to share the judgment against me. I'll be alone, and I'll be held accountable. I am responsible for what I write. No one else is. Just me.

Works Cited

Barthes, Roland (1978). *Image, Music, Text*. New York: Farrar, Straus & Giroux.

Corder, Jim W. (1989). *Chronicle of a Small Town*. College Station, TX: Texas A & M University Press.

Fish, Stanley (1980). *Is There a Text in This Class? The Authority of Interpretive Communities*. Cambridge, MA: Harvard University Press.

Sharing Ideas

- Search through your own pockets, purse, bookbag, jacket. What do you find, and what does it tell you about your identity?

- Sit in your writing area and pretend to be a stranger. What do you deduce about the writer who chooses to work there?

- This book has focused on writers and writing although several authors look particularly at reading and reading processes. Jim mentions a long standing tension, maybe even an academic battle, that pits writer against readers. What do you know about this issue; does it ever influence you?

- How does it feel to publish writing—in a class peer group or book, by sharing it with family and friends, through your own desktop publishing, or by winning a literary contest and having your piece read aloud?

- Have you had the experience of being "misread" by a friend or by class members?

- Should writers argue with readers about their intentions?

- As a writer, discuss the methods you use for assuring that your readers will understand you and read you the way you hope to be read.

- What do you make of Jim's claim that as a writer you are always writing alone and with others?

- Producing a text means producing a physical document that can be used by others in legal or in emotional arguments. Does that fact make you more or less willing to write?

- Jim ends by claiming his own accountability; what are your thoughts on writers' responsibilities?
